P9-CDZ-064

RUSSIA AND AMERICA

Dangers and Prospects

RUSSIA

and

Published for the
COUNCIL ON FOREIGN RELATIONS
by
HARPER & BROTHERS, NEW YORK
1956

AMERICA

Dangers and Prospects

by HENRY L. ROBERTS

foreword by JOHN J. McCLOY

The Council on Foreign Relations is a non-profit institution devoted to study of the international aspects of American political, economic and strategic problems. It takes no stand, expressed or implied, on American policy.

The authors of books published under the auspices of the Council are responsible for their statements of fact and expressions of opinion. The Council is responsible only for determining that they should be presented to the public.

RUSSIA AND AMERICA: DANGERS AND PROSPECTS

Copyright, 1956, by Council on Foreign Relations, Inc.
Printed in the United States of America

All rights reserved, including the right to reproduce this book or any portion thereof in any form.

For information address Council on Foreign Relations, 58 East 68th Street, New York 21

THIRD PRINTING

American Book–Stratford Press, Inc., New York

Library of Congress catalog card number: LC 55-11968

E
183.8
.R9R6

COUNCIL ON FOREIGN RELATIONS

OFFICERS AND DIRECTORS

JOHN J. MCCLOY
Chairman of the Board

HENRY M. WRISTON
President

FRANK ALTSCHUL
Vice-President & Secretary

DAVID ROCKEFELLER
Vice-President

ELLIOTT V. BELL
Treasurer

WALTER H. MALLORY
Executive Director

GEORGE S. FRANKLIN, JR.
Executive Director

FRANK D. CARUTHERS, JR.
Assistant Treasurer

HAMILTON FISH ARMSTRONG
WILLIAM A. M. BURDEN
ARTHUR H. DEAN
ALLEN W. DULLES
THOMAS K. FINLETTER
JOSEPH E. JOHNSON
DEVEREUX C. JOSEPHS
GRAYSON L. KIRK
R. C. LEFFINGWELL
PHILIP D. REED
WHITNEY H. SHEPARDSON
CHARLES M. SPOFFORD
MYRON C. TAYLOR
JOHN H. WILLIAMS

COMMITTEE ON STUDIES

HENRY M. WRISTON
Chairman

HAMILTON FISH ARMSTRONG
GORDON DEAN
BYRON DEXTER
GRAYSON L. KIRK
WILLIAM L. LANGER
THOMAS H. MCKITTRICK
STACY MAY
WHITNEY H. SHEPARDSON
JOHN H. WILLIAMS

91591

EMORY AND HENRY LIBRARY

FOREWORD

BY JOHN J. McCLOY

IN THE autumn of 1952 the suggestion was made that a group of men of varied experience and background, not burdened with the responsibilities of government, should come together to discuss problems creating world tension, especially as they concerned Soviet-American relations, and try to identify policies and actions to provide conditions for peace. Government officials and representatives of both political parties supported the proposal.

The group, as it was later constituted by the Council on Foreign Relations, included men who had formerly served in responsible governmental positions in Washington and abroad, scientists with knowledge of atomic developments, scholars and experts in the area of Soviet studies, and men with large experience in the business and industrial life of the nation.

It was understood that the group would concentrate on long-term problems and not allow itself to be lost in the labyrinth of immediate issues and policy. People outside the government, without access to the cables, are not in a position to deal with the day-to-day decisions of foreign policy. Even in respect of long-range problems it was appreciated by those who took part in the discussions that there might be no result other than the self-education of the participants.

The search assumed organized form in May 1953 when the group met at the Council on Foreign Relations in New York. This was the first of many meetings, held over a period of more than two years. During the course of its work individual members of the group had many opportunities to discuss major international problems with officials and others in this country, Asia, Africa and Europe. Throughout, the group had the support of an able research staff brilliantly headed by Professor Henry L. Roberts of Columbia University.

One or two aspects of the group's deliberations demonstrated the complexity of the problems we discussed. During our first meetings it was apparent that the scientists, who knew the atomic developments, were looking to the men of public or diplomatic experience for solutions to the problems, while the latter looked across the table to the scholars and experts for the answers. The measure of understanding that we achieved came the hard way. Individual members of the group presented logical, well-defined views which frequently failed to endure the analysis made by their colleagues. Positions on the German problem or on atomic requirements gave way before penetrating criticism. Many of my colleagues would agree with me, I believe, that our group approach, though sometimes confusing, clarified points which individual opinions frequently overlooked.

As the discussions proceeded it was concluded that it might be worth while to submit some of the thinking to the judgment of a wider public. Mr. Roberts was asked to undertake the difficult task of exploring and developing the implications of what was said and drawing systematic conclusions from the discussions. The members of the group deeply appreciate the important contribution he has made in writing this book. Though he has, where feasible, made specific recommendations, he has been particularly concerned to analyze the complexities of the problems presented and to state the advantages and disadvantages of the various possible courses of action.

In place of a conventional foreword, I have been asked, as chairman, to outline a few perspectives on American foreign policy as they appear to me after having had the benefit of the group's exchange of views. I agreed to try to do so, with the understanding, however, that these remarks should be taken as the personal exercise of only one individual. What I have to say owes much to the intellectual companionship of the men who met together, but they bear no responsibility for the views expressed, which are my own. Nor do my remarks attempt to summarize Mr. Roberts' findings, though much of what I say has been stimulated by his remarkable work. These, then, are the personal and current views of one member of the group, neither the most representative nor the most expert, on some of the problems confronting the United States.

I should begin these remarks by saying that I do not believe the new leaders in the Kremlin have abandoned long-range Communist objectives. I do believe that some very radical and important changes have taken place in Soviet methods. However, Khrushchev's opening speech last February before the Twentieth Congress of the Soviet Communist Party should put us on guard against illusions. Though he avoided Stalin's inelegant language, Khrushchev did not renounce the objective of one Communist world. He gave no indication that he was discarding a parochial belief in the mid-nineteenth century concepts of capitalism which Marx nurtured. Moreover, he did not renounce force. He merely gave a more elastic definition to the old Lenin-Stalin doctrine of the "inevitable transition to Socialism." (Incidentally, we should not be misled by Khrushchev's special use of the word "socialism.")

In his speech Khrushchev's adherence to old Communist goals was clear and firm:

> It is quite likely that the forms of the transition to socialism will become more and more variegated. Moreover, it is not obligatory for the implementation of these forms to be connected with civil war in all circumstances.
>
> The enemies are fond of depicting us, Leninists, as supporters of violence always and in all circumstances. It is true that we recognize the necessity for the revolutionary transformation of capitalist society into Socialist society.
>
> This is what distinguishes revolutionary Marxists from reformists and opportunists. There is not a shadow of doubt that for a number of capitalist countries the overthrow of the bourgeois dictatorship by force and the connected sharp aggravation of the class struggle is inevitable.

There are other passages in his declaration which give the impression that, if at any stage the route to world Communism was blocked, revolutionary methods would not be excluded.

Khrushchev's words are a warning that a discussion of policies for peace must begin with the recognition of two basic uncertainties which confront the world: the dangers of the Soviet Communist outlook and intentions, and the tremendous growth of man's destructive power. In this situation the United States and its partners must maintain military strength and vigilance. No other course is conceivable, yet military power, however fundamental and important for defense, is not the full solution to the problems. What emerges for me at the end of our discussions is the sense that though our strong deterrent power may prevent Soviet aggression, we could lose the struggle for freedom because of failures in the non-military area. To prevent such failures there is a compelling need for fresh perspectives in our foreign policy.

I do not mean that our policies in the past have been inadequate. There have been mistakes, but there have also been noble achievements in American policy since 1945. The economic and social aid that began with the Marshall Plan helped to give hundreds of millions of men, women and children a new start and a chance for a decent life. Our non-vindictive and humane settlements with Germany and Japan furthered the course of peace. Our resistance in Korea helped to save a large part of the world from totalitarianism. Our atoms-for-peace proposals have stimulated hope in the future.

The need for new perspectives arises not from past errors, but from the fact that the nature of the struggle with the Soviet Union is undergoing a change. The need, as I see it, is to understand this change and then to face frankly what kind of world the United States wants to see develop. Once clarity on this question has been attained, we may have a vantage point from which to view the major problems which confront us.

Briefly stated, it seems to me that the struggle with Soviet Russia now extends beyond the military to the political, economic and social areas. To be sure, the military threat must never be allowed out of sight, and we and our partners must develop the required military strength to deter the Kremlin from aggression. But we must take more seriously than we have the economic, social and political implications of Soviet actions.

The Soviet leadership is competing with us in the non-military areas. Soviet scientific and engineering achievements are remarkable. Soviet production is rising rapidly, and we must face the possibility that twenty years from now Communist Russia may be challenging the position of the United States as the first industrial power in the world. Moreover, the new leaders of the Kremlin appear to understand what Stalin failed to see—that their influence in the world increases as they decrease their bellicosity (though not their military capabilities). Accordingly, it seems, for the time being at least, that they are unlikely to jeopardize their considerable gains and influence by resorting to open war.

If this is so, we may be too prone to evaluate our situation in terms which were more appropriate to the context of 1950–1951 than to the present. At that time the Korean war was going badly, an invasion of Yugoslavia seemed imminent, and Stalin was spearheading his intensive "hate America" campaign. Though we may assume that the present "collective leadership" of the Kremlin bears us the same basic ill-will as did Stalin and supports fanatically the same long-range objectives of world domination, the new leaders have shifted their line of attack. Soviet aggression is now being carried out by Soviet diplomats, salesmen and technicians and by Kremlin politicians on propaganda and business visits all over the world—both to the uncommitted nations and, as well, to nations associated with us.

It is a mistake, however, to describe and evaluate this situation exclusively in military terms as a contest or to score everything that happens as either a gain for the United States or a gain for the U.S.S.R. We should guard against the tendency to attribute all political and economic developments in this unsettled world to Soviet deviltry and cunning, and we should be more willing to view them on their own terms and conditions. Soviet power looms large, but it is not the only key to an understanding of world developments. It has often been pointed out, and quite rightly, that if the Soviet Union were to disappear or have a complete and convincing change of heart with respect to world domination, we should still have to face and solve many problems which we now consider to be aspects of the Soviet threat. Large segments of the world's population would still be struggling for better living standards, economic security, and viable institutions. Hyper-nationalism, authoritarianism and other dangers to free institutions would persist. Indeed, it is partly because these and other issues exist in the world today that Communism has large opportunities for initiative. The Soviet Union did not create, in Asia, the Middle East, North Africa and Europe, all of the problems which now confront us. It has taken sharp advantage of them to press its own policies forward. Although it has tormented and aggravated the issues to new and more ominous dimensions, it is nonetheless misleading to regard these issues as of moment to us only insofar as they concern Soviet aims and policies.

I do not suggest that a realistic foreign policy for the United States can ignore the existence of the Soviet Union and the threat it poses. But our policy must avoid the defensive, negative mood which results from exclusive preoccupation with the Soviet threat. Our chances of achieving our purposes—and they are the purposes of peaceful peoples throughout the world—will be increased if we do not always look over our shoulders to find the Soviet shadow. If we merely try to counteract Soviet moves, we may fall victim to Soviet strategy. Our policies, our budgets, our statements before Congressional committees, will lack vitality and imagination if justification is made only in terms of the Soviet threat. In the present situation to be negative is to invite failure.

It is compelling, therefore, to identify in clear and unmistakable terms what the United States seeks for itself and the rest of the world. Fundamental to these objectives are three axioms: the United States seeks no territorial aggrandizement; the United States will not seek to impose its rule on others; the United States will never embark on an aggressive war.

The affirmative objectives of the American people which they wish to have expressed in their foreign policy are to promote the ability of all peoples to manage their internal affairs in a way satisfactory to them without outside interference and without damage to others; to open the channels for economic and cultural improvement so that all men may have a chance to live a free and better life; and to promote the peaceful settlement of conflicts and a wider understanding of common interests throughout the world. Such are the things that Americans want for themselves and for other peoples. These are American purposes regardless of the conflict with Soviet totalitarianism.

Do we not have here common ground with men everywhere? Would not Mr. Nehru, for example, make the same answer, identify himself with us on this platform? It is true that some peoples of Asia and Africa are more concerned at the present time with industrialization than they are with civil liberties, with national independence than they are with individual freedom. We understand that people cannot feel free without independence, but we believe that independence is only a step toward the greater objective of individual freedom.

In advancing beyond a merely anti-Soviet attitude, the United States must also recognize that America's fundamental interests are identical or at least consistent with the interests of the free community of nations. The task of preserving and extending freedom and independence for all peoples demands that we forge a community of interests, enlarge the scope of foreign policy. To enter upon a community of interests means that the interests of the community must become a large and embracing criterion for testing policy and program. Obviously such a test is not to be taken as excluding, or opposing, the interests of the United States. It does mean adopting a faith that improvements in the welfare of the community of free peoples also promote the national interest of the United States. Consequently, when we talk of "our" side in the present world situation, we must think of the word in a more than national sense. We cannot ask for allegiance to the United States by those who owe it none, but we can ask for allegiance to freedom. We should recognize that a nation which is "neutral" can be on "our" side if it works persistently toward the type of international community which is written into the United Nations charter. Such, I think, must be the overall perspective and the general purposes of American foreign policy. They are valid regardless of the conflict with Soviet totalitarianism. They give us a fixed point from which we may develop our regional relationships in the Atlantic Community, in Asia and generally in the world.

The Atlantic Community

No objective of American foreign policy is more important than that of strengthening the solidarity of the great Atlantic coalition, which reflects both common interests and common aspirations. This requires us to give thoughtful attention to the differences in interest and policy within the coalition. We sometimes tend to forget that these coalitions were not easily born, that they were formed with great effort by the subordination of secondary issues to primary objectives, with genuine sacrifices from many of the participants. The NATO coalition was the careful work of devoted men of many political parties in many countries who recognized that the unity of the free peoples was itself a major objective to which lesser policies must make their contribution. It is of the utmost importance that we realize that it is not dishonorable to compromise with a friend in the interest of unity and of improving the common position.

The strength of the Atlantic Community, of NATO, a strength not yet fully realized and developed, lies in a broadly shared set of political and cultural values: respect for the autonomy of the individual, commitment to the principle of the balance between the rights enjoyed by the individual and the duties owed to the state. The tendency to regard the Atlantic Alliance as an emergency device for military protection alone must give way to an appreciation of its potentiality as a community of political, economic and cultural interest. I should like to see us give close thought to the establishment of annual interparliamentary sessions, even if only advisory in character, to bring together representative segments of the legislatures of the Atlantic countries for a common discussion of problems and outlooks. The more the Atlantic Community reaches into the lives of the various peoples who have joined in it, the more it will be nourished and the stronger it will grow.

The Atlantic Community and its sub-grouping, the European Community, are ripe for new advances. Modern economic developments are such that, even if there were no Soviet threat, there would be an incentive among the European countries to pool many of their resources and activities to provide wider opportunities for all. The initiative in this must lie with Europe, but the United States can take practical measures, at the request of the Europeans, to help them on their way. On our side, I think we should examine and develop our policies in the light of the question—do they help or hinder European and Atlantic cooperation? This question has a broad meaning in the years ahead for American policies concerned with nuclear development, tariffs and trade, and for passport, visa and immigration practices. Here again we will face the problem of community interest and national interest. Just as our peace, freedom and prosperity will be endangered unless freedom and economic progress are strengthened in Asia, so they will be jeopardized unless Europe is enabled to expand its development. The political problems of France, the economic problems of Italy, the general European problem of social and economic stratification are more than national questions; they have a far better chance of solution within a free, prospering and mobile community of peoples. I should not like to see the United States remain aloof from the endeavor, cheering or criticising from the grandstand. It ought to be an active participant on the field.

Our relations with Europe do not exist in a compartment separate from Asia and the rest of the world. Although it always seems easier to manage a particular problem within a narrow regional framework, and our allies in Europe are generally less interested in the problems and risks which the United States encounters in Asia, our community approach requires that we consult with them before we take actions in Asia. Such wider consultation within the structure of an alliance is not simple, but compartmentalization of policy-thinking and policy-making brings great dangers. Discrepancies in outlook serve to undermine the potentiality for united action on a major problem. The leadership of the Soviet bloc is always seeking to probe these areas of discrepancy, in the hope of breaking up the unity of will and action among the free-world powers. A community perspective will minimize its chances of success.

In our policies of defense it is necessary to give more attention to the relation between the economic strength of many of our allies and the burdens which large-scale armaments place upon their economies. In a community all members must share responsibilities and costs. Our allies can and must carry economic burdens if they wish to protect their own freedom. Some of them are clearly in a position to do more than they are now doing. At the same time, overly heavy military budgets and inflation can impair the attachment of peoples to the governments which we are assisting through military aid. If that happens, military defenses erected at great cost and effort may be undermined from within, especially if the Soviet bloc chooses to avoid sharp crises in the next few years. American opinion and the American Congress should be prepared to extend the emphasis from aid for military purposes to a more comprehensive concern for healthy all-round economic development. To do this we must actively re-examine the relations between military strength, political solidarity and economic health.

If we are prepared to reconsider, as I believe we must, the strategic concept upon which NATO is based, the economics of defense in Europe will be changed considerably. Current concepts underlying NATO strategy are not likely to meet the requirements of 1960. By that time the Soviet Union may have matched the NATO tactical atomic capability in Europe. The problem is to devise a strategy which will create a strong European deterrent to any form of Soviet attack in Europe, which will strengthen the solidarity of our friendships with other NATO countries, which will encourage common European efforts, and which will hold the economic costs at a reasonable level.

What, for example, is the significance of the possibility that the European nations will possess—whether through American equipment or through their own technology and industry—an intermediate-range ballistic and nuclear capability sufficient to retaliate instantaneously and effectively against Soviet Russia west of the Urals? Such a capability could have a strong deterrent effect upon any Soviet thought of direct atomic aggression in Europe. In giving the European community a responsibility for making the decision whether or not to respond to such aggression, it might release Europe from the sense of a somewhat helpless dependence on American strategic decisions and put it in a better position to be an equal though more independent partner within the NATO community.

Germany and the Soviet "Satellites"

Our foreign policy cannot ignore the millions of peoples living in East Germany and in the so-called satellite states. The Soviet leaders are trying to deprive them of all hope of recovering control of their own affairs. Here is colonialism—Communist colonialism—stark and ultimate. The Poles, Czechs, Slovaks, Hungarians, Rumanians, Bulgarians, East Germans and many other peoples are living under the autocratic, colonial rule of the Kremlin. Their tragic condition should be a warning to the leaders of Egypt, India and of other countries in the Near, Middle and Far East who fear colonialism but who fail to recognize that its present and powerful source is in Moscow, not in London or Paris. Even though we cannot now foresee how and when these peoples of Eastern Europe will again be free, it is our task to keep that hope alive without raising false notions of easy or military solutions.

Is there more that we can do than merely to express our sympathy? For one thing, I believe that advantage should be taken of every opportunity to re-establish ties with these peoples, who have long participated in and contributed to the general development of European civilization. Whenever the United States admits a "farm delegation" from the Soviet Union, we should also call for the sending of a delegation from each of the satellite states. When we discuss the exchanges of literary, historical and other cultural materials with the Soviet Union, we should take equally energetic steps to try to re-establish the channels of communication with the peoples in the satellite countries. We should, I believe, facilitate a revival of trade in peaceful goods between the European satellites and Western Europe. While this trade is bound to be smaller than before the war, it can help to keep alive numerous contacts between the people of these states and the people of the free world.

A special and vital issue in the cause of self-determination is that of Germany. Our efforts hitherto to achieve German unification have failed, yet we must continue, with the Federal Republic and our European friends, to press for free elections so that the Germans can decide their own future. Here again this is a step not exclusively in the interests of one country, Germany, but advisable and necessary for the future stability of Europe. As long as Germany is divided and under threat of Communist domination, all Europe and the world will be kept on tenterhooks. It is inevitable that one day Germany will be reunited, and meanwhile contacts between the people of West and East Germany should be encouraged.

Military considerations have played an important role in Soviet resistance to a solution of the problem of German reunification. There is evidence that the Soviet Union, propaganda effects aside, has no present intention of giving up its position in East Germany. If the Soviets were prepared to permit German reunification, a resolution of the military question would have to include two guarantees: a guarantee of the freedom and independence of the German people and of the other free peoples of Western Europe against Soviet aggression and a guarantee to Soviet Russia against German expansion to the East. The NATO community, including the Federal Republic of Germany, should be prepared in future, as it has been in the past, to make such a commitment to the Soviet Union.

Certain pledges would have to be given by the German people. The maintenance of Soviet control over Eastern Europe is assisted by the fear of the Poles and Czechs of losing their present boundaries in the west. The free people of the German Federal Republic may have to consider the desirability of renouncing claims to some former German-held territory as a step to reunification of East and West Germany. The understandable desire of the Germans to recover the territories placed under Polish provisional administration in 1945 makes it all but impossible for people in Poland, regardless of their attitude toward the Communist regime in Poland, to support wholeheartedly cooperation with the West. The people of the Federal Republic have already demonstrated their ability to re-establish a healthy national life within their present more limited boundaries.

It might be political wisdom to make it clear that Poland and Czechoslovakia, if they achieved independence, need not fear a reunited Germany. This is a decision which only the German people can make. A Poland and a Czechoslovakia, reassured concerning their territorial status as independent states, would be more difficult for the Soviet rulers to dominate. The Communist rulers of those countries would no longer be in a position to pose as defenders of the national-territorial interest. The line between the ruling Communist group and the majority of the people would be sharpened.

I say this without condoning in the least the provisional territorial decision which was made at Potsdam. The problem, however, is to achieve the maximum freedom for peoples everywhere. A united Germany and a free Poland could become partners within a united Europe. Within a united Europe boundaries and old animosities would lose their ancient divisive significance, and all Europeans would have a chance for a better life.

Uncommitted Nations and Colonial Areas

There is need for a new perspective on our relations with the so-called uncommitted areas in Asia and Africa where there exists great misunderstanding and mistrust of our country and of our European friends. We must, to begin with, clarify our own ideas and then adhere to policies which we believe to be right.

We must strive for a community of understanding and effort with the uncommitted nations. In the past we have taken little time and made small effort to understand the people, religion, philosophies, policies and objectives of the East. The population statistics alone of the Eastern countries are compelling reasons to enlarge our knowledge and interest: India, Pakistan and Burma, 460 million; Indonesia, 80 million; Africa to the Cape of Good Hope, 200 million; and China, which is now dominated by the Communist ideology, about 500 million. It is clearly a matter of great moment to us and to the world which direction these peoples will take in the second part of the twentieth century.

The war in Korea, the controversy over our China policy,

Mr. Nehru's criticisms of the United States and many other factors have made it difficult for Americans to take a dispassionate view of the East. It is not easy for us to listen to criticism from peoples whose independence we stimulated and maintained by many actions throughout our history, not excluding the stand we took in Asia against aggression in Korea. We find it difficult to understand governments and peoples who so vociferously declare their passion for independence, yet studiously insist on being "objective" in regard to Soviet aggression and domination of non-Russian peoples.

I doubt, however, that our aid and other positive actions should be expected to gain military allies in the East. We should accept the prospect that the vast area stretching from the China Sea around the crescent of Southeast Asia, South Asia, the Near East and North Africa, is likely to remain neutral or uncommitted except in self-defense against a direct military threat from the Soviet Union or Communist China. As the depolarization of power continues—as I believe it will—the uncommitted nations are likely to be strengthened in their belief that they do not have to come under close protection of the United States in order to survive. Whatever the United States does or wants, a policy of diplomatic neutrality is likely to remain a popular concept among these peoples.

We must also face the fact that the neutral and semi-independent nations are likely to try to play off the United States and the Soviet Union and Communist China in an effort to achieve maximum political and economic advantage. Though this course may be short-sighted, we should recognize that such attitudes are not inherently inimical to the objectives of the United States. The fact that these nations have or are likely to have diplomatic relations with the Soviet Union, and will do business with it, will not necessarily harm the United States. In any event, it may do little good to continue to warn these nations against Communist penetration. Our major effort among these nations must rather be to do the things we feel should be done regardless of the Soviet Union. With our great resources, our political strength based on the ideals of freedom—which I think these people share—we can win in the competition if we focus on constructive political and economic solutions rather than on propaganda. I have confidence that the Soviet attempt to marshal the Islamic, Hindu and Buddhist peoples against Europe and the United States will fail if we are consistent with our own ideals and if we work to fulfill them. Unlike the Soviet Union we are not seeking to exploit Asia and Africa for purposes of control, power or ideological domination.

A larger moral interest, as well as physical security, is served if India, Burma, Indonesia and the other peoples in the East wish to maintain their own freedom and develop the political, economic and social structures that will help them do it. The objective is not that these nations should be committed to us, but that they and we should both be committed to the same goals of peace and freedom. If they commit themselves to these objectives, the Soviet, not we, will suffer a defeat.

As for areas which are not yet self-governing, the American repugnance to seeing peoples governed by force, against their will remains just as strong as ever. Where peoples still live under simple community organizations and are not yet conscious of larger national unities, our natural tendency is to leave well enough alone. But while we have often taken the side of the colonial powers, who are also our allies in Europe, we are not happy when this puts us into conflict with peoples who have become aware of their own power and national identity and are determined to govern their own future. Sometimes we have tried to take both sides of the issue, with consequent loss of friendship everywhere.

We must always remember, however, that the peoples of Asia and Africa, whether self-governing or not, have not had our good fortune. They are still struggling for minimum standards of economic development. They are still seeking fuller liberty and independence. Nevertheless, though the Indian peasant and the Iowa farmer are separated by enormous differences of conditions, objectives, needs and wants, they have a common bond: the desire for a decent life. Our actions in future must demonstrate that we ask nothing from these peoples, that we genuinely desire their own free progress to a higher standard of living. We must show that we understand and respect their cultural individualities.

It is natural for Americans to sympathize with peoples who have achieved or are striving to achieve effective control of their own political destinies. This does not mean that we can go about giving gratuitous and often resented advice. It does mean that we can do far more, directly and through the United Nations, to help the ambitious peoples of Asia to acquire from the free world those bodies of administrative, technical and economic experience which will help them in making their independence strong and genuine. New administrative functions of government arise wherever people assert control over their own national lives. Much more can be done, too, in assisting in the creation of educational systems to meet the actual needs of the people and to help them to make their lives richer and more productive.

The Middle East

Perhaps a few words on the Middle East will not be out of place, especially since our group at the Council on Foreign Relations was unable to give as much study as it wished to the problems of that area. In the first part of 1956 I had occasion to visit the Middle East and to talk with many of the political and economic leaders of the Arab states. While my impressions on the tour were so rapid and so kaleidoscopic that no conviction as to a clear and definite line of action emerged, I did find that the diplomatic representatives of the United States in these countries are alert to the dangers prevalent in the region. They are deeply concerned, and they are striving to protect the interests of the United States and to contribute, within their power, to the welfare of the Middle East peoples and to the maintenance of peace.

My visit, however, reinforced my view that the Middle East today is of such political and economic importance that it is imperative for the American people to increase their knowledge of an area, which for centuries was the link between the East and the West. Here are found old paths along which conquerors rode, old routes along which caravans and trade flowed, old sites of flourishing civilizations. If the development of other lines of communication served to make the Middle East something of a bypath, this part of the world has recently gained new significance from oil, and oil in such quantities that it almost dwarfs the other known sources of supply. The realization of the extent of these reserves of power comes at a time when Western Europe and the British Isles are increasingly dependent upon the continuous flow of oil from the Middle East. More and more the basic industries of Europe and Britain rely upon Mid-East oil as the source of power for their future economic expansion. Even though a new age of atomic power may be dawning, it is apparent that for the immediate future, and indeed even after the coming of the so-called atomic age, oil is going to be of supreme significance to the future of Europe and the British Isles.

One of the consequences of the dependence upon the oil of the Middle East is that royalties exceeding the mythical wealth of Araby are pouring into the hands of people and nations as yet unprepared for their most efficient or wise use. This has produced a revolution or rather an explosion in the desert. Yet while this situation has been developing, we have seen the diminution of British and French political power in this section of the world, an influence and power long unquestioned.

The mere existence of a power vacuum creates many problems, but unrest in the Middle East is increased, of course, by the sharp antagonisms which have arisen as the result of the establishment of the Israeli State. Abandoned refugees, fierce passions and outright warfare have revived old and generated new hatreds. Extreme nationalism and anti-Western attitudes, stimulated by many indigenous problems, have also made the pot boil.

All this would not be so ominous were it not for another factor, and that is the penetration of the Soviet Union and its agents into the politics and into the life of the area. The bold and strong assertion of Soviet interests, with the follow-up of arms, propagandists, engineers, technicians, and the other tools of Soviet penetration, has created a very dangerous situation. Soviet blandishments here fall on fruitful territory. Old resentments and newly found freedoms, superimposed on poor economies, give considerable resonance to the promises of the Soviets. One might suppose that the Arab peoples would be particularly wary of the interposition of any new power complexes in the area, having so recently seen the diminution of old ones. The urge, however, to find short-cuts, to improve living standards, to achieve industrialization and economic progress is great, and in the midst of these preoccupations the political dangers of Soviet penetration are apt to be overlooked.

This set of events in the Middle East—the tremendous flow of oil, the diminution of Western European prestige, the Arab-Israel conflict, and the exploitation of the situation by the Communists—can lead to disastrous results. To avoid them certain things appear necessary. The British and ourselves must adopt a definite and integrated policy in respect of the Middle East. There are those on both sides of the Atlantic who feel that we should go our separate ways, but the consequences of such a divergence of policy seem to me to be too obvious to require comment. Our combined policy should be one with which the Arab states can advance their political and economic growth. At the same time that policy must take into account the enormous contribution and investment which the Western powers have made in the area and in whose benefits these states have shared and will continue to share. With the new power resources of the area and the stimulus which Western investments have given, there is today, for the first time in centuries, an opportunity for the improved economic conditions and living standards that the Middle East so badly needs. It is in the interest both of the Arab countries and of the West that this part of the world be peaceful and stable economically.

There is little hope that the Arab nations can achieve their aspirations if they do not have security against aggression or infiltration. Today the strength of the West provides this security. If they did not have this protection, the Arab states, after a turbulent assertion of extreme nationalism, might well find themselves facing a new Communist colonialism, oppressive, exploitative and permanent.

A central condition of peace in the Middle East is, of course, a settlement between the Arab nations and Israel. A combined British-American policy in the Middle and Near

East must serve not only to advance the political stability and economic growth of the Arab states but also to maintain the independence of Israel. The Arab states and Israel can and must live together. A firm, consistent British and American policy could help to bring about the end of hostilities and a rational compromise between the two. Notwithstanding the immense difficulties involved, I cannot consider a peaceful settlement of the Arab-Israel conflict to be beyond the capacities of British and American statesmanship.

Control of Armaments and the UN

It is a foregone conclusion that at present we must continue to develop our atomic strength. No policy which permits any considerable lag in development vis-a-vis the Soviet Union is likely to be permitted by the administration, Congress, or the public, nor would it be anything but dangerous to act on such a program. Whatever the dangers of an atomic race—and they are considerable—the alternative for the immediate future is even more hazardous for this country and for the free world. It is, therefore, axiomatic that in the present circumstances we are committed to giving a high priority to maintaining superiority in atomic weapons.

I do not believe, however, that the whole of our policy can be restricted to this commitment. Sooner or later some alternative to the race for armaments will have to be found. United States policy planning should devote utmost energy to devising such a break-through. Our willingness to call off the armaments race if a bona-fide plan for control and reduction can be found should constantly be emphasized, and our search, on both the technological and the political front, for such plans as are likely to be considered by the Soviet Union should be at least as vigorous as our development of strength.

In other words, breaking the atomic deadlock ought to be a major policy objective. The initiative we can develop lies in the field of peace rather than in preparation for war. Nor should the search, I must emphasize, be confined to the atomic field. In fact, reduction of conventional armaments will have to accompany, or perhaps precede, atomic reduction, control, or prohibition. Plans which promise success in this field should be carefully explored.

In my view we must be ready to consider the most far-reaching proposals, including those for total disarmament—universal, enforceable and complete with international control and inspection. Although in the past such plans for peace through disarmament have seemed to some unrealistic and unobtainable, our present perspective encourages a serious study of these and related proposals.

In line with a consideration of the problem of disarmaments, I should like to see renewed attention given to the United Nations and the part it can play in bringing about a more peaceful situation. Considerably more can be done to strengthen it as a center for discussion of differences and conciliation of disputes. It offers, after all, the only established meeting ground for representatives of peoples from all continents. No better international instrument exists for the peaceful resolution of tensions. In our foreign policy we can give recognition to its importance to our objectives, both by direct support and by greater use of it as an agency and channel for our foreign programs.

Economic and technical assistance channeled through the United Nations is generally more acceptable than direct aid from individual countries. Direct aid arouses suspicions. Assistance through the United Nations would demonstrate to the receiving nations that the United States has no purpose other than the raising of economic and social standards. Such action on the part of the United States and of Britain, Germany and other industrial nations might work to eliminate rivalries among themselves and make a more profound impact on the peoples receiving aid.

There is another aspect of aid to underdeveloped countries that should be kept in the forefront. Aid to individual countries, without consideration for the needs of neighboring nations, may create dislocations and jealousies. This can be partially avoided by extending assistance with a regard to the needs of an entire region. The cooperation of the European nations in the O.E.E.C., which developed a combined program for Marshall Plan assistance to Europe, provides an example to follow. In the future, through United Nations agencies, it would be desirable if the governments of Southeast Asia, the Middle East and the Near East, developed regional programs to meet their needs. Such an approach would help to create understanding among the nations concerned for the needs of their neighbors. It would serve to develop a community outlook.

Image of Ourselves

Popular images which nations have of themselves and of one another are notoriously superficial. Foreign policy cannot be based on such clichés, though there is sad and plentiful experience to suggest that governmental officials seem to embrace views which are on an only slightly higher level of information. To be effective a foreign policy must be based on the best understanding of other nations that can be obtained. In addition, a nation must have a clear understanding of what others think of it, and take this image into account. Finally, a foreign policy must be based on the highest degree of self-understanding that is possible. This is no easy task. Self-understanding is even more difficult for nations than it is for individuals. Historians have no difficulty in finding examples of nations which did not understand themselves, which did not know what they were, what they could do, or what the times required of them.

The image which we Americans have of ourselves, and which others have of us, is therefore a powerful factor in the common affairs of mankind today. In this connection I should like to cite an example which seems to me to be pertinent:

We commonly think of the Soviet Union as the revolutionary force in the world today. In doing so we run the risk of allowing the Soviets to pre-empt the role of the symbol and inspiration for constructive change in the conditions of hundreds of millions of people throughout the world. We have forgotten, or we fail to remind others, that less than two centuries ago the American people helped to ignite a great revolution which is still sweeping over the earth. The blazing idea of this revolution is that governments derive their just powers from the consent of the governed. We have had hardship and tragedy on our way. But nowhere in the world has a people faced and come up so adequately with answers to such problems as ordered society, peaceful change, freedom of expression, constitutional protection of citizens against privileges of the few. Throughout our history the decision has consistently been against tyranny. Ours has been a remarkable achievement in advancing individual dignity and in providing decency for the average man. The story of the choices we have made should give us renewed strength and provide bearings for others who are in the midst of, or who are just emerging from, their own revolution and who have similar choices to make. This is the world revolution with which we should be associated and which we should be proud to sponsor. The Communist movement is actually a counter-revolution which has stolen the language of democracy and perverted its ends to project a society which would scrap the heritage of liberalism.

Our achievements cannot conceal the fact that there are many shortcomings in this country and that our open society parades these shortcomings to the rest of the world. There is no way to hide them and no reason to do so. Our reply to others is that we recognize them and that we are trying to overcome them. We have problems of race relations, slums, intolerance. We are not the perfect society. But the gradual, consistent, positive solutions to our problems, arrived at in a society constantly expanding its freedoms for all, is a powerful example, and the determination to continue to improve our own society will have its effect throughout the world. It is essential that our domestic affairs be so ordered as to give the world a picture of a free, tolerant, progressive society which practices what it recommends. Thucydides quotes Pericles as saying: "For I am more afraid of our own mistakes than of the enemy's designs."

It is important to keep before us the fact that the basic, long-range aspirations and policies of the American people are directed toward aims which we share with a vast majority of mankind. These aims are well stated in the Preamble and Articles One and Two of the United Nations Charter. That these are widely shared is demonstrated not only by what representatives do and say in one international forum after another, but also by the vast cooperative effort now under way to get at a long list of specific jobs ranging from malaria control to safety in the air and at sea. An empirical examination of what people are doing will disclose common ideas and common interests in a multitude of practical actions.

We are among the prime movers in this joint endeavor. Our friends abroad must learn to distinguish what we do from much of what we say to each other here at home while we are doing it. We are a turbulent and sprawling democracy; our power hooks loudspeakers to what we say and it is heard around the globe. Our policy, since the days of isolation, requires action, and a democracy is mobilized for action through debate, some of it harsh debate. We roar at each other, and the roaring sometimes frightens our friends and encourages our enemies. It can detract, in the eyes of others, from the essential quality and purpose of our policy. It leads to superficial rather than to serious discussion of foreign policy here at home. It deprives us of subtlety and flexibility. But the significant fact is that the policy which emerges is generally a policy good for ourselves and for the peoples of the world.

As we go forward we must not be afraid of the Communists, though we must always be alert to their subterranean motives and actions. We should encourage rather than discourage contacts with the Soviet Union and with the satellite states. We must not allow the question to arise: "Whose Iron Curtain?" For ten years Churchill's magnificent figure of speech has been a weapon in the hands of the West. Now that the Soviets appear to recognize the disadvantage of their own policy we should not allow our fears for our own internal security to block an exchange of persons, views and contacts with the Communists. We should encourage the establishment of relations between our libraries and universities and the libraries and universities within the Communist area and give a chance to the power of free ideas. The American public has good reason to guard against subversion, but we must not shrink from our own faith that free exchanges of ideas are our strength and that ultimately they will prevail. No people has yet voted voluntarily for the Communist way of life.

The United States has no designs on Communist Russia. Coexistence which is more than the present uneasy peace will depend, however, on the willingness of the Soviet leaders to recognize and act in accordance with the realities. If the men in the Kremlin want peace they will abandon their blind adherence to the dated Marxist concepts of the decadence of Western industrial society; they will abandon their ambitions of Communist world rule.

The Soviet leaders are not going to be successful where Alexander and Hitler failed. The free peoples will not permit domination by a system in which the law of the jungle prevails. By Khrushchev's own admission, one man in the Kremlin was in a position so to terrorize his immediate associates that from one day to the next they were not certain of their own lives. Even though the apotheosis of Stalin has now arbitrarily turned into his damnation, the darkly unpredictable nature of the Communist regime must keep the free peoples on the alert.

Opposed to this opaque method of government, we have the great, compelling and open idea—freedom. With freedom we have the preponderance of moral and physical power on our side. And we also have the economic and the military might to keep people who are presently free from being subjugated by the Communist powers.

The primary tests by which we shall be judged will include the following:

1) Whether or not we are using our military power exclusively to protect and defend and not to provoke or threaten; whether our power is shielding regimes accepted by the bulk of mankind as legitimate and indigenous;

2) Whether or not we are genuinely willing to reduce our military power once appropriate control and inspection safeguards are assured;

3) Whether or not we are willing to employ our economic resources and direct our economic policies so as to help the free peoples and those who want to be free to make steady progress toward material well being;

4) Whether or not we are prepared to act steadfastly as a member of a community of peoples.

A heavy and unavoidable obligation rests on the leaders of our government and of our parties to clarify American foreign policy. The central fact of that policy is inescapable. America's safety and freedom cannot be assured unless we act in community with all nations which are working toward greater freedom.

In the next decade, the great opportunity and the great need is to communicate to peoples throughout the world our sense of partnership in the liberal revolution which began two hundred years ago.

AUTHOR'S NOTE

WHILE this book, as it now stands, is in large part the outcome of my own reflections, it had its origins in, and is based upon, the discussions of a study group at the Council on Foreign Relations during the years 1953–1955, a group which met under the chairmanship of Mr. John J. McCloy. In the early stages my task as director of a research staff was to organize the preparation of papers for the members' consideration. Subsequently the research staff worked closely with a number of sub-committees which addressed themselves to the principal topics making up the substance of this book. After the findings were assembled and discussed, I undertook, in the spring of 1955, to write a comprehensive draft report, developing and interpreting the conclusions which, in my judgment, had emerged from the preceding discussions. Toward the end of the summer the study group reviewed and criticized the draft in a two-day conference. I then revised the report and prepared it for publication.

A study of this kind does not fully correspond to the ideas of any one person, though I, as the responsible author, have not written anything to which I could not subscribe in good conscience. While I believe that each of the conclusions reached would be favored by the majority of the participants, but not by all, it was not the purpose of the study group to render a collective judgment. In particular, the organization of the material into a single body of observations and recommendations is my own responsibility. The use of "we" in the text is purely editorial. I should add that the Council on Foreign Relations, which sponsored the project, and the Ford Foundation, which provided the financial support, have no responsibility for the opinions and conclusions here expressed.

I owe a great debt to the chairman and to the members of the group, with whom I had the good fortune to be associated in these two years. The following participated in most of the discussions: Frank Altschul, Hamilton Fish Armstrong,

Chester Bowles, Arthur H. Dean, William Diebold, Jr., Ferdinand Eberstadt, Merle Fainsod, William T. R. Fox, George S. Franklin, Jr., W. Averell Harriman, Howard C. Johnson, Devereux C. Josephs, Milton Katz, Mervin J. Kelly, William L. Langer, Walter H. Mallory, Philip E. Mosely, Geroid T. Robinson, John D. Rockefeller, 3rd, Dean Rusk, Charles M. Spofford, Shepard Stone, Jacob Viner, and Henry M. Wriston. These members would, I know, join me in thanking those who participated more briefly or in individual meetings of the group or its sub-committees: Abram Bergson, McGeorge Bundy, Herbert Feis, Gregory Grossman, Kenneth Hanson, J. Robert Oppenheimer, Lucian Pye, Walt W. Rostow, Frank Trager, and Phillips Talbot.

The group is deeply obligated to observers from various branches of the Government: Robert Amory, Jr., Brigadier General C. H. Bonesteel, 3rd, Robert R. Bowie, and General L. L. Lemnitzer. This report, however, is in no way a statement of the views of these observers or of the United States Government.

I have an especially intimate obligation to my associates on the research staff, for their cooperation in preparing the materials, for their important contribution in ideas and methods of analysis, and for their very good companionship: Marina Salvin Finkelstein, Perry Laukhuff, Gerhart Niemeyer, A. David Redding, Donald Urquidi, and Paul E. Zinner.

HENRY L. ROBERTS

CONTENTS

Foreword, by John J. McCloy vii
Author's Note xxxiii

INTRODUCTION 1

PART ONE

THE NATURE OF THE PROBLEM

I. THE ATOM AND COMMUNIST TOTALITARIANISM 9
The Atom 10
Communist Totalitarianism 18
Some Continuing Problems 29

II. STRENGTHS AND VULNERABILITIES 37
The Application of Maximum Physical Power 38
Power for Securing Limited Territorial or Other Material Advantages 46
The Tactical Use of Nuclear Weapons 51
Guerrilla and Irregular Warfare 52
Future Economic Prospects 53
Political Warfare 56
Ideological Conformity 60
Revolutionary Zeal 61
Duplicity 63
The Communist Party 64
A Controlled Society 65
Soviet Vulnerabilities 66
The Balance 71
Annex: Note on Prospects for Soviet Economic Growth 74

PART TWO

AMERICAN POLICY REQUIREMENTS

III. MINIMUM REQUIREMENTS 79

IV. DEFENSE POLICY AND ARMS CONTROL 91
Control of Arms 101

V. ALLIES AND NEUTRALS 112
Neutral and Uncommitted Nations 124

VI. ECONOMIC POLICY: THE PROBLEM OF GROWTH 128
The Expansion of the United States Economy 128
Foreign Economic Policy 135
Reduction of Trade Restrictions 142
Trade with the Soviet Bloc 143

VII. SOCIAL POLICY: THE PROBLEM OF MODERNIZATION AND REFORM 146

PART THREE

AREAS OF CONFLICT

VIII. DIRECT RELATIONS: THE PROBLEM OF POSITIVE OBJECTIVES 159

IX. GERMANY 174
A Divided Germany 178
Efforts at Reunification 180
Reunification without Alliance 182
Forward Pressure 186
Requirements for a German Policy 188

X. THE EASTERN EUROPEAN SATELLITES 195
Acquiescence in the Status Quo 198
A Policy of the Free Hand 201
Pressures Short of War 203
A Note on Yugoslavia 207

XI. COMMUNIST CHINA AND ASIAN SECURITY 212
Communism in China 212
Asian Defense and Construction 220
Policy toward Communist China 232

XII. THE OUTLOOK 240

INTRODUCTION

THIS report rests upon faith in the democratic process as a means of meeting the complex problems which confront the United States in the mid-twentieth century. We take it that foreign policy is a part of democratic politics, a continuing play of debate and consensus, of divergent interest and common cause. Foreign policy is not outside politics, nor should it be. Although we frequently meet complaints that the delicate work of the statesman or diplomat is made more difficult by the clamor of politics—as indeed it is—we should guard against the view that the statesmen of other times and other regimes were better able to pursue rational policies. A royal master, with his whims and courtiers; an oligarchy, with massive protected interests; an entrenched bureaucracy, with departmental concerns and prejudices; a modern tyranny, with its irrational compulsions—these have proved at least equally disruptive, and certainly less responsive than voters and majorities to the correctives of time and discussion.

It is true, of course, that in its foreign policy the nation is supposed to be speaking as a whole to other nations. One can understand the plea that "politics should stop at the water's edge," that consensus rather than dissent should mark the formulation and execution of foreign policy, especially when this concerns cooperation with allies or a position toward an opponent. A deeply divided nation whose ability to determine a particular line of foreign policy depends upon narrow and uncertain majorities speaks with far less authority than one that can count on the support of the great body of the national community. Still, at any given time, this consensus must be hoped for rather than demanded. If the nation is in fact split on a major issue of its foreign policy, this issue must be aired. A prolonged suppression of divisions for the sake of demonstrating a solid front to the outside world could only backfire, and would ultimately undermine even the possibility of speaking as a united nation.

The fact remains, however, that the foreign policy of an American administration must command general support; hence the repeated appeals for "bipartisan" or "nonpartisan" cooperation. Accompanying these appeals is a strong impulse to seek compromises, to blunt the sharper issues, or to seek verbal formulas which can blur the differences. Unfortunately, this impulse, which is an essential lubricant to a harmonious society, may run counter to a real need for clarification, particularly in a time of rapid change and crisis.

It is doubtful whether we can find any wholly satisfactory resolution to this dilemma. It can be overcome only if a society enjoys an abiding unity regarding ends and the broadly appropriate means of achieving them. Without that unity two perilous paths are open: either the group, party or faction capable of marshalling some margin of superiority, in numbers or in will, seeks to enforce its views on the rest of the nation; or policy and policy commitments must be scaled down to a point where general agreement can be rediscovered. In periods of emergency either of these courses carries with it the threat of tyranny, civil strife or paralysis.

While the possibility of these extreme cases, which illustrate the old truth that any form of human organization contains its own potential forms of self-destruction, should not be disregarded even in our own society, we seem to have little occasion for despair in this regard. On the basis of our experience in recent trying decades, the United States does appear to possess that basic unity which is prerequisite to a positive and democratically arrived at foreign policy. At times this unity is strained, at others it lacks adequate means of expression. Problems shift, and real issues often are debated in terms of earlier arguments now become unreal.

A primary concern of the present report is to find the more fruitful lines of discussion, to define and examine what seem to be the major issues, with the final purpose of promoting through such discussion and definition an informed and positive consensus concerning policies to be followed. It is, of course, the duty of democratic political leadership to present to the public, from its vantage point of responsibility and information, the content and import of foreign policy issues as it best understands them. Without such leadership the nation will falter. But it is also the duty of the public to participate in the process of policy formulation.

The political scene in the United States is something far more complex than the act of voting periodically for one of the two major parties, or even than the sum of arrangements, maneuvers and compromises of the legislative program or harmonizing the work of the executive, legislative and judiciary branches of the government. Intimately associated with the whole process is the activity of private groups and organizations. Broadly speaking the function of these groups is to get a particular point across: to feed it into the machinery of public discussion and political decision and press for its successful adoption. A multitude of interests are constantly involved. The actions may, of course, seek the personal advantage of their proponents, or they may aim at measures deemed necessary to the public welfare. This multitude of shifting, contending, articulate foci of opinion and concern undoubtedly provides much of the dynamism and vigor of our democratic form of government. The United States has shown a genius for voluntary association, and, while the individual stands taken are at times one-sided or downright erroneous, in their totality they are indispensable to the life of a healthy democracy of the continental size and complexity of the United States.

It is an unwarranted presumption for any citizen, or group of citizens, to make the claim of standing above politics, as wholly detached observers. The present report, therefore, is a part of the political process and should be recognized as such. Put most simply, this report is a communication concerning Soviet-American relations, derived from the discussions of one group of citizens, a study group, and addressed to another group of citizens, the readers.

We start from the belief that the general lines of American foreign policy, as they have evolved in the past and as they are now, are representative of the American people, its thought and aspirations. The changes in our foreign policy, sometimes quite sharp and abrupt, correspond, in the main, to those movements of American opinion when it is adapting its fairly stable basic concepts to the demands of new situations.

But while we affirm the representative quality of American foreign policy we do not thereby leap to the conclusion that it has been right on all occasions or that it is necessarily adequate today. One may say that a policy is good because it reflects the wishes of the people, or one may say that it is good because it corresponds to the demands of the situation, including, among other things, a regard for the interests of other peoples and a correct assessment of the intentions and capabilities of an aggressive power. These two statements may be synonymous or they may be antithetical. One may not be speaking of the same thing. For example, we may defend Neville Chamberlain's appeasement policy or American neutrality as accurate expressions of a prevailing mood of the 1930's, and yet criticize their utter inadequacy in meeting the menace of Hitler. Any successful policy, in a democracy, must come to terms with both these requirements, which together determine that elusive entity we call the national interest.

Policy, then, must also be examined and criticized in light of its foreseeable or probable consequences; the various other possible courses of action must be weighed; and, if some alternative course seems preferable, the reasons for that preference must be set forth and defended. This may lead to rejection of certain existing policies and to advocacy of policies concerning which public opinion may currently be thought to be apathetic or even hostile. Such advocacy should not be made irresponsibly and must always recognize that it is a part of the political process—one voice among many in the continuing act of forming and re-forming the national opinion.

How are we to reconcile these two sets of requirements: to harmonize actions, which we consider called for by our external relations, with public opinion, which may or may not be inclined to support such actions? Ultimately it is a matter of persuasion; if the evidence is set before them, we may hope that people will, in time, recognize it and act accordingly. Yet this necessary article of democratic faith should not lead us to underestimate the difficulties of its application. Innumerable perfectly "reasonable" programs, for which the term utopian is most appropriate, have been rejected or simply ignored, because they could not pass the test of political acceptability. At any given moment there are limits to the foreign policies a democracy may follow, and a policy proposal which exceeds those limits is little more than an intellectual exercise. In general these limits are determined by the extent to which actions in the area of foreign policy can make a reasonably concrete appeal to people's moral, rational and material concerns.

As the outcome of the discussions over two years of a number of people of varying background, outlook and party affiliation, the present report has been concerned from the outset with the question of consensus, of finding interpretations and policies that gain acceptance and of eliminating those which fail to appeal. We cannot claim that all views on all matters were presented, and the reader may find (as did individual members of the group) a number of analyses and conclusions to which he may not subscribe, in whole or in part. But the important point here is that the report itself does represent a step in the process of finding or creating a consensus, a process that must be continued in the larger public.

In this process certain things are lost: the statements lose the drama and vigor of personal advocacy; they may lack the penetrating vision of the single thinker. In compensation, we can offer a body of views and conclusions which has been extensively discussed and criticized and which reflects the method by which opinion comes to bear on problems of foreign policy. These views and conclusions may also help in identifying the limits of United States policy regarding the Soviet Union and give strength and stability to those actions that are both salutary and possible.

Part One

THE NATURE OF THE PROBLEM

CHAPTER I
THE ATOM AND COMMUNIST TOTALITARIANISM

THE WORLD would have problems enough even if those provided by the Soviet Union and the international Communist movement were to disappear entirely. An exclusive preoccupation with Soviet-American relations would seriously warp our foreign policy, which must deal with the interests, ambitions and needs of many nations, some of long-standing importance in the international scene, others newly come to independence. Still, having said this, we must admit that nearly all international issues have been affected by the emergence of Soviet Communist power. There is practically no part of the globe where our inquiry could not lead us, no major problem without some bearing on our subject. The boundaries we have adopted are often arbitrary and have been set for reasons of time and competence.

Even more difficult than to determine the limits of our subject is to describe its particular characteristics. Many of our present troubles with the U.S.S.R. would have been familiar to statesmen of earlier periods. Issues of war and peace, of power politics, of economic and social tensions, of ethnic and cultural friction: these are all hardy perennials, and a number of them have had much the same appearance for the last generation or two. Most will persist in one form or another as long as there are human societies.

We should, of course, beware of thinking that the identification of a problem as belonging to a familiar species is the same as solving it. The world's continuing problems are not "solved"; at best they are moderated, contained, circumvented or transformed. Nevertheless, it is a distinct gain to discover oneself on reasonably familiar ground, where the accumulated precepts and experiences of our history may find profitable application. For that reason an understandably strong impulse exists to seek recognizable patterns and analogies in our relations with the Soviet Union.

The most disquieting features of the present international situation, however, are novel and unfamiliar. Certain problems seem without adequate precedent; customary tools of analysis fail to measure them. The statesman finds it hard to play by ear because he cannot recall any appropriate tune.

Perhaps we can best start by plunging in at this most difficult point: see what really new elements we are dealing with and try to isolate and describe them. Without such an effort it is only too easy to pile up "background information" and historical antecedents which may be irrelevant and may even obscure rather than clarify the basic issues. We can begin by grappling with two terms that have come to symbolize the more disturbing aspects of the present international crisis, the "atom" and "totalitarianism." Neither is exclusively a monopoly of the Soviet Union. The first represents an international advance in science and technology, the second a political and social phenomenon of which Soviet Communism is but the most formidable and contagious example. Yet the fact that the Soviet Union possesses atomic power and is possessed by Communist totalitarianism expresses most starkly the singularly refractory and unprecedented nature of our tense relations with that regime.

The Atom

Ever since the explosion over Hiroshima the atomic (and more recently the thermonuclear) bomb has been the symbol of a new, strange and fearsome age. We are still trying, however, to grasp the nature of this novelty and its impact on its human creators. To be sure, the enormous multiplication of power, the "quantum leap" to a new order of magnitude of destruction, is something very real and comprehensible. One thermonuclear bomb can have several times the TNT equivalent of all the bombs dropped by the United States in the whole course of the Second World War. This tremendous power of destruction, when combined with existing, and presently forthcoming, methods of delivery, means that even the greatest nations can be reduced to a shambles in very short order, a reduction that may be mutual. For the first time man possesses the physical means to bring about the abrupt reduction of an entire society to a primitive and anarchic level.

This greatly increased destructiveness is said by some to have altered radically the cost-gain ratio in warfare, to have made war exorbitantly unprofitable, and hence to have eliminated war as a rational instrument of national policy. Such a conclusion could be accepted, however, only if there were a guarantee of *mutual* destruction, and this cannot be established as a lasting certainty, though we shall have to return to this point in more detail later. Moreover, it rests on the dubious premise that wars have been started as the outcome of cost-risk calculations. This may have been the case in some wars; it was not in others. We cannot assume that the advent of the atomic or thermonuclear bomb has fundamentally altered the conditions causing conflict between nations. The possibility remains of a collective decision to accept death rather than real or imagined servitude, dishonor or loss of status.

In addition to the magnitude of destruction, certain other characteristics of the new weapons (or more exactly, weapons systems, to include means of delivery and guidance) appear to be without precedent. The devastation they deal promises to be so highly automatic and impersonal that the prospective human victim feels reduced to meaninglessness, since he cannot even have the satisfaction of going down fighting. Although the popular notion of "push-button" warfare is a misleading simplification, this threatening reduction of the individual to a nullity can have a paralyzing effect upon the will, an effect we find, too, in totalitarianism.

A second feature is the "invisible" effects: death by radiation and the possibilities, as yet undetermined, of widespread gene mutation or sterilization. The possibility of a build-up of radioactivity has led a number of people to the view that, as Bertrand Russell said not long ago, "a war with hydrogen bombs is quite likely to put an end to the human race." Now, while there may be a question whether the literal eradication of mankind is within the range of the possible, the continuing rapid advances being made in the arts of scientific destruction prevent us from dismissing this possibility out of hand. In any event it warrants our attention as an extreme case.

In what sense does the possibility of extending obliteration from the individual, or even the society or the nation, to the whole of humanity make a difference? What new problems does it present to the statesman or citizen? Under this danger it is obviously necessary to try to persuade one's potential enemy of the need not to embark upon the course of universal suicide. But then any nation or community facing annihilation must always for its own sake attempt to dissuade its assailant from attacking. In the present situation the dissuasive arguments which can be advanced may be more telling in convincing the potential assailant that his own existence is also at stake, but the question remains whether the dissuasion will be successful or not. The consequences, if it should not, must be faced. Can the statesman or citizen admit that rather than fight a nuclear war his national cause should succumb, if need be, to some other order, more particularly to a totalitarian order? It would seem that the problem of reaching a decision here is essentially the same as any life-or-death decision which societies have been called upon to make. If the question is put purely in terms of the biological continuation of the human species—that this is the ultimate and overriding requirement, above all considerations of social values and community or national survival—one discovers that it cannot be given an answer that provides the statesman or citizen with any guidance in his capacity as statesman or citizen. To affirm, without any qualification, that the human race must go on is to accept, if it proved to be necessary for the race's survival, the obliteration of one's own nation, community, family or self. The human individual can make such an affirmation for himself. The statesman or citizen cannot, at least not without denying the state he is serving or the society of which he is a member. As a political act it would mean an absolute, unconditional surrender. This not only would be the last political act but would of course make nonsense of all policy, since the opponent, if he so willed, could safely impale all proposals, negotiations or bluffs on this ultimate renunciation.

Rather than pursue our inquiry along these lines, which carry us beyond the realm of politics, it is probably wiser to limit ourselves to examining the challenge of the atom to that particular complex of political and social institutions, practices, and sciences which produced it: modern Western civilization. Considered thus, while not presenting the human individual with an unprecedented problem, it still poses quite new strategic, political and organizational problems. By so defining the atom's novelty we do not reduce its significance but try rather to look at it apart from its apocalyptic associations, though we must recognize that the way it is regarded by many people is itself a political fact of no little importance.

In the military field the "pure" rules of strategy may not have been overthrown, but actual military planning and organization, concerned with such things as balance of forces, the employment of space, manpower requirements, etc., have been subject to a real revolution. Habits of military thought based on previous wars of our experience may prove seriously misleading; familiar phrases, such as dispersal or concentration of firepower, take on entirely new meanings.

Similarly, in the field of international politics, a "pure" theory of power, if such there be, might be unchanged, but traditional power politics—usages and principles regarding balances, buffers, alliances, pressure, etc.—have lost the familiar meanings they enjoyed over several centuries. For an example, and we shall find many in later pages, it is difficult to know what constitutes a "balance of power" among powers in ample possession of thermonuclear bombs. How does one define, much less "shift" or "restore," such a balance?

Or again, in the field of economics, what, in the light of the new weapons, is the bearing of economic strength upon military strength? What does it mean to measure the industrial potential of a country if that potential can be wiped out overnight? Answers can be given to these questions, we believe, but they are certainly not the same answers that were arrived at in the past.

An individual may not realize, until confronted with such a challenge, the extent to which his thoughts and actions in practical affairs are habitual, conditioned from the ground up by the institutional forms and practices within which he has worked. The major test we face today is whether we as a nation are capable, at this level of institutional and practical thinking, of adjusting and adapting ourselves to the atomic age. If our thinking, our strategy and our institutions fail to absorb this enormous novelty, the whole structure of Western society may collapse.

To try to grasp the challenge at what we can call the operating level we might briefly sketch some of the facts and prospects of atomic power, leaving a more detailed consideration of them to the next chapter. A 20-megaton [1] bomb—which does not represent the upper limit—is capable of damaging all structures within a radius of fifteen miles of ground zero, and, under certain conditions, of releasing a radiation "fall out" which could seriously threaten life in an elliptical area of about 7,000 square miles. Atomic and thermonuclear bombs can range in explosive power from such multi-megaton weapons to "tactical" bombs of a few kilotons, capable of being used by ground and naval forces. The bombs do not deteriorate or become obsolete and may easily be concealed from inspection. Both the United States and the Soviet Union are, or shortly will be, in plentiful possession of this whole range of weapons. Though the American stockpile is estimated to be considerably larger, this becomes of decreasing importance as the Soviet stockpile grows and as the arms race increasingly centers on the means of delivery and defense. The means of delivery are becoming extremely varied: aircraft, artillery, land-based antiaircraft, surface and subsurface vessels, and—within the next few years—intercontinental ballistic missiles. While the atomic activities of nations other than the United States, the Soviet Union and Great Britain are limited currently, and perhaps for some time to come, to nonmilitary projects, it is likely that an increasing number of nations will be capable of developing, in greater or lesser degree, an atomic military force.

From this résumé of present and promised features of the atomic age it is evident that the major practical problems

[1] In expressing the power of the thermonuclear weapons, a megaton is equivalent to 1,000,000 tons of TNT, a kiloton to 1,000 tons of TNT.

which they raise relate to the employment, modulation and control of power in the realms of politics and war. No matter how one defines political or military power—and the term "power" has been notoriously confusing—there is no question that the advent of atomic weapons has complicated things enormously. Underlying any debate concerning the development of the thermonuclear bomb, the strategy of "massive retaliation" and the "tactical use of atomic weapons" are conflicting sets of propositions, one supporting and one opposing further military thermonuclear development. They may be summarized as follows.

Against emphasizing further military thermonuclear development:

1. The competitive race among states for the development of thermonuclear weapons, and their means of delivery, can only lead, if the weapons so developed are employed without restraint, to the mutual destruction of the states themselves. The completeness of the destruction will mount steadily with the passage of time. The avoidance of total destruction will no longer rest on limited capabilities but only on intentions and discretion with respect to the use of the weapons.

2. Quite apart from the unfriendly intentions of Soviet Communism and the possibility that at some time in the future someone with a nihilistic bent may gain power in some country—it would take only one such person—the arms race itself is not productive of good intentions.

3. As for discretion in the use of weapons, the integration of tactical atomic weapons into the armed forces of the nations means that it is increasingly probable that they will be employed in any future war. This will be especially the case when both sides have a full range of weapons and each must make its strategic and political plans on the assumption that the other may use them.

4. Once the atomic weapons are employed, their limitation to "tactical" use—in theory not an impossibility—becomes highly problematic, either because the strictly military requirements in a battle may argue for an extension of the area and intensity of atomic strikes, or because of emotional demands for ever greater retaliation. At the very least we cer-

tainly cannot state in advance that the use of atomic weapons *can* be limited; we do not know.

5. From this the conclusion would follow that the mutually determined pattern the United States and the Soviet Union are following promises to be, in time, utterly disastrous, and any stalemate a most precarious and fragile one, likely to break down at some time or other. We cannot afford even one such breakdown. The continued development of atomic weaponry only carries us further along this path and should be checked. In so far as the bombs are in existence, they should be used only in response to a strategic atomic assault upon us. The use and development of power for other purposes should be along different lines.

For continued emphasis on thermonuclear and associated developments:

1. If the other side gets ahead in this competitive race, the party lagging behind will be at a fatal disadvantage, since it will face defeat either through military action or through the threat thereof. Hence it is imperative that we develop as fast and as far as we can. Outpacing the opponent is the only way to give us a chance of surviving, since the opponent may not use the weapons against us if he knows we can retaliate effectively. A stalemate, in which each side has and knows the other to have full capabilities, may be more stable than one where the capabilities are limited or in doubt.

2. As far as intentions are concerned, we cannot afford to assume, for this purpose, any but potentially hostile ones. Even if the Soviet intentions of the moment appear good, the line may switch abruptly. The development of thermonuclear arms is necessary precisely because we cannot afford to count on intentions to prevent an outbreak of hostilities.

3. The tremendous technological advances of recent years have made possible the construction of increasingly powerful weapons. Ours must be no less efficient than our opponent's. Because to develop such weapons takes time we obviously cannot afford to follow his lead. Moreover, these technological innovations are extremely costly. It would be impossibly expensive if we were to try to keep advancing on this very broad scientific and technological front without making a

selection, on the basis of comparative military effectiveness, of the items to be developed.

4. As far as limiting war is concerned, that depends upon our opponent. He can start a war, he can expand it and, if he is willing to swallow his losses, he can limit it. We cannot control his decision, but we must be able to meet successfully whatever he tries. If we tie our hands (either through failing to develop the appropriate weapons or through deciding in advance not to use them) in order to limit the conflict, we should only succeed in losing it. Granted that a limited war might get out of hand, it can be argued that knowledge on all sides of the ultimate consequences of spreading the conflict—thermonuclear retaliation on their homelands—is as great a deterrent as there can be. In any event we cannot prevent the opponent from expanding a local war into a global war if he is willing to pay the price.

5. From this the conclusion would follow that in face of a powerful and determined opponent we have no choice but to build up our own strength in the most effective directions. To be prepared to fight only with weapons or methods more antiquated [2] than those which are available to the opponent (and we cannot be sure in advance whether in fact he will or will not develop or use them) would seem to insure our defeat.

The arguments on both sides of this debate appear valid, but they fail to meet since they are based on essentially different points of view. The first tries to judge the situation from *outside* the conflict, the second from *within* it. This explains in good part why the weight of events has largely favored the second line of arguments. In our capacity as statesmen, military leaders or citizens, we inevitably act and decide inside the framework of that conflict, and within that framework the steps which have been taken and which seem to be in train appear absolutely necessary. It should be noted, however, that this does not dispose of the problems raised by the first line of argument; we are certainly faced with the dangers suggested.

[2] This does not mean that atomic weapons are necessarily the most effective militarily in all cases; "conventional" weapons might be in a number of circumstances, but this is a quite different and essentially technical question.

It is an open question whether these two lines of argument are capable of reconciliation. It is never easy simultaneously to pursue actions which will both improve our relative situation in a power struggle and mitigate the struggle itself. We shall not at this point attempt to resolve this issue, which is, of course, a great deal more complex than this general presentation might suggest.[3] One fact does stand out, however: that the possibility of accepting the first line of argument and its conclusion—the ability to take a stand *outside* the power struggle—may depend decisively upon the nature of the opponent with whom we are dealing. If he is determined to regard our relations as a struggle, and is strong enough to make that struggle one of life-and-death, it is hard to see how we can take a position outside it without running the most dangerous risks. For this reason it is necessary to explore now the second of the challenging novelties of our time: Communist totalitarianism.

Communist Totalitarianism

Among students of totalitarianism there is no firm agreement on its definition, its origins and drives, or its future prospects. We cannot hope here to resolve their differences; the most we can do is to arrive at a few characterizations to help us with our particular problem.

From our present vantage point the twentieth century appears to have produced a type of regime—most notably in the cases of Nazi Germany and the Soviet Union—which is peculiar to our epoch. To be sure, one can find antecedents for certain features of both Nazism and Soviet Communism, as well as significant differences between them, especially in the range and types of discontent they are able to exploit in their striving for total power. Moreover, in the ordering of the Soviet society and economy one can discern an almost Pharaonic atavism, as though the dialectic had somehow gone in reverse to resurrect the bureaucratic-servile societies of oriental antiquity. Still, it is difficult to conceive of these regimes being able to entrench and maintain themselves without the instrumentalities of the twentieth century: the industrial machine, the means of communication and trans-

[3] See also below, p. 101.

portation, the weapons, the state apparatus. Even more, the totalitarian ideologies are intimately related—though in a complex and debated fashion—to dominant currents of thought and expression of contemporary Western civilization. It is this combination of the advanced with the retrograde, of the familiar with the totally alien, that makes totalitarianism so perplexing.

Classical political nomenclature—such terms as state, party, tyranny and dictatorship—tends to break down when it tries to encompass totalitarian movements and regimes. Religious terminology may seem more appropriate, though it must be admitted that a "secular religion" is not an altogether obvious entity. It is not surprising that some of the most penetrating and persuasive insights into the nature of totalitarianism have been achieved in literary or imaginative constructions, but to find such a creation as George Orwell's society of 1984 the truest embodiment of totalitarianism is not really very helpful when it comes to meeting concrete problems of international or domestic politics.

Perhaps the most serious danger arising from our inability to grasp with any certainty the nature of totalitarianism is that we are inclined to regard its practitioners as either superhuman or subhuman. Since totalitarianism does not seem to conform to known "rules" of social or political organization, we are tempted to draw one of two erroneous conclusions. We may feel that the totalitarian regimes have somehow overcome the limitations of other social orders and promise to be the irresistible wave of the future. Or we may feel that they are "against nature," or simply an expression of criminality in individuals, and are bound to collapse sooner or later. Neither view is healthy. We are dealing with fallible mortals, not with some Lysenko-bred super race. On the other hand, we must not make the error of the scientist who proved that the wing area of the bumble bee was too small to support the creature in flight. Our knowledge of society is still so limited that we cannot say, for example, that the issue of succession and legitimacy *must* bring the members of a ruling group in a totalitarian regime into self-destructive conflict among themselves or that collectivization of agriculture *cannot* work. Even less are we able to attach timetables to such prospects. There is no question but that the Soviet regime has made some remarkable achievements, and has been able to exploit the potentialities of twentieth-century technology and organization to a degree greater than we might have thought its cumbersome system and doctrinaire outlook would permit.

How, then, are we to approach this phenomenon, as manifested in the Soviet Union, in a way useful to the United States in determining its lines of policy?

The central attribute of Soviet Communism has been its aggressive and persistent hostility, in theory and in practice, toward those features of the contemporary world embodied in the economic, cultural and political life of Western Europe and the United States. Many things have contributed to this enmity—Marx's vision of inevitable conflict and struggle, the traditionally ambiguous Russian attitude toward the West, the personalities of Lenin and Stalin, the Bolshevist doctrine of revolution, the course of Soviet-Western relations since 1917—and there has been a good deal of argument about the weight to be attached to these or other components. But the decisive fact is that in 1917 a highly self-conscious revolutionary group, fully intent on making a break with the continuity, not only of Russian history but of modern world history, succeeded in gaining political power.

A program for revolution, no matter how uncompromisingly or dogmatically conceived, is subject to modification and adaptation so long as it remains in the realm of ideas or is without controlling power in the political arena. The history of German Social Democracy is the classic example. When, however, the program becomes a reality in a successful revolution, when it possesses power and determines the political framework rather than being determined by it, a new situation results. Modification and adaptation are still possible but in an altogether different setting. New institutions and practices are created to embody and carry out the intentions of the revolution. This break in continuity in turn raises new problems and, in the case of major revolutions which involve a change of political and social systems of more than local or national significance, quickly extends to international ruptures and strains. And whereas a revolutionary idea or even a revolutionary opposition party may in time be reabsorbed into the main stream or suffer erosion, it can be argued, though not proven, that once such a major revolution has occurred some sort of "restoration"—as in the cases of the English and French revolutions—is required before the rift between the old order abroad and the new order at home can be ended. This rift, it should be stressed, is not just a line of demarcation between two dissimilar societies; the relationship is by its origins one of intimate antagonism.

Apart from an externally imposed defeat, a number of things may promote a restoration: inertia of people and institutions to abrupt change, the tendency of even the revolutionary leaders to rely on habitual and familiar ways in dealing with the problem of government, and the ebbing of the initial revolutionary élan. Perhaps the most singular feature of Soviet Communism is its special awareness of, indeed its intense preoccupation with, the possibility of a "restoration." The self-consciousness of the Hegelian-Marxist tradition, the much pondered lessons of the nineteenth-century revolutions, the concepts of party and leadership developed by Lenin in the years before the revolution, and the political instincts of both Lenin and Stalin—all these combined to instill a permanent fear of backsliding and a determination to maintain the revolution and to extend it territorially. This very sophisticated and self-conscious quality of the Russian revolution sharply distinguishes it from earlier revolutions and lies behind much that is totalitarian in the Soviet regime.

Since the "mass" of the people are always apt to back slide into customary ways, all the instruments of technology education, organization and terror must be used to chec this tendency or divert it into harmless channels. Even th party members may succumb, hence the tight organization the doctrinal concern, the continual purges. Moreover, the institutionalization of this fear and determination serves to establish a built-in "deviation corrector": the system itself is geared to maintaining the revolution and to creating a compulsory ideological orthodoxy, if not the original faith and zeal of the movement.

Initially state power was captured for the services of the

revolution; the maintenance and completion of the revolution required the instrumentality of the state. In consequence a number of earlier goals, especially those concerning the territorial spread of the revolution and the withering of the state, had to be modified. But these modifications, and even the significant revisions in Marxist theory (begun by Lenin well before the revolution), do not mean that *raison d'état* has superseded revolutionary aims; the two have become completely identified.

The fear of backsliding has also complicated the chronic problem of dictatorships: how to regulate succession and change in the ruling group. The danger that any settled or normal procedure regarding promotion, security of tenure, or replacement, especially with respect to key posts, may lead to complacency is counteracted in the Soviet Union by the hectic practice of periodic purges. Since we have 38 years' evidence that this system is capable of maintaining and perpetuating itself, it would seem that despite the appearance of increasing the traditional instability of dictatorships the Communist purge system may have helped to surmount it. Precisely because the system is devised to prevent backsliding or individual adventurousness, and has developed its own peculiar categories of left and right "deviational" heresies, the contenders for office, even the highest, have been forced into line.

Connected with this is a curious wave-like or pendulum pattern which seems to provide a good deal of the dynamism of the Soviet system. If backsliding toward "normalcy" presents one threat, so does the opposite tendency to seek so rapid an advance toward revolutionary objectives at home and abroad as to threaten the safety of the revolutionary base. Soviet policy has tended to undulate between these two limits. This undulation may be consciously manipulated, or it may reflect conflicts within the ruling group, or both. In any event, it has remained, up to the present, within controllable limits.

The foreign relations of the Soviet regime reflect all these characteristics. In the West the hostility of Soviet foreign policy is frequently explained in one of two ways. Either it is that Soviets intend to "conquer the world" or that the

Soviet leaders must conjure up an external enemy to keep their subjects under control. Both of these explanations can be misleading. Admittedly, Communists anticipate the eventual world-wide victory of Communism and do not believe that this will come about either peacefully or automatically. They must further the process with whatever means they possess, including military means, and they must be prepared for decisive clashes which will bring the downfall of the capitalist world. To this aggressive bent, however, is joined a strong sense of defensiveness, born in part of the revolution and dread of backsliding and defeat. This strain of defense-mindedness may explain why, on occasion, the Communists have not pressed forward as "world conquerors" might be expected to do.[4] But while the caution they have sometimes displayed appears to involve more than the simple prudence of a rational aggressor who is covering his base, and could for that reason be of some political significance, we have little way of judging from Soviet behavior thus far whether this defensiveness is in any way separable from the aggressive ideology which underlies it. The fear of "capitalist encirclement," though not merely a propaganda phrase, has been a self-fulfilling concept, constantly creating its own object. In the Soviet reading of the international scene, advancing the revolution and meeting the capitalist threat have been two sides of the same coin.

If Soviet foreign policy is thus simultaneously geared to the fear of backsliding and to the maintenance and territorial expansion of the revolution, it is not necessary to set up an antithesis between foreign policy and domestic policy; in the Communist mind both are part of the battle against one continuing obstacle, and threat, to the revolution that will last until the day when the revolution is made to prevail in the major powers of the world. The challenge is not identical at all times on both fronts. In general, the home front has appeared, quite reasonably, to be of primary importance, although in the mortal crisis of 1941–42 there was a marked

[4] The Russian failure to overthrow Tito by force and the Chinese Communist failure to occupy Hong Kong have been cited as examples of this; in both instances it seems that they could have moved in without real danger to themselves.

"retreat" to nationalism until the immediate external enemy had been defeated. All in all, however, it is more realistic to regard the relation between domestic and foreign concerns as one between different sectors of a single battlefield than to see foreign policy a function of domestic policy, or vice versa.

The international Communist movement provides a link between the Soviet domestic and foreign fronts. Its organization and methods are derived from Soviet domestic practices, but its primary function has been to reinforce Soviet foreign policy. Since the early days of the Soviet regime the immediate revolutionary interests of Communist parties abroad have frequently been subordinated (so far as the Soviet leaders were in full control of them) to the defense and strengthening of the Soviet base. But while this subordination at times has caused severe strains and even schisms, it does not follow that from the point of view of the Soviet regime any contradiction is involved; revolutionary efforts abroad which would imperil the indispensable base for the long-term expansion of world Communism are just as impermissible as leftist deviations on the home front. If the local Communists fail to see this they cannot be true Communists any more than if they fail to press actively for revolutionary expansion when the occasion demands.

There is no question that international Communism, symbolized by the Comintern and the Cominform, has caused the deepest alarm among non-Communist nations in indicating that the U.S.S.R. is not like other states and is not guided simply by normal "national interests." Repeatedly in the years after 1919 the non-Communist powers, in an effort to establish normal relations with the Soviet Union, sought to have the regime break its ties with international Communism, but to no avail. This was partly because the U.S.S.R., through a variety of devices and arguments, contrived to circumvent such efforts. But it is difficult to see how the Soviet Union could honestly disavow the international complexion of Communism since this would be to deny, in the face of the capitalist enemy, the meaning of the revolution. Soviet leaders can, of course, abandon or sacrifice foreign Communist parties to some pressing need of the U.S.S.R. They are expendable outposts, and it is doubtful whether Stalin had much faith in the foreign Communist parties alone as tools for extending the revolution. Indeed, it is conceivable that should the occasion warrant it, and the stakes be great enough, the Soviet Union would acquiesce in the destruction of all foreign Communist parties if that alone would preserve the home base. Still, such acquiescence is quite different from "honest disavowal," and would not prevent the Kremlin from reorganizing the parties when the opportunity arose. It might be added that even a "disavowal" would not prevent the local Communists from following the Soviet line on their own. So long as they were Communist parties this would be the only reasonable course, unless, to press it to the ridiculous, the Soviet Union *instructed* them to oppose it.

While international Communism, as a symbol of the universal pretensions of the Soviet system, is a challenge to the non-Communist world, to what extent does it represent more than a symbolic danger? There are, of course, the specific dangers of espionage, sabotage and, in some countries, armed insurrection to cooperate with a Soviet invasion or to set up a pro-Soviet regime. But beyond these we encounter the difficult and ill-defined area of subversion. One of the novel and most appalling features of twentieth-century totalitarian movements and regimes is their capacity not only to subvert but to engender an obsessive preoccupation with subversion. Certainly in the case of the Soviet Union itself there is a direct connection between the Communists' efforts to infiltrate and manipulate non-Communist bodies abroad and Soviet fears of subversion at home. The belief that secret, inimical forces are at work, plotting and undermining, evokes counterforces. And just as in the game of espionage, agents are met by double agents who in turn may prove to be triple agents, so the totalitarian miasma of subversion seems to spread to other nations.

But we must be careful not to become fascinated by this nightmare. It is not surprising that it should prevail in a totalitarian regime: it is a natural companion of the break in continuity, the limitless ambition to recreate the world. To the extent, however, that we participate in the nightmare, as distinct from recognizing the real but certainly manageable perils, so far are we in danger of succumbing to morbid doubts about our own society and diverting our attention from the main job.

What are the expectations for a change in the Soviet regime? This is an unanswerable question. The only other full-fledged totalitarian regime, the Third Reich, was abolished only by complete military defeat. But we cannot safely draw a conclusion from such a single piece of evidence. Speculations concerning a less catastrophic dénouement have been concerned with several possibilities.

1. It is not to be excluded that the Russian people, or perhaps the non-Russian nationalities, might some time rise against the regime. Positive evidence of such a will is naturally very difficult to establish. Moreover, the massive military force, the ubiquitous controls and the tremendous propaganda at the command of a totalitarian regime make it unlikely that a large-scale uprising could be launched in the absence of a powerful external attack and a considerable occupation of Soviet territory.

2. It is also possible that the regime might become even more extreme, to the extent of destroying itself by a *reductio ad absurdum* of some of its tenets and practices. Conceivably it could press its impulse to atomize the individual to such a degree that the intellectual and moral personality would collapse. We have seen the kind of madness that impelled the Nazis to embark on mass genocide at a time when they desperately needed manpower to carry on a war. The Soviet regime, however, has shown little inclination toward suicidal extremes (unless, of course, its actions bring on a nuclear war). It has had the wit, for example, to refrain, despite some experimentation, from the dissolution of the family unit.

3. It has been suggested that the regime might be disrupted internally through some kind of schism, or palace revolt, in the ranks of the Communist élite. This may be more likely than the preceding possibilities. But, while there have been vigorous purges and bitter struggles for power in the Soviet era, they have not got out of control, and it is certainly not predictable that they will. Stalin's death and the subsequent turn to the form of collegial leadership have once again raised the question whether government by committee can

survive in such a society or whether a single person must eventually come to the top, as did Lenin and Stalin. The evidence thus far is that none of Stalin's successors monopolizes power as he did and that the appearance of collective management has some real substance. But this tells us neither that one or another of the inner group will not eventually get complete control, nor that committee rule will lead to a further fractioning and decentralization of authority and decision. We do, then, have some evidence of a change but little notion of what, if anything, it may portend.

4. It has been suggested, too, that a) the regime might "regress" to a more traditional Russian pattern, or b) the bureaucrats and technicians (including the military) might come to outweigh the party and produce a managerial or technocratic system. With regard to the former, it is hard to envisage just what this "regression" would result in, especially since the Soviet regime in the course of its existence has taken over and utilized a number of traditional Russian patterns without having its purposes perceptibly diluted. At most, such traditionalist tendencies are likely to be more of a drag on the regime than an active force for change.

5. With regard to the latter possibility—the domination of bureaucratic elements—there is ample evidence that the vast state, military, and party apparatus has created a managing élite which now has a large social and material stake to preserve, and hence a motive for being relatively conservative and cautious. This drift toward "normalcy" and administrative rationality has been particularly apparent in the time since Stalin's death, and it has been argued that with the passing of the generation that made the revolution this trend may prove to be the most powerful in determining the character of Soviet society. Against this, however, it should be observed that while the Communist regime has been bureaucratized the bureaucracy (including the military) has been Communized. If one can get rid of the quite inapplicable mental image of the wild-eyed, bomb-throwing Bolshevik of early cartoons, the divergence of type and interest between Communist and bureaucrat may prove to be much less than it would be in a setting other than that of the Soviet Union. The bureaucrat may have no real enthu-

siasm for advancing the cause of world revolution (though there is no reason why he should not believe in that as much as in raising workers' living standards, in increasing production or in any goal beyond his own immediate comfort and security), but his status is certainly tied to the continued success of the Soviet system, which in turn is scarcely to be understood except as an organization to advance the purposes of the Communist party.

If this possibility, for which at least there is some tangible evidence, develops to a degree to promise a real change in the aims and structure of Soviet Communism, it remains to be seen if it can be realized as a gradual, natural, unnoticed process and without a major crisis. In the Communist mind such a drift represents precisely the kind of backsliding toward a "restoration" against which the regime has tried to guard itself since its inception. No matter how "bureaucratized" or "Russian" the political leadership itself may become, it cannot avoid challenging such tendencies. In the final analysis they call in question the whole regime and all the people who have made their careers in it.

6. Finally, it has been suggested that over a long period of time the regime, while not markedly altering its structure and even without specifically repudiating its ideology, might let the ideology become nonoperative for want of conditions to nourish and vitalize it. Such a withering away of ideological aggressiveness could conceivably be the outcome of a situation in which the Communists' control over their own territory was unchallenged, from within or without, and the non-Communist world afforded them no weak spots for attack, probing or subversion. In circumstances where the ideology would have nothing to feed upon but its own fantasies, it might cease to have even the appearance of relevance as a guide or stimulus to action. The conditions, of course, for any such dissolution of the unity of theory and practice at the heart of the Communist ideology are peculiarly exacting, especially since any untoward shift in either the domestic or the foreign situation could stimulate the regime to renewed aggressiveness.

With respect to possible changes, then, we can offer only a few general conclusions. First, we do not know which direction the changes will take or even that they would necessarily be preferable to the present system. Second, more than most systems, Soviet Communism is built to resist such changes. Its leaders, by their training and by the nature of their office, are thoroughly conditioned to recognize and to oppose actions which might unravel the fabric of the regime. This self-correcting tendency may fail some time, but the breakdown is not demonstrably inherent in the system. Third, the likelihood of such changes is so uncertain that, while the United States should try to bring about those which seem most favorable to American and free world interests, it cannot let its security or its hopes for the future rest on confidence in an advantageous change in the Soviet system. We must not, of course, conclude that change is out of the question or is quite beyond our influence. The world does move, new things appear and the old succumbs or is transformed. We cannot, on peril of falling into the belief that the Marxist-Leninist analysis of social and historical processes is the whole truth, conclude that the Communists have an answer to every problem. Forces, which neither we nor the Communists are even aware of, may be at work to alter their regime. In this sense the situation is altogether open-ended and we must not, because of our relative ignorance or our total dismay, try to close it.

In practical terms what does this all amount to? Briefly, we confront a regime the ultimate fate of which is unknown, which has created an appalling social and political structure that has held together for nearly forty years, which does not conform to our modes of thought and behavior, which has unlimited expectations and intentions regarding its eventual expansion, and which is profoundly hostile to us.

Some Continuing Problems

In discussing Soviet totalitarianism one runs the risk of stressing the strange and often horrifying features to the exclusion of all else, especially when one sees the regime in its chilling aspect of labor camps, trials, police raids and deportations. The "univers concentrationnaire" is real enough, of course, and it is not "compensated for" by some good features. The danger is rather that we may fail to realize that a human society can still exist and adapt itself to such a background—the most shocking features are normally in the shadow, out of public sight—and that social relations, customs, ambitions and loyalties continue to weave their patterns. The Soviet Union is not a monolith despite ideological and organizational pressure to make it so. The Russian people are still the Russian people. The individual Communist remains a human being, committing venial, and venal, as well as mortal sins. Our capacity to judge and estimate not only the direction but the tempo and intensity of Soviet trends depends in part on our ability to recognize the complexities of life and society. A characterization can be useful in setting the terms of our problem; it does not exhaust the problem.

When we descend from the arduous and uncertain terrain of the atomic and totalitarian challenges to the more familiar reaches of "normal" international affairs we encounter a sufficiency of tough questions. One could construct a model of post-1945 Soviet-American relations which omitted both the atomic bomb and Communist totalitarianism and yet was extremely dangerous and troublesome. Indeed, this model has been the occasion of some misgivings: may we not, in our minds and in our policies, be placing false emphasis on the atom or on Communism? Are they the real culprits? Before trying to deal with these misgivings let us briefly examine some of these "normal" or continuing problems.

In the first place, it is reasonably clear that the international states system has been undergoing major changes over the last several decades. The relative importance of the Western and Central European powers has declined and that of the extra-European powers has increased. Two world wars brought about a progressive reduction of the number of great powers that "counted," until by 1945, although Britain remained one of the Big Three, it appeared that the world was progressing toward a bipolar situation, with the two great continental powers, the United States and U.S.S.R., towering over the rest.[5] In so far as the "balance of power"—and we need not here judge its adequacy in explaining in-

[5] But see below, p. 120.

ternational relations—classically finds stability in a multi-power system, it could be argued that this bipolar line-up was inherently unstable and would of itself, independently of any ideological differences, promote Soviet-American hostility.

In the second place, the Soviet Union has entered a phase of full industrialization, as Britain and then Germany and the United States had earlier done in their turn. In each case this sudden increase in economic growth and power has been reflected in a change in international power relations; Germany's industrialization, for example, appeared as a threat to Britain at the end of the nineteenth century. Moreover, the later each state moves into full industrialization the faster its rate of acceleration can be, partly because of the improved technology it is able to command. Doubtless, compulsion and economic planning have had an effect on the Soviet rate of growth, though it would be impossible to tell how much, but there is evidence that, before the revolution, Russia was already picking up speed as an industrial power. We cannot say what would have been the extent or nature of the Russian power challenge to the United States in the absence of Communism, but it is not unreasonable to suppose that there would have been a challenge, based on Russia's new industrial stature.

In the third place, armament was certainly a threatening problem before the atomic bomb and was the inevitable accompaniment of modern industry and technology. The Hague Conferences and the protracted disarmament negotiations of the 1920's and 1930's attest to the mounting seriousness of the problem and also to the failure to find any solution. Even without the atom we would be faced with this long-standing sense of insecurity resulting from the competitive build-up of military strength.

Fourth, nationalistic conflicts are a persistent feature of modern history. It is questionable, for example, whether Poles and Russians would have entertained warm feelings toward one another even had the revolution not brought the Communists to power. Indeed, in the interwar years Russia's western neighbors tended to feel that Bolshevism was just the sort of thing the Russians were capable of producing. Consequently, even without Communism Russia's quest for "friendly" regimes on its frontiers was likely to be unrewarding unless the friendliness was enforced. This in turn would have produced an imbalance of major proportions in Europe.

Fifth, it should be remembered that Lenin did not invent the word, "imperialism." While the Communists have exploited the term, colonial-European friction was a quite independent problem that would undoubtedly have been a major issue in world politics. How this would have affected United States-Russian relations in the absence of Communism is impossible to say.

Other factors might be added—relative demographic growths, domestic social conflicts, pan-Slavism, etc.—but the items we have enumerated, when taken together, obviously amount to a formidable set of issues.

It may be submitted that it was the anticipation of these issues which, toward the end of the war, led many non-Communist Western statesmen to feel so urgently that an arrangement with the Soviet Union had to be made, especially since wartime alliances were known to have a way of falling apart once the common enemy was defeated. To avoid such a breakdown, it was deemed necessary to avoid starting a chain reaction, to try to meet the Soviet requirements, and even to give in on some points in order to maintain a propitious atmosphere for a mutual effort to work out these very thorny problems.

Perhaps the most illuminating single statement of this mood is expressed in the document Harry Hopkins brought to the First Quebec Conference in August 1943:

"Russia's postwar position in Europe will be a dominant one. With Germany crushed, there is no power in Europe to oppose her tremendous military forces. It is true that Great Britain is building up a position in the Mediterranean vis-à-vis Russia that she may find useful in balancing power in Europe. However, even here she may not be able to oppose Russia unless she is otherwise supported.

"The conclusions from the foregoing are obvious. Since Russia is the decisive factor in the war, she must be given every assistance and every effort must be made to obtain her friendship.

Likewise, since without question she will dominate Europe on the defeat of the Axis, it is even more essential to develop and maintain the most friendly relations with Russia."

What is it in our present perspective that makes this model so unconvincing and produces the sense of a startling non sequitur between the first and the second paragraphs of the preceding quotation? The problems envisaged are real, are continuing, are grave and have to be met. It is quite possible that they alone would have led to serious American-Russian tension.

Nevertheless, it now seems clear that viewing American-Soviet relations primarily in terms of customary power politics, economic rivalry and military competition would be a serious mistake despite the apparent advantage of providing us with a more familiar, if still difficult, setting. As we have said already, the power of the atom is so overwhelming as to make any analysis based only on such concepts of doubtful value. The whole problem of physical power in politics requires rethinking.

With respect to Communist totalitarianism, while we may never know until the Kremlin archives are open, if then, what motives lay behind the various Soviet moves of the last decade, it has become increasingly apparent that they are not to be explained by traditional notions of the national interest or by the maneuvers, à la Bismarck, of a competitive sparring match between great powers. Recent research on the Soviet system has shown that the presumed reversions to normalcy of the later 1930's and early 1940's—the Popular Front as a form of multiparty cooperation, the 1936 Constitution, the fostering of Great Russian nationalism, the announced dropping of the Comintern, the adoption of a new national anthem to replace the Internationale, etc.—did not affect the basic structure of the state, the party or the Communist ideology. Soviet foreign policy has remained an instrument of the total system. In 1943 and 1944, well before the postwar chilling of the alliance, the U.S.S.R. was setting up the conditions for the cold war, warning the faithful that the basic conflict between capitalism and Communism remained at the core of the historical process, that the wartime cooperation should not lead to illusions.

This does not mean that the Soviet leaders had everything planned in advance; there is quite evidently a good deal of reciprocity in the particular steps by which the postwar enmity developed. In the first year or so after the end of the Second World War, the United States and Great Britain were baffled at the way the Soviets were destroying the wartime alliance—to all appearances the best guarantee for lasting Russian security—by pressing westward and southward in Europe and the Middle East; the Soviet leaders were perhaps equally perplexed by the American and British refusal to grant the U.S.S.R. the plums of victory, to acknowledge Soviet hegemony in the areas it had conquered and occupied or to allow a Soviet advance into the power vacuums. This interplay of cross-purposes created the specific historical pattern which we call the Cold War. Yet two remarks by leading Soviet figures cut through the impression that the Cold War was therefore an unnecessary product of mutual fumbling and misconceptions. At the Potsdam conference Stalin is reported to have said: "A freely elected government in any of these countries [in Eastern Europe] would be anti-Soviet, and that we cannot allow." A year later, in June 1946, an American correspondent asked Maxim Litvinov, then in deep retirement, whether the West's granting Moscow's demands regarding Trieste, the Italian colonies, the Danube and the rest would lead to an easing of tension. Litvinov responded: "It would lead to the West being faced with the next series of demands." Quite evidently no happy outcome could be expected from such premises, premises which ultimately derive from the character of the Soviet regime: the Communist order, in battle against the capitalist order.

Finally, when we examine Soviet actions in the foreign field there are a number that simply are not to be explained by power politics alone, or even by the more sophisticated suggestion of ideology being employed in the service of power interests. They clearly show the harnessing of power to ideology. Here we can only list some examples: the gratuitous, and unsuccessful, introduction of ideology into the

Soviet-Finnish war of 1939, by the creation of the Finnish People's Republic on the border; the Communization of the Eastern European satellites to a degree far greater than was necessary to assure their benevolence in any traditional diplomatic sense (some of the satellites, especially Czechoslovakia, were prepared to be friendly, and even to have Communists in coalition governments); finally, and most conclusively, the break with Tito in 1948, which makes no sense in terms of conventional power politics: Tito was eager to be pro-Soviet in his foreign policy and even tried to remain so after the break.

It may seem that this is an altogether unnecessary demonstration, to show what is very generally accepted. Nevertheless, in face of the very bleak prospects of the contemporary world and the possibility of a universal catastrophe, any reasonable man may be impelled to ask himself whether the present situation could have been avoided. Did we at some point fail to do what we could to put Soviet-American relations on a more normal basis? In so far as such doubts may reduce our ability to think clearly about the present or the future they may be a real disadvantage. Now, while we can never know what course history might have followed had the United States taken different actions in the recent past, it is possible to feel reasonably certain that normal relations between the Soviet Union and the United States were out of the question and for reasons beyond our power to control. The Soviet Union, like Nazi Germany, does represent a new order of regime, and all the continuing and familiar problems which come in contact with it are transformed into something unfamiliar, though still continuing.

It is not easy to digest the full implications of this fact, much less to devise adequate means of coping with it. Still, it may prove to be salutary that we are being forced to confront dangers as explicit, undisguised and novel as the atomic bomb and Soviet totalitarianism, and to try to relate them to the continuing problems of human relations. For neither of them is a *deus ex machina,* an inexplicable intruder into our world. Both are products of modern man. At the same time these fearful novelties are clear markers of the limits of our course, limits beyond which human or at least humane existence is not possible. The limits may have been there before, perhaps have always been there, but today there is no mistaking them. Now we must see what there is for us to do.

CHAPTER II

STRENGTHS AND VULNERABILITIES

The Soviet relationship with the United States has been antagonistic, implicitly antagonistic in the Communist attitude toward all capitalist and pre-capitalist societies, actively so since the defeat of the common enemy in 1945. Antagonistic relations with a totalitarian regime which has universal pretensions are without any evidently prescribable limits. The objectives may be total victory, and the means may encompass the whole range of power available to the contenders, a range that has expanded enormously with the advent of atomic energy. Whether the aims and means actually do become "total" or whether the antagonism can in practice be kept within limits or brought to an end depends upon the intentions, actions and capabilities of both parties. The United States alone cannot set the limits; it remains to be seen whether a mutually agreed upon limitation of the form and objectives of the antagonism is feasible.

In this chapter, however, our primary concern is with the strengths and vulnerabilities of each side. These will affect both the outcome of the relationship and the arena, or arenas, in which the contest is held. Because of the elusive quality of power, because of the tendency of the Communist regime to convert any issue into a power struggle, and because of the engulfing nature of atomic power, the task of measuring the strengths and vulnerabilities of the United States and the Soviet Union is of utmost difficulty. The measurements, to be relevant, must be set against possible contingencies, yet the likelihood of these contingencies may in turn depend upon our and the Soviet interpretation of the measurements.

To simplify, as a first approach, we can envisage three forms the antagonism might assume. The first would rest purely on the maximum application of physical power, the function of which would be to achieve the destruction of the opponent's effective physical power and potential. In practical terms, a full thermonuclear war. A second, and more conventional, would be based upon the employment of physical power to impose one's will on the opponent in gaining limited territorial or other tangible objects. This could cover a variety of kinds of military and economic warfare. It differs from the first in being directed not at destroying the enemy's power but at securing material advantages. A third would be based on the intangible forms of power, pure political warfare in which the possession of physical power (economic or military) would be for a primarily political purpose: to threaten, to bluff, to disarm, to discourage (this should be distinguished from traditional psychological warfare which is an adjunct to military strategy). No sharp line divides these three forms, and conflict could move from one to the other, but they do express three different contingencies against which strengths and vulnerabilities may be measured.

The Application of Maximum Physical Power

Under this contingency we have in mind the possibility of a war initiated by atomic and thermonuclear strikes aimed at knocking out the opponent. With respect to the strengths the picture, while constantly changing, is fairly clear in its broad outlines. As was indicated in the preceding chapter, it is to be expected that each side will shortly possess a stockpile of weapons and means of delivery sufficient, if they are able to get to their targets, to damage the other to a degree beyond any early recovery. Each has exploded thermonuclear devices of multimegaton power, capable of destroying the heart of the largest cities, wreaking serious damage in outlying areas, and—depending on wind conditions, the composition of the bomb and the debris, and the height of the explosion—creating over an area of several thousand square miles a radioactive fall-out that would threaten the lives of all persons unable to take adequate protective measures.

While the American stockpile of bombs is estimated to be considerably larger,[1] the ingredients for the creation of the

[1] "Published estimates of comparative nuclear strength, including some by atomic physicists, have indicated that the United States stockpile of all types of nuclear weapons is probably more than 5,000. The Russian stockpile may

thermonuclear bomb, triggered by an atom bomb, appear to be relatively inexpensive. Both the United States and the Soviet Union are probably capable of delivering on target several hundred atomic bombs by piloted aircraft; within a relatively short time they could probably deliver an even greater number of both atomic and thermonuclear bombs. The number of aircraft capable of two-way missions (with or without air refueling) is currently greater in the United States, even though the Soviet development and production of intercontinental heavy jet bombers has been considerably more rapid than anticipated. Moreover, American overseas bases are much closer to the major Soviet targets than Soviet bases are to the United States. With the completion of the American early warning network, this advantage in overseas bases could make it possible, even if the Soviets initiated an attack, for American planes to reach major Soviet targets before Soviet planes could reach American targets. The advantage, of course, rests on the very important condition that the United States enjoys the right to use these bases which are not on American soil.

If the United States, on balance, enjoys an advantage, it is an uncertain and diminishing one, uncertain because of the inevitable range of error in intelligence estimates, diminishing because of the Soviet approach to atomic plenty and sufficiency of means of delivery. We certainly must face the prospect that within a matter of two to five years both sides will be able to deliver a "knockout blow." It is, of course, difficult to define this knockout. It is possible that an exchange of thermonuclear strikes, however devastating, would not be decisive in determining the outcome of the conflict. It has been argued, though it seems progressively less likely, that after such an exchange both sides might still have the will to continue the struggle with whatever means were left to them. But those elements of strength that might come into play in any "post-atomic" phase of conflict can best be exam-

---

be more than 500, perhaps as many as 1,000. . . . [However] the combined power of available Russian weapons today is between 20 and 40 megatons. . . . One United States thermonuclear test device, detonated a year ago in the Pacific, released the equivalent of 20,000,000 tons of TNT." Hanson W. Baldwin in *The New York Times,* March 4, 1955.

ined in connection with the military forces discussed in the next section.

Apart from stockpiles of nuclear weapons and the means to deliver them, the relevance of other elements of strength to a general atomic war would depend in part upon the way the war was fought. If cities and industrial targets were the primary targets, industrial potential would be of relatively little significance after the fighting started. Under these circumstances military forces in being, placed in strategically critical areas—including offshore bases—together with the weapons, equipment and supplies in being and not destroyed on D-day, would be of utmost importance.

We shall discuss military forces in being in the next section. With respect to stocks of weapons and strategically important equipment and finished goods, Soviet central reserves, not in absolute quantities but relative to military and "essential" civilian needs, are believed to be greater for most commodities than are United States and NATO stockpiles. The Western powers have greater supplies in their production pipelines, but these might be disrupted.

It is quite possible, perhaps most likely, that the primary targets would not be cities and industrial areas but would be the opponent's air-atomic bases, launching sites, stockpiles, and atomic bomb and airplane plants. In such an event, the general industrial potential might have better chances of surviving, which would clearly be to the advantage of the United States. Even so, however, under conditions of full atomic war, it is probable that stocks of finished weapons and supplies would be the most significant factor. The importance of reserves of raw materials and of processing equipment would depend not only on the nature and extent of the devastation but on the plans made ahead of time for continued functioning of the economy.

Concerning vulnerabilities, the United States and the Soviet Union confront problems of a similar order of magnitude. It is impossible to say anything very specific about military vulnerabilities, except that in the short run the United States with its wider distribution of air bases, including those overseas, probably presents a more dispersed military target and is less liable to be prevented from making an effective retaliatory attack. Against this, however, the Russians probably enjoy an intelligence advantage in having more of our military targets accurately spotted. But with the coming of intercontinental ballistic missiles, which would require much smaller bases, this whole picture may be altered considerably, and to our disadvantage. The air base structure of both powers would then be a good deal less vulnerable, dispersal of weapons easier to achieve, and our overseas bases of relatively less value.

Owing to the greater degree of urbanization in the United States, the destruction of comparable numbers of the largest metropolitan areas in both countries would produce greater casualties here than in the Soviet Union. For example, nearly 20 per cent of the total United States population lives in its 25 largest cities, as contrasted with only 10 per cent in such cities in the Soviet Union. (Equivalent destruction of life in the Soviet Union would be accomplished only by bombing nearly 150 of their largest centers.)

As for industrial targets, output in both countries is approximately equally concentrated in vulnerable areas. For example, 10 metropolitan areas in the United States, each 25 miles in radius, account for 82 per cent of total iron capacity, 77 per cent of coke, and 73 per cent of steel ingot capacity. In the Soviet Union, 10 metropolitan areas account for just under 75 per cent of the total iron and steel production. Key production, particularly of military end items, may be somewhat more widely dispersed among (although still within) the major target areas in the Soviet Union than in the United States.

Soviet urban and industrial targets are at present a good deal more accessible to American bombers—provided overseas bases are available to the United States—than are ours to their bombers. Weighing against this advantage, however, is the greater experience of Soviet industry in operating under conditions of uncertain supply of raw materials, semifabricates and equipment. This experience was gained not only during World War II, but also during most years of Soviet rule. Less integrated, less specialized and using subcontractors less than does American industry, Soviet industry may be better able to function under conditions of large-scale destruction. Further, subsistence possibilities are probably better in the U.S.S.R. since a larger proportion of the population is in agricultural or rural areas, its agriculture is less mechanized and more self-sufficient, and the physical endurance of most of its citizens would be greater under primitive conditions.

The impact of thermonuclear destruction would place tremendous strains upon the organization of a country—upon its ability to maintain communications, to get things done, to have orders carried out. Because of the great differences in the two societies, the adequacy under attack of the Soviet and American organizations can be estimated only in general terms. Despite the centralization of the Soviet system the Russians have demonstrated their ability, in situations of extreme crisis, to decentralize and create centers of local initiative and improvisation. Moreover, the whole Soviet system of government and organization was created and developed in an atmosphere of crisis, attack and anticipated attack, and it has had the practical experience of absorbing and surviving the massive German assaults of 1941 and 1942. With respect to the American system we have little experience to go on. There is undoubtedly a real tradition of "Minute Man" improvisation in time of emergency, but it is by no means certain what role this could play in the complex, interdependent, industrialized organization of twentieth-century America. This organization developed in the relative immunity of our hemispheric isolation and was not designed for conflict. Despite the events of the last decade we have not moved very far toward being prepared for war in this respect.

On balance it would appear that under conditions of equal destruction the Soviet organization may enjoy an advantage since it has had this experience and has met it successfully, though we should not overlook Great Britain's extraordinary achievement in World War II. The balance could perhaps be tipped, however, by the presumably greater American attacking power; by our relative economic advantage, which could compensate for a degree of disorganization; and, of course, by the hoped-for performance of spontaneous initiative which we take to be part of the American character.

Of crucial importance to a nation's ability to survive an atomic war is the morale of its citizens. It is impossible, however, to predict with any confidence how morale will stand up in either the United States or the Soviet Union in face of the unprecedented violence of thermonuclear attacks if they are directed against centers of population. In the wars of the last two decades aerial bombardment generally proved to be less damaging to civilian morale than anticipated, partly because people could do something to help. But blockbusters, V-1's and V-2's were not multimegaton explosives. It is evident, however, that the forces bolstering or sapping morale under such a test are inseparable from their foundations in the period prior to hostilities, and hence are intimately bound to the whole of American and Soviet policy, domestic and foreign. The maintenance of morale depends upon the citizen's belief in the rightness of the cause to which he may be sacrificed, his acquiescence in the fact that war came, and came in such a fashion, and finally his willingness to persevere in the face of the risk of physical obliteration.

In the preceding paragraphs we have been considering Soviet and American vulnerabilities in the event the bombs were actually delivered on their targets. What of active defense against the bombs and their means of delivery? One form of defense, of course, is to prevent the bombers from taking off by destroying them on the ground along with their bases. As has been stated above, the United States has had a marked advantage on this score, both because of the dispersal of its air bases and because of the capacity of SAC to strike at Soviet bases. Whether such strikes could prevent the opponent from carrying out a coordinated and effective counterraid may be debated. It is a very complex problem, the elements of which are constantly shifting with improvements in aircraft, missiles and base structures. It seems likely, however, that this preventive possibility will diminish with the development of mobile launching sites and of missiles not requiring long or exposed runways.

With respect to defense through warning systems and the

interception of planes or missiles before they reach their target, the United States does enjoy a marked advantage. Soviet bases are much further from our frontiers than our bases are from their frontiers, and this advantage in space can be used for defense. In addition to spotting Soviet planes as they cross their frontiers the United States has the opportunity of utilizing the far reaches of the Arctic, the Atlantic and Pacific Oceans to receive warnings, send up interceptors, and have some time for civil defense and perhaps for evacuation. The details of the job of realizing this potential advantage are enormously complicated. It has been estimated, however, that a fully developed warning and defense screen, properly manned and employing atomic warheads, could hope to destroy, *as an optimum,* from 75 to 80 per cent of the attacking planes (barring changes in offensive weapons).

This should not be taken as very encouraging since the remaining 20 to 25 per cent that came through could, if the initial attacking force was a large one, knock out the major urban centers of the United States. Moreover, these prospects will constantly change with time. In the first place it would take some time to develop such a complete screen; one is not in existence now. The task of the defending force in knocking down the attackers is likely to become more difficult. For example, a jet bomber, with a speed close to that of sound, forces the defense to move into the supersonic range to intercept it. Finally, the figure of 75-80 per cent interception does not cover the day of the intercontinental ballistic missile, rising to a height of 600 miles and attaining a speed about 20 times that of sound, against which no effective defense has been developed and which constitutes a problem of a quite new order of difficulty.

In other words, the task of reducing vulnerability through passive and active defense measures seems to be operating, over time, at a distinct handicap against the powers of offense. This does not mean that at any point in the process improvements in defense are without significant marginal importance, especially since within this uncertain range of defense possibilities the United States does appear to have an advantage.

One major question has to be raised: the advantage of surprise attack. These advantages are doubtless very great in permitting the attacker to bring his forces to full efficiency, to alert his defense system against a counterattack, and even to make arrangements for civilian and official evacuation, though too much activity in advance would reveal his hand. The object of the attack is at a corresponding disadvantage since defensive and offensive forces cannot possibly be maintained at top efficiency and strength at all times.

If the party attacked, however, had brought the defenses of his strategic air force to a high pitch of efficiency, it is quite doubtful that the advantages of striking first would be so great as to prevent the party attacked from making an effective and damaging retaliation. Under these circumstances, it is at least certain that the attacker could not be *sure* he could avoid devastating retaliation. In general the risk element seems so high that a surprise attack would be a very dangerous gamble. The same may be said of the concealed planting of atomic weapons in the opponent's territory in advance of an attack. While such concealment is technically feasible, the risk of discovery is great, especially if a significant number are brought in, and one could never be sure that the enterprise had not been discovered.

Within the limits just mentioned, the Soviet system is far better designed than ours for deciding upon and planning a war initiated by a surprise attack. The United States is simply not organized to make, in the necessary secrecy, the political decision to launch an unprovoked atomic strike. Indeed, we should write off an American-initiated surprise attack as impracticable; it is not—and should not be—our way of doing things.

To summarize this section on strengths and vulnerabilities: both the United States and the Soviet Union are very strong and very vulnerable and promise to become increasingly strong and increasingly vulnerable. The differentials, however, are of importance, as they might constitute the margin between a very painful victory and an even more painful defeat. On balance the United States seems to have an advantage, which will probably diminish but which, at least until the advent of the intercontinental ballistic missile, can be retained despite the political practicability of surprise attack by the U.S.S.R. This rests largely on our advantage in weapons, delivery system, dispersed bases (including aircraft carriers and bases in the territory of allies) and geographic location, and on our capacity to keep our vulnerability at about a par with that of the U.S.S.R. Beyond this we cannot speak with any certainty about the condition in which we would emerge from a mutual thermonuclear mauling. The odds are great that we would be very badly hurt, and these odds will be greater as time passes.

Power for Securing Limited Territorial or Other Material Advantages

In this section we may seem to be on more familiar ground, the traditional arena of power politics and war, in which strengths and vulnerabilities are more easily measured than in the atomic field. But nothing is really familiar about our problem; the atom, in the form of tactical nuclear weapons, and Communism, in the form of infiltration, guerrilla warfare and political subversion—both of these render the "conventional" highly unconventional. Moreover, we are here confronted with a much more extensive range of possible actions than in the case of a thermonuclear slugging match. The importance of one or another type of strength may largely depend upon the form and location of the conflict. The strengths and weaknesses of other nations—the satellites and associates of the Soviet Union, the allies of the United States, and the uncommitted nations—assume considerably greater importance. In the face of such complexity, strength can be measured only very approximately and in aggregates that seem from experience to be the most significant ones.

We may start with the economic strength of the two sides. While the material power of a nation does not rest exclusively on its economic base, its productivity and output can give us a general notion of its ability to develop the sinews of war. Any precise measurement of strength would require detailed knowledge of the uses to which it was to be put, but a few broad and relatively undifferentiated economic estimates, if used with discrimination, can be helpful in giving a picture of the general stature of a nation, its ability to meet reasonably well a variety of contingencies.

The United States currently produces roughly three times as many goods and services as does the Soviet Union. This and the following economic comparisons remain about the same when they are extended to include NATO and the Soviet bloc. Use of this measure (gross national product), however, presents our position vis-à-vis the Russians in a considerably more favorable light than it actually is relative to economic support of war.[2] If the comparison is made for industry only, the ratio of United States to Soviet Union production is whittled down to about 2½ to 1. If we eliminate from consideration production of goods for private consumption—a sector in which we excel but which is less immediately relevant to war-making, though it would include such things as the automobile industry—and measure only output in the war-supporting industries, the United States-Soviet ratio is reduced to somewhere between 2 to 1 and 1 to 1. In some of these industries, such as machine tools, the Soviets produce approximately the same number as we; but our belief is that our tools are generally more productive and can work with finer tolerances, that a larger percentage of them are multiple-purpose, and that even our special-purpose tools are more flexible. In other war-supporting industries, such as steel and petroleum, our production ratio is more than twice theirs. On balance the production ratio is probably closer to 2 to 1 than 1 to 1.

In terms of resource cost, our production of military end items is about 1½ to 2 times that of the Soviet Union, though the ratio of military effectiveness is probably somewhat less. That is, we may not get full value, in terms of military effectiveness, from some of the extra features (and costs) built into our equipment. If we measure numerical output of military end items, the United States-Soviet Union ratio reaches its lowest point—probably just over 1 to 1. In certain specific hard goods, such as light bombers, medium-

[2] The gross national product—a "promiscuous aggregate"—would include, for example, the volume of passenger transportation in and out of large cities, though this might add less to war-support capabilities than "transportation" of passengers by bicycle or on foot—which is not included in GNP.

weight tanks and medium-range artillery, the U.S.S.R. may even be outproducing us. Such a narrow comparison, however, probably presents the United States-Soviet relationship in an unduly unfavorable light, much as the GNP ratio suggests a rosier picture than actually exists. In general, though, we find that the more immediately relevant the economic measurement is to actual military capabilities, the less favorable is the ratio to the United States.

With respect to manpower the Soviet Union appears to have a considerable advantage. The population of the United States is only three-fourths that of the U.S.S.R. If we add China and the satellites, and Canada and Western Europe, to the comparison, the balance tilts far more heavily toward the Soviet bloc. At the moment, however, this advantage is potential rather than actual, largely because of the heavy manpower requirements in Soviet bloc agriculture,[3] but also because of the generally much lower level of Soviet labor productivity. As a result, the United States, despite its smaller population, outproduces the entire Soviet bloc. In the Second World War it was able nearly to match the Soviet Union in numbers of military personnel—a peak of about 11 million as against an estimated 12 million. It seems unlikely that the United States could in the immediate future duplicate that experience, or that the NATO forces could match in numbers those of the Soviet bloc, but this disparity would probably not be *the* most important factor, even in conventional warfare.

Regarding conventional military forces, the Soviet bloc appears to have a considerable advantage in forces in being. The Soviet Union and its satellites could throw into a European conflict, for example, from 100 to 150 divisions, including 50 to 75 mechanized or tank divisions, and could

[3] If the Chinese and the Russians could substantially increase agricultural production and labor productivity, so that they could withdraw men from agriculture and still have sufficient food both for the increased numbers of military personnel and for the urban and rural workers, they would have removed a major obstacle to the military use of manpower, and they could then train and equip forces in much larger numbers than is presently possible. The chances of the Russians being successful in their current endeavors substantially to increase agricultural output have been variously assessed by Western experts—mostly negatively—but the possibility of their success should not be ruled out. Chinese prospects in this respect seem even less favorable.

mobilize and equip an additional 150 to 200 of their own and satellite divisions in about a month's time. Against these forces, the NATO command has at its disposal about 50 active divisions and an additional 50 in reserve; but, since the NATO divisions are scattered from Norway to Turkey, probably no more than 20 divisions would be located where they could be thrown quickly against an attacking force.[4] Offsetting this apparent locational deficiency, however, is the fact that (in General Gruenther's words, January 1954) "We have . . . an air-ground shield which, although still not strong enough, would force an enemy to concentrate prior to attack. In doing so, the concentrating force would be extremely vulnerable to losses from atomic weapon attacks . . . [Further] we think that it [the NATO defense] is of such strength that the Soviets do not now have in occupied Europe sufficient air and ground forces to be certain of overwhelming this shield. Of course, the Soviets can move in additional forces to overcome that deficiency. But if they do, we should be able to get some warning of an impending attack . . . we should [then] be able to alert our air forces."

In the Far Eastern theatre, the Communists appear also to have an advantage in ready manpower (including active reserves), as well as in proximity to certain areas of likely conflict. This advantage is heightened by their control of the military and political initiative. Further, in both Europe and the Far East, the Communists have fewer problems of coordinating their forces; there is greater unity of command, fewer language problems in any particular theatre, and less likelihood of effective opposition developing within the bloc (unless the allies actually occupy bloc territory).

An over-all balance is difficult if not impossible to strike, prior to a test of arms. However, the balance may not be as much in the Soviet favor as it appears from the two preceding paragraphs, since the quality of troops and of weapons is still missing from the picture. For example, to judge from the American record in Korea, it is not unlikely that the allied forces could establish air supremacy over Western

[4] The difference in actual numbers of troops may be somewhat less. Any close comparison by divisions can be misleading since divisions are of differing size and quality.

Europe, even though NATO is alleged to have fewer jet fighters than the Soviet bloc. Further, the United States probably has at its disposal considerably greater numbers of nuclear weapons for tactical use—weapons which would add greatly to its firepower.

A close comparison of these aggregates of Soviet and American economic and military strength could be made only in relation to a particular situation in which the theatre of conflict, the scope and intensity of the fighting and the presence or absence of allied forces were known. In the most general terms, however, and omitting the strategic atomic factor, we would conclude that despite the economic preponderance of the United States and its NATO and other allies, the combination of ready manpower and military supplies currently gives the Soviet bloc at least an initial advantage, which could in time be compensated for by our generally higher technical level and our great conversion potential.

We must avoid simplified views of this balance of forces, and in particular the prevalent notion of the Communist bloc commanding countless hordes, holding interior positions and able to flood out and overwhelm the defenses of any peripheral area. While it does enjoy a population advantage, this does not indicate, for the immediate future at least, a formidable superiority in effective manpower. Moreover, when an "interior" position becomes virtually hemispheric in extent, the principal advantage of being able to shift forces and supplies rapidly from one front to another is largely lost. To be sure, China and Russia do have a local advantage in bordering on certain Middle Eastern and South Asian countries close to their military or supply bases. But Russia would probably not have a logistic advantage over the United States in its ability to shift men and supplies back and forth between Europe and the Middle or Far East. (The problem in Southeast Asia is complicated by the extreme weakness of local forces and the distances from existing concentrations of Western power). Admittedly, Soviet *willingness* to use manpower freely and its possession of the military *initiative* in deciding where the next blow should be struck can give it an advantage, but this represents political rather than physical strength.

The Tactical Use of Nuclear Weapons

In the early postwar years the Soviet military advantage, especially in its large ground forces, was checked by the American atomic monopoly. Because of the incommensurate nature of these respective advantages it was difficult to know just how they balanced one another, and perhaps this uncertainty worked for stability since it made the power calculations difficult for both sides. The approach of Soviet atomic parity has altered this relationship, however, and has forced the question of the tactical use of nuclear weapons.

It must be said that this is one of the most intricate problems with which our leaders and military strategists have to deal, and about which there appears to be no unanimous expert opinion. Our judgments must be regarded as very tentative, and the most we can hope for is not to fall into any seriously misleading conclusions.

There is no question that the possession, by one side only, of tactical atomic weapons can more than compensate for a great deal of manpower and conventional armaments on the other side. If, however, both sides are able to develop a range of tactical atomic arms, deliverable by plane or by artillery, the situation becomes extremely uncertain. Because of the need for dispersal, it may be that more manpower is required rather than less. The concept of a military front changes greatly, especially with respect to strong points, depths and maneuver. The communications system and the battle disposition and direction of troops have to be reorganized. Indeed, even the expectation that the other side *might* have and employ atomic weapons forces a radical revision of organization and planning well in advance of any conflict.

This problem is far too complex and delicate for any but trained experts, with full access to all the facts, to work out in detail. It is not our task here to dabble in strategy. But for our present task of describing strengths and vulnerabilities the following conclusions seem warranted:

1. The *functions,* if not the quantitative requirements, of

manpower will be radically altered, as will the type of military leadership. Intensive prior training will be of utmost importance.

2. The more it is open to *both* sides to develop tactical atomic weapons, the more *each* side must develop its plans and tactics accordingly if it is not to be hopelessly outclassed. Consequently, there seems to be an inescapable impulse toward the increasing integration of atomic weapons in the total weapons systems of the powers involved. To the present, at least, the United States has apparently gone further in this direction than the Soviet Union, partly because of a greater initial need to balance the manpower and conventional arms advantage of the other side.

3. In the short run, the United States does enjoy an advantage in the employment of tactical atomic weapons.

4. As for the outcome of a war fought with tactical atomic weapons and the possibility of its staying within restricted geographic limits and not leading to general thermonuclear warfare, this question is not, so far as we can see, answerable with certainty. The answer at any point in time would depend upon the relative atomic capabilities of the contestants; the importance each attached to the area being fought for; the military possibility, especially with reference to bases and logistics, of keeping a battle confined to a limited area; the relative risk or advantage to each side of allowing the limited war to become an all-out one; and the capacity of both sides to maintain self-control and not set off the general war through excitement, revenge or hysteria.

Guerrilla and Irregular Warfare

There are situations in which tactical atomic weapons may not be militarily effective. In general such situations are those where, because of the terrain or the political situation, warfare by infiltration or guerrilla tactics is most effective, areas where there is no clearly defined front, no obvious concentration in or near the battle area. It seems evident from recent experience that the Communists here enjoy a marked advantage. They have had much practical experience, in Europe and Asia, with guerrilla and partisan warfare. They have been adept at exploiting discontents, mobilizing forces, turning a political into a civil conflict and converting civil conflicts into minor wars, through which they have achieved territorial gains.

Irregular warfare suffers from some inherent limitations. The ability to maintain it usually depends upon support and supplies from outside the area. In modern warfare, purely guerrilla fighting in isolation can, sooner or later, be choked off by a strong opponent. Consequently, the importance of this advantage in the over-all picture depends upon the balance of strength in other sectors and areas. But if these tend to cancel out one another, and if irregular warfare comes to be the major active form of conflict, it could be of great importance.

Future Economic Prospects

The preceding comparisons are based on the present situation or that of the relatively near future. What can be said of longer-run prospects? First, it should be emphasized that we cannot regard the future as fixed or determined, either by past rates of development or by the current levels of strength. The relative strength of each nation in the future will be significantly and perhaps decisively affected by a whole range of human decisions. Nevertheless, rates of development are of importance in indicating possible future trends which the policy maker may wish to change or reinforce, in suggesting certain limits to actions by either side or in giving some clues to the timing of strategy.

In the discussion of rates of development bearing on the future strength of the United States, or NATO, and of the Soviet Union, or the Soviet bloc, attention has focused chiefly on economic growth during the next decade or two. Population changes seem to be of less immediate relevance; if population growth were accompanied by increased production, it might add to strength; if not so accompanied, it might lead to enfeeblement. Changes in the size and quality of military forces are so dependent upon human decisions that long-run projections seem out of the question.

The relationship of economic growth to future strength is an elusive one. As we have seen, not all of the components of the economy which are reflected in measures of gross national product or even of industrial production contribute in the same measure to current strength. On the other hand, these indicators are not irrelevant, since it is possible, if time is available, to redirect resources so as to hasten growth in the particular sectors deemed most important to national strength.

Reduced to simplest terms, the evidence indicates that the Soviet Union has expanded at a significantly faster rate, both industrially and in gross national product, than has the United States in almost all years since 1928, the start of the Soviet planning era, and even faster than the United States did during the period of the latter's exceptionally rapid growth from 1860 to 1900.[5] If the comparison is restricted to the postwar years—and here the picture varies according to the years chosen—it appears that the Soviet Union's gross national product expanded at a rate of about 7 or 8 per cent from 1947 or 1948 to 1953, whereas the measure for the United States during those same years was between 4½ and 5 per cent.[6] The disparity in industrial growth for the same years appears to have been even greater, the rates being estimated at about 12 per cent for the Soviet Union[7] and about 5 per cent for the United States.[8] The figures cited, especially those for the Soviet Union, are questionable, but most Western students of the Soviet Union would not, we believe, question the conclusion that the Soviet economy has expanded in postwar years at something like 1½ times the rate of our own.

Introduction of postwar economic growth rates in the satellites and NATO would have little effect on this compari-

[5] By use of a shorter time period embracing World War II—for example, 1938 to 1953, as in a recent Library of Congress publication—conflicting conclusions could be drawn. That comparison would be misleading, however, since the United States data would reflect the stimulating effects of World War II on a depressed economy, whereas the Soviet data would reflect the considerable destruction suffered in that war. See *Trends in Economic Growth: A Comparison of the Western Powers and the Soviet Bloc* (Washington: GPO, 1955).

[6] The United States rate was between 3½ to 4 per cent if the period chosen is 1947 or 1948 to 1954, or over 6 per cent from 1949 to 1953.

[7] Data compiled and adjusted by Hodgman (*Soviet Industrial Production, 1928–1951*) yield an average of about 15 per cent for the same period.

[8] The United States rate was between 3 and 3½ per cent for the period 1947 or 1948 to 1954, and over 8 per cent from 1949 to 1953.

son, because the ratio of Eastern European satellite growth rates to those of NATO (excluding the United States) does not appear to have differed significantly from the ratio of Soviet to United States growth rates. China excluded, the Soviet satellites appear to have expanded since 1948 at an annual rate of about 5 per cent for gross national product, and a rate of 10 per cent for industrial output.

How likely is it that the postwar trends will continue? There are a number of reasons for expecting the Soviet and Eastern European rates of economic growth to diminish.[9] This, however, does not preclude Soviet-bloc growth rates from leveling off at a figure considerably in excess of any of those usually projected for the United States and its allies. A likely rate of economic growth for the United States during the next decade or two is from 3 to 4 per cent, barring a major depression or a succession of minor ones such as that in 1954. A likely rate of Soviet growth is about 5 to 7 per cent for the same period. Although "forecasts" for the Soviet satellites and for the allied nations would differ somewhat from these estimates for the United States and the Soviet Union, there appears to be general agreement among Western students of Soviet-type economies that the Soviet bloc will continue to grow economically at a rate greater than that of the allies—perhaps half again as fast, if a single figure has to be chosen.

The implications of these estimates for United States economic policy will be considered in a subsequent chapter.[10] In concluding this section, however, we may touch on one problem of interpreting the meaning of growth rates for the future relative strengths of the United States and the Soviet Union. Although the Soviet rate of economic growth may continue at a higher level than that of the United States, the size of the increment will be smaller because the Soviet level of production, to which the higher rate is applied, is much smaller than that of the United States (roughly one-third). In other words, while the ratio of American to Soviet production is decreasing, the absolute difference between Amer-

[9] For a discussion of this point, see the Annex at the end of this chapter, p. 74.

[10] See below, p. 134.

ican and Soviet levels of production is still increasing. Obviously, if the higher rate of annual increment persisted, the Soviet Union would eventually catch up with and outproduce the United States. In the long run all the advantage goes to the nation which is expanding more rapidly. In a shorter run, however, there might be some question as to the relative advantage because of the increasing quantitative gap between the two economies. Under certain circumstances this might provide the United States with an increased surplus of economic production available for implementing a particular policy. It is an interesting question whether this potential advantage could counterbalance the increasing maneuverability and flexibility which the Russians will enjoy through their relatively larger if absolutely smaller increment of output.

Political Warfare

In estimating the strengths and vulnerabilities relating to political warfare, we are concerned with manifestations of power which, though real enough, are hard to define and are usually expressed metaphorically: strength of morale, political pressure, force of public opinion, social stresses, etc. Physical power also plays a role, but primarily as a means of influencing the will of the opponent, as a potentiality in the background rather than as a force in action.

In trying to compare the political strengths and vulnerabilities of the United States and the Soviet Union we may refer to our interpretation of their relationship: that the antagonism between them derives primarily from the *fact* of the Bolshevik Revolution, from the seizure of state power and the development or transformation of institutions by a group of men intent upon maintaining and preserving that revolution, and expanding it territorially, in face of a world which, by their definition, was, is, and will continue to be necessarily and ineradicably hostile until it is fully absorbed into their system. In consequence, the whole of the Soviet system, its ideology and its organization have been designed to exploit this antagonism, and, indeed, make very little sense without it.

In view of the fact that the Soviet system is thus directed

toward antagonism, it would appear at first glance as though it had a clear advantage over the American system, which rests on entirely different foundations. As a result of its history and relative geographical isolation, the structure of American society has been less adapted than that of other great powers to dealing with antagonistic relations. Because of the apparent disadvantage we suffer in this regard, we may tend to accept one of two opposing conclusions. The first is to maintain that, even though the Soviet system is designed for conflict and ours is not, the American nation is perfectly capable of meeting the challenge on its own terms. In this view we hear an echo of Pericles' comparison between democratic Athens and regimented Sparta:

> Where our rivals from their very cradles by a painful discipline seek after manliness, at Athens we live exactly as we please, and yet are just as ready to encounter every legitimate danger. . . . If with habits not of labor but of ease, and courage not of art but of nature, we are still willing to encounter danger, we have the double advantage of escaping the experience of hardships in anticipation and of facing them in the hour of need as fearlessly as those who are never free from them.

Such assumption of a "double advantage" disposes of the problem by denying its reality.

The opposing conclusion is that the methods of Communist political warfare are so highly effective against a soft-shelled society such as ours that it is necessary to employ weapons from their arsenal in our struggle against them. Borrowing and adapting effective weapons developed by the enemy has been customary and indispensable in the history of warfare, but in political warfare, where the devices developed may be intimately related to the ethical norms of the society, it requires a good deal of discrimination to make the distinction between developing political counterweapons and creating of one's own society a mirror-image of the opponent.

Neither of these conclusions, in our view, can be accepted as it stands. While the first has the merit of displaying the necessary confidence in democracy's ability to meet the world's challenges, it fails to express the all-important fact that democracy is not something we can regard as attained, as a static achievement; it is itself a never-ending task and challenge, and only through our continued and strenuous efforts to satisfy its demands on us do we create the dynamism which is indeed capable of meeting the threats of our time. The opposing conclusion, while acutely aware of the dangers of complacency about democracy's past achievements and successes, may err in equating our goals with the opponent's. Estimates of political strength are likely to be empty unless we ask, strength for what? If the purposes of the two opponents differ, we may be obliged to use different yardsticks for each in measuring the effectiveness and adequacy of their political strengths.

From our general experience, a party which, in a relatively stable situation, is trying to force a change is at a disadvantage vis-à-vis the party of stability, since it must possess and be able to exert additional will and strength to break through habit and inertia. If this party is at the same time physically weaker, it must overcome a double disadvantage. In other words, its requirements in political strength, for the achievement of its particular goal, are greater than those of the party of order and stability.

In some measure—we will introduce qualifications presently—the United States in the past has enjoyed a double advantage in this regard. While we may feel that our mobile society and expanding free economy are in fact constantly generating change and that we are not frozen to any unchanging *status quo,* the United States does not have, as a political objective, the aim of breaking the continuity of developments, of forcing change; the distinction is between evolution, no matter how rapid, and revolution. The Soviet leaders, at least, have considered the United States the principal upholder and beneficiary of the *status quo*. Moreover, they have always been preoccupied with overtaking and surpassing the American productive level, which they consider a decisive long-run factor in world politics. This difference between American and Soviet objectives and physical capabilities has meant different requirements. To give an example, American interests are satisfied if the geographic areas lying between the U.S.S.R. and the United States remain independent. We are not obliged to exert the energy and will that would be necessary if our interest were to bring them under our political domination. We are not driven to take the risks—however great or small they may be deemed—of planning and initiating such adventures as the Berlin blockade or the Korean invasion. Nor are we impelled to create the explosive dangers of an enforced domestic conformity, since a diversity of political views is itself in conformity with our interests.

But these advantages which the United States has enjoyed are subject to some important qualifications in the present and probable future international situation.

In the first place, when two powers approach parity in their physical strength and resources, the stronger's margin of indifference with respect to political strength diminishes. Today the Soviet Union may not have the revolutionary enthusiasm of the 1920's but from our point of view this is more than balanced by the enormous increase in power and territory which the Soviet Union controls today as against Lenin's time. This great shift in the ratios of physical power reduces our ability to regard the political strength of the opponent as a matter of relative unimportance.

In the second place, when conditions are unstable, when social habits are under criticism and are disintegrating, the party of change has the opportunity of exploiting this instability. In many parts of the world today where, for a variety of reasons, the existing social order is in a state of more or less rapid change, the Communists are not battling the solid wall of a self-assured society but can ride along with, and stimulate, the tides of anticolonialism, anti-westernism and anti-capitalism. This opportunity is enhanced when the party of change is eager, as the Communists are, to accept and even to promote social chaos as a prelude to the imposition of the new order. One of the distinguishing features of Leninism-Stalinism is its patent willingness to reduce a society to a rubble heap for the sake of gaining power; this is in marked contrast to the earlier Marxian notion of the revolution as the historical climax, the capstone, of a capitalist structure to be taken over largely intact.

In the third place, while the party of the *status quo*, especially if it is materially the stronger, in general need not take the risks required of the revolutionary, at those points where the antagonism becomes an explicit and definite challenge—as in the case of the Berlin blockade—it must be prepared to stand up to the risks imposed on it by the other side. If it fails at these points of encounter, its potential advantages will in time be eroded away by blackmail and bluff.

Finally, if the party of order has, as a consequence of the conflict, taken up thoughts of a "roll-back" or liberation, then its requirements obviously increase, since it, too, has become engaged in an effort to force an alteration of the *status quo*.

If the above analysis is correct, a comparison of the political strengths of the U.S.S.R. and the United States depends upon a double estimate of their adequacy in achieving the particular, and dissimilar, objectives of the two systems in the setting of the clash of these objectives in the international scene. In this light let us examine some Soviet strengths and vulnerabilities as compared with our own.

Ideological Conformity

The possession of a thoroughly developed, universally imposed body of theory and practice—Communism—can be considered an indispensable element of political strength in determining and supporting the aims of the Soviet Union. The persistence of the revolutionary order and the justification for its universal pretensions depend upon the maintenance of this ideology. Part of its appeal lies in the certainties it purports to offer. The United States and the non-Communist world have no such unifying philosophy, and, even if they were all agreed upon anti-Communism, such a negative premise could not itself create an equivalent system. In terms of American society, of course, there is no need for such conformity, but in this situation of antagonism can such a loose-jointed, relatively nonconformist order hold its own? In reviewing the experiences of recent years the answer would appear to be affirmative. Although many Americans have been troubled by discovering the impossibility of absorbing Communism as one among many political systems in the international community of their aspirations, the very insistence on conformity and the doctrinal nature of Soviet Communism have also served to isolate it and to reduce its appeal. In the United States, at least, Communism had its greatest appeal precisely at the time of the Popular Front when, in appearance, it had dropped its rigidly defined and uncompromising individuality. Given the differing tasks of the two systems, then, it would appear on balance that the self-isolating quality of Communist conformity rather largely negatives the advantages it may gain through its dogmatic certitude.

Revolutionary Zeal

In a contest of wills a great advantage obviously accrues to the party with the greater belief and enthusiasm in its cause. Certainly the expansion of the Soviet empire from a small nucleus of revolutionaries in 1917 is not to be explained without the presence of this zeal. Enthusiasm alone, of course, did not bring the Communists to power; in every case, historically, their seizure of power has been in the wake of a state apparatus destroyed or weakened by war (Russia, Yugoslavia, China) or with strong military support (East Central Europe). Moreover, we have to make a sharp distinction between the zeal of the Communists themselves and the state of social ferment which may produce a revolutionary mood.

With regard to the former, the style, comportment and outward appearance of the upper party hierarchy in the Soviet Union today seems very different from that of the early days of the Bolshevik Revolution, an alteration that some have ascribed to a loss of élan and belief. But we should do well to recall a remark by the late Carlo Sforza, that this transformation was analogous to the difference between the early Christians and the medieval Papacy; a change in temper had taken place, but one could hardly regard Innocent III as lacking in faith and zeal. In the case of the Communist leaders, they are obviously "professionals" of long standing, with much experience behind them, and doubtless some cynicism, but it would be a romantic fallacy to take this as necessarily marking a loss of dynamism. Moreover, when we look at the Communist leadership in areas where Communism is still striving for power, we are made fully aware that the movement has not lost its ability to imbue its adherents with great passion and energy.

When we consider the social temper we find very important differences between a) countries where Communism is in power, b) the economically advanced non-Communist countries, and c) the so-called underdeveloped countries. In the countries which have been Communized, and especially the U.S.S.R. itself, we have reason to doubt the presence of enthusiasm in the bulk of the population, though it is difficult to separate the obligatory and simulated fervor from the real product. Still, these countries are not our major concern in this connection; with enthusiasm or without it they have been effectively harnessed to the goals of the Communist leadership.

With respect to the more advanced and industrialized non-Communist countries, the situation, though by no means uniform, is hardly one of revolutionary turbulence, even in countries with large Communist parties. In 1918–1920 there was in many of these countries a great deal of real ferment. The Second World War, in contrast, was much less productive of social and political turmoil in Western Europe and America. When this diminution of spontaneous movements for revolutionary change is combined with the quite remarkable decline of Marxism as a guide to action where it is not a state-imposed doctrine (the history of the German and Austrian Social Democratic parties is most illuminating in this regard), one sees the possibility that we may be approaching, in the industrialized parts of the world, the end of a powerful but time-bound wave of radical socialist enthusiasm.[11]

In the underdeveloped or economically backward areas—and these cover a very wide range of conditions—there is still enormous ferment, which may be subsiding a bit in some regions but which is only beginning in others. From our point of view this is undoubtedly the most vulnerable area and one where the zeal of the Communists can find sympathetic response. But while we must not underestimate this danger, we should remember that the aims and goals of the

[11] But see also below, p. 146.

Communists and of these peoples are not identical, or need not be. For example, the most striking thing about the objectives which emerged from the Bandung Conference of Asian and African nations in 1955 was their familiarity; they were not of Communist origin but were goals born of the democratic tradition, our goals, with which we should not feel at all embarrassed.

We should not overlook the fact that while the area of Communist control has greatly expanded since 1945, so has the area of democracy, not only in the former Axis powers that were our antagonists in the Second World War, but also in many formerly colonial or dependent countries of the Near and Far East. Our preoccupation with the outthrust of Communist power and influence must not blind us to the tremendous continuing force of the democratic ideals: self-government free of foreign control; the dignity of the human individual whatever his race, creed or color; material welfare and betterment as the product and symbol of that dignity; the fraternity of all men. Thus we return to our earlier observation that democracy is a challenge, not an achievement; if, *but only if,* we work to realize the demands of democracy itself, we can achieve the dynamism and zeal to meet the Communists in these important parts of the world.

Duplicity

The fact that Communist tactics—as explicitly set forth, for example, in Lenin's "Left Wing Communism"—make use of any and all forms of deceit and deception in dealing with the capitalist enemy has been taken as a singular advantage for the U.S.S.R. In terms of Communist objectives Lenin is quite persuasive in showing the need for such unrestricted and unsqueamish use of means. We must be careful, however, not to make too much of this advantage. It is a wasting asset that loses its effectiveness with repeated use. Indeed, one could argue that the rather naive blatancy with which the Communists from the start announced their intended double-dealing may have done them as much damage as good. It has meant, of course, that other nations, at each step in their dealings with the Soviet Union, have had to develop the habit of looking for potential treachery in every statement, a possible breach in every engagement. This has reduced international dealings with the U.S.S.R. to a pretty sterile level. But while the Soviets have scored some points, we can conclude that if we keep our wits about us the Communist reputation for congenital duplicity is probably as great an advantage to us as actual or intended duplicity may be to them.

The Communist Party

Closely associated with the question of duplicity is that of international Communism. In the Communist parties and their fronts the Soviet Union possesses instruments to penetrate and influence other societies. We have no corresponding political tool. But it may be incorrect to rest the comparison upon the ability of one or the other party to create fifth columns. It is not an inherent requirement of our society to subvert others (whether it is expedient to do so under conditions of war is quite a different question). Rather the comparison should be based on our ability to thwart the activities of the Communist parties. In the United States, at least, it seems fairly evident that we have proved able. The case of the American Negro is perhaps the most striking example. Despite the social and economic disadvantages suffered by American Negroes, the Communists have been singularly unsuccessful in influencing them, in part because of the duplicity of Communist tactics, which were soon seen through, but basically because the Negroes have not lost confidence in being able to realize their aspirations within our system. Consequently, instead of seeing this as an American vulnerability, or comparing it with our relative inability to manipulate, say, Ukrainian nationalism in the U.S.S.R., we should feel that this particular sector of the conflict affords a definite indication of American political strength, and a most important one.

It is true, of course, that in a number of the parts of the world the story is not the same; the infiltrated society is not demonstrating the capacity to resist and shrug off the efforts of the local Communist parties, and in these areas, some of which are of major strategic importance,[12] the Soviet Union has gained a significant political advantage which we must work to counteract.

A Controlled Society

The police state, with its centralization of authority, its ability to reach decisions in secrecy and without public debate, its controls over its citizens and over news and communications, has a number of apparent political warfare advantages over a free society. This is reflected in the tightening of controls in the free society under conditions of national emergency. Among the presumed advantages are the ability to reverse a policy overnight (as in the case of the German-Soviet pact of 1939); to avoid evidence of internal debate and disagreement over a line of policy; to prepare surprise moves and *faits accomplis;* to let the people hear only what the government wants them to hear, and prevent alien or disruptive ideas from entering the society; to prevent the opponent from sampling the state of public opinion and morale; and to give the appearance of unanimous support for a policy. In a word, such controls give the rulers a freer hand for decision and a simulacrum of public opinion to support it.

When these advantages are set against the pulling and hauling of American party politics, the transparency of most of our political decisions, the openness and variety of public opinion and the volubility of dissenting views, it is easy to conclude that the advantages of the controlled system are overwhelming. We are constantly tipping our hand; the masters of the Kremlin play close to the vest. We write letters to our newspapers worrying about the wisdom of our ways; the Soviet people acclaim their confidence in the infallibility of the party's higher leadership.

Yet some of these advantages are more imaginary than real. By and large, the noisy floundering of our political process does in time produce a rather wide consensus concerning the main lines to be followed. Conversely, manipulation to create opinion (even when successful) and the lack of real communication between ruler and ruled create prob-

[12] See below, p. 220.

lems of their own, especially the danger of undertaking a policy which in application proves to be more than the traffic can bear. Abrupt changes in the line can leave the population bewildered and unprepared, as seems to have been the case in the early months of the German invasion of 1941. Moreover, it is incorrect to assume that the decision-making process is simplified merely by taking it out of the public domain. When it is confined to a co-opting body such as a Politburo, where political responsibility, personal dependence and departmental interests are hopelessly intertwined, the process can become very tortuous.

As far as the tipping of hands is concerned, in some respects Soviet policy may be more predictable than our own because of its attachment to the Communist ideology. Our debates are in the open, to be sure, but for that reason new views, new demands, new realignments create a constant possibility of new policies, which even we cannot anticipate. On the Soviet side there is by now a pretty well identified bag of tricks. They may try a "hard" line, they may try a "soft" line, but at least we are in a reasonably good position to anticipate their range of choices, though the particular choice may be concealed until it occurs.

Nevertheless, with all these reservations it remains true that we do feel at a disadvantage when we face the Soviet regime, wondering just what may turn up next and where, and how we should best be prepared for it. This sense of dismay is itself a political fact of importance, especially when it creates the myth of the opponent as an inscrutable, unhampered, all-controlling chess player. While this Soviet advantage does derive from the structure of their society and government, it is, in the last analysis, a reflection of the basic intent and meaning of the regime; it is not an adventitious advantage.

Soviet Vulnerabilities

In the preceding paragraphs we have touched on some of the strengths, in the area of political forces, which the U.S.S.R. seems to enjoy. On examination we find that, while the Soviet Union does possess attributes and instruments largely lacking to us, they do not necessarily create a corresponding comparative advantage, since they must be set against the exceptional kind of requirements the Communist ideology and the Soviet regime have set themselves. Still, the Soviet leaders do have some advantages, even if they are not overwhelming. Nor is this surprising, for it would really be a sign of incredible mismanagement if all the sacrifices and discipline the Soviet rulers have imposed on their subjects, and on themselves, had brought no dividends whatsoever. It is only to be expected that a society geared to conflict from its very inception, and fighting to overcome an initial material disadvantage, should have developed these advantages in the political sphere.

But what of the vulnerabilities, since a system such as that of the Soviet Union is not created without its costs? Perhaps they can be lumped under the general headings of "disaffection" and "sterility."

Disaffection is regarded by many as the Achilles' heel of the Soviet system and the principal hope for its early demise. The disaffection has been real enough and widespread. It has been particularly strong in the satellite nations where anti-Communism is compounded with anti-Russian feelings and hatred of alien rule; among the Ukrainians and certain other non-Russian nationalities within the Soviet Union; among the millions of inmates of the concentration camps and their relatives and friends outside; among the social groups marked for liquidation; and among the peasants. But it is also to be found in the more favored groups and even within the Communist party. Indeed, the threat of schism, of palace revolt, has been a constant worry of the Soviet leaders. Moreover, the system seems automatically to create disaffection as it operates, in part precisely because of its efforts to impose uniformity and create a monolithic order of society.

Perhaps the most striking evidence of disaffection is provided by the behavior of Soviet citizens in areas where the regime's control was removed or greatly weakened during periods of the Second World War: the German-occupied territories and Moscow itself during the 1941 retreat. In both instances disaffection came strongly to the surface. Some have argued that the Germans could greatly have increased this disaffection had they behaved other than they did. The unifying effect of the war itself, the horrors of the German invasion and the eventual Soviet victory may subsequently have served as important counteragents. Still, we have, from this historical experience, an unmistakable glimpse of an important inner weakness of the regime.

But just as we were obliged to make some qualifications about Soviet strengths, so here we must be cautious about overestimating vulnerabilities. Again we should not confuse our requirements. For a nation like the United States, evidence of such widespread disaffection would be a clear sign of approaching disaster. Yet we cannot judge the Soviet system in this light. The most formidable feature of totalitarian regimes is not that there should be disaffection—that is axiomatic in a system trying to remold human nature and society—but that they can build, and build successfully, upon such a foundation, that the human subject can be geared to the purposes of the regime, that the skilled use of the stick and the carrot can prevent disaffection from crystallizing into real resistance. We can gain some satisfaction from the fact that so many Chinese Communist prisoners of war in Korea refused to be repatriated. The Communists can probably gain equivalent satisfaction from the fact that such disaffected soldiers had been induced to fight so effectively for the regime up to the time they were captured. There have been disturbances, in East Berlin, among the Vorkuta miners and elsewhere. But when one recalls the tradition of revolt, of peasant, worker and nationalist uprising, that was such a feature of Eastern European and Russian history in past times, one is struck by the significant fact that since the Kronstadt rebellion of 1921 there have been no major organized upheavals within Communist-controlled territory.

So while this is a real vulnerability, and must be a constant concern of the Soviet leaders, it is hard to assess its importance, at least until such time as the regime, for whatever reason, shows signs of cracking up. As was the case in the Second World War, it might be that disaffection cannot come into play as an active force except on Soviet territory occupied by an enemy.

By "sterility" we mean that deadening of creativity which

appears to be one of the self-defeating consequences of imposing a total ideological system upon a society. From time to time even Soviet "self-criticism" has shown an uneasy awareness of this drying up of the creative springs. The history of Soviet art, music and letters, as well as such episodes as the Lysenko controversy in the field of natural science, affords some very illuminating case studies of the ill effects of enforced conformity. This feature of Soviet Communism lies very close to the heart of our conflict with it, since it is the antithesis of our ideal of the free society, unfettered inquiry and uninhibited creation. Freedom is not just a good in itself but promotes a vigorous society with better chances of healthy survival.

But again we must enter a reservation, and one that could be of decisive importance. Despite the heavy ideological burden we see lying on Soviet thought, art and science, the fact of the matter is that in a number of fields, and most notably in natural science, pure and applied, the Soviets have been making some spectacular achievements. Their accomplishment in the nuclear field is very much more than just copying, or spying upon, Western developments. In their training of scientists and engineers the evidence seems clear that they are doing an impressive job, in numbers and in quality. For the time being, at least, and in this vital area of science and engineering, they have avoided being hamstrung by their ideological preconceptions,[13] and we would do ourselves no good to belittle their efforts.

Even more important, we must not neglect the fact that the United States, for all its goals of free inquiry, is not doing as well as it should. It is chastening but useful to realize that virtually every new weapon of the Second World War was the outgrowth of European, not American, thinking. To be sure, we have displayed our customary ability in organizing, applying and mass-producing the products of this thinking, but a roster of the personnel connected not only with the Manhattan Project but with the subsequent development of the thermonuclear weapons will show the extent of our dependence

[13] It has been suggested that because this field is less burdened by ideological controls it has, for that reason, become particularly attractive to the best students in the U.S.S.R.

upon foreign scientific thought and theory. At a time when weapons become ever more complex, when higher mathematics rather than Yankee ingenuity may be the key to our survival, this is not a matter for indifference or indulgence.

The American situation regarding the training of its scientists and engineers is far from reassuring. Not only are we facing a shortage, not only are we training too few teachers of science, especially at the critical high school level, but in our national education the decline of mathematics—the product in our view of a general weakening of the liberal arts tradition—is not easily or quickly to be remedied. We cannot in the present report make an analysis of the American educational system and the formidable problem of improving the quality of mass education. But it is highly relevant to our present concern to stress as vigorously as we can the importance of this problem and the need to meet it, a task that will take time, goes far beyond *ad hoc* or "crash" measures, and ultimately means—for our kind of society if not for the Communists'—reinvigorating and adapting the great liberal arts tradition to the demands of the times. In any event, this example does demonstrate that we cannot let our notion of what Soviet vulnerabilities *ought* to be blind us to their achievements or our own shortcomings.

When we set Soviet strengths against Soviet vulnerabilities we reach the conclusion that their advantages, which are real but not overwhelming, are primarily at the points of contact in political warfare, that their disadvantages, which are also real but not overwhelming, are behind the scene as a potential, and that the two are related; their vulnerabilities are in large part the inescapable cost of the political weapons they have created. When we go beyond this, however, and ask more generally whether the Soviet system *with* its costs possesses a political warfare advantage over our own—in the broadest sense of the comparative ability to win in a conflict of will and intellect—this question is equivalent to asking whether Soviet Communism, with its aims and its methods, represents a more realistic and hardheaded appraisal than our own of the needs, impulses and potentialities of contemporary human nature and society. This question, of course, is to be answered not by estimates or conjecture but by actions, now and in the future, actions which—in our view—will be made by the free will of men, not by the inexorable working out of a historical process.

The Balance

In concluding this chapter on strengths and vulnerabilities we must emphasize the need not to regard the comparisons we have made as data in a problem in mathematics or chess. Even the physical factors are not just "givens"; for the most part they are also the creation, past, present and future, of the human mind and the human will, and their meaning depends upon human decisions concerning their employment. To illustrate, we may look at some types of situation in which the kinds of force we have discussed separately above—atomic power, conventional military and economic forces, political strength—can overlap and merge with one another.

It seems likely that as the United States and the Soviet Union reach what has been called atomic parity—when each is capable of devastating the other with multimegaton weapons, but at the cost of being subjected to devastating retaliation—there will be a mutual inclination not to become involved in such an exchange. At the same time, so long as the Soviet regime's relation to the United States is one of antagonism, the play and counterplay of force in its different manifestations may be expected to continue. This thermonuclear "ceiling" can itself become a factor in the contest, with each side trying to use it to paralyze the other's will, either by demonstrating greater willingness to approach the ceiling or by inducing the opponent not to face the risk of any resort to force. This contest could take a number of forms.

Perhaps the least likely, as time passes, will be the expressed threat to set off a full-scale, mutually devastating exchange as the first response to a local encounter or aggression, since such a threat is more and more apt to be taken, or expected to be taken, as an empty bluff.[14]

A more likely form of competition will be the progressive incorporation of a full range of nuclear weapons in the devel-

[14] See below, pp. 92-94.

opment of "conventional" strategy and tactics. In this case the test will be in the capacity of the opponents to face the risk of engaging in a limited war that may see the use of nuclear weapons. While a localized nuclear war is not impossible in theory, no one can be sure, before the event, how such a war—or any war in these days, for that matter—might develop once it has started. It is certainly not difficult to imagine a local war building up and expanding, in area and intensity, until the massive thermonuclear exchange seemed to be only the next step, and not a very long one. While it is certainly not to be excluded that such a potential build-up might induce both sides to call off the fight and come to some arrangement to avoid their mutual destruction, we must also reckon with the fact that it provides good opportunity for piecemeal or "creeping" expansion, under the threat of *atomic blackmail.*

We must recognize that a Communist strategy for progressive expansion can involve numerous devices: diplomatic seduction, subversion and political warfare, supported by the threat, or actual employment, of military force. These many devices could be brought to bear with considerable sophistication and local tailoring to achieve the conquest of one after another of the vulnerable countries on the periphery of the Communist bloc. In this subtle and deadly game the centralized direction of the Communist order is a serious challenge to the will and determination of the loosely organized, often disorganized, non-Communist world, with its divergent interests, differing vulnerabilities and disparate capabilities.

In face of these extremely unstable possibilities, the role of political warfare is of utmost importance: to make use of the expectations and uncertainties implicit in a conflict carried on under the thermonuclear ceiling in such a way as to keep the opponent from engaging in the conflict at all, partly through the fear that it may get out of hand, or to induce him to engage in a manner disadvantageous to himself.

We cannot here develop this difficult problem in greater detail,[15] but it does point up the question of determining the relative strength of the United States and the U.S.S.R. in

15 See below, p. 248.

dealing with a challenge in which all the components of their power may be involved, actually or by implication. As we have suggested above, the answer to such a question, despite appearances to the contrary, cannot be reduced simply to a measurement of capabilities, even if all the relevant facts were known. To be sure, the outcome would depend in part upon the possession of military, atomic and economic strengths. But it would also depend upon their use—how they were used and, above all, whether they were used.

It can be maintained that the willingness to use certain weapons is itself a manifestation of political strength. But it is doubtful whether we are here dealing with something that can be measured or compared. For example, the statement that the Soviet leaders, an unusually tough and case-hardened group of men, are better able than we to make the difficult and risky decisions about using atomic weapons—such a statement, as soon as it is made and propagated, has an immediate tendency to create its own refutation, since it conveys an immediate obligation to the American to be quite as tough or tougher. If you tell another man he is a coward, he can immediately prove your statement false by punching you in the nose. In other words, when our analysis of strengths and capabilities impinges upon self-awareness, which is the unique characteristic of human societies, we are no longer dealing with facts and figures alone but with tasks and requirements.

ANNEX

Note on Prospects for Soviet Economic Growth

The considerations for and against a declining rate of Soviet economic growth can be summarized as follows:

1. Technological problems. The Soviet Union started from a much lower technological base and has been able to take over, directly or with modifications, technology developed in the West. With the narrowing of the technological gap, this advantage will be lost. Soviet technological progress has remained rapid, however, even as the gap has narrowed, and has made significant advances independently, particularly in areas of high interest to the Communists. Further, there are still many opportunities for applying existing technology in backward economic sectors and activities, e.g., in light industry, industrial services and construction, if Soviet authorities should so choose.

2. Potential labor shortages. There has been a slowing up in the rate of increase of the nonagricultural labor force. This *could* be remedied by substantial increases in agricultural labor productivity, and the resultant release of manpower to industry. Such large-scale releases, however, seem unlikely in the near future.

3. Declining rate of increase of industrial labor productivity. The rate of increase of industrial output per worker has slowed down in recent years, and there are many reasons for expecting this to continue: current rates of increase are still high by the standards of most countries; a declining rate of increase has normally accompanied industrial maturity; fixed capital per worker may not increase as rapidly as in the past; and technological advances may be slower. However, the decline in the Soviet rate of increase, if it continues, will probably not reach the United States level, for the following reasons: a slower rate of increase in the nonagricultural labor force would allow more training of entrants (this is already taking place); there are still oppor-

tunities for rapid productivity advances, especially in capital-starved light industries; less rather than more capital may be required per unit of output now that the Soviet Union has improved its technological and managerial base; rectification of the imbalance between males and females in the labor force might also contribute to greater labor productivity; and, finally, Soviet investment is expected to continue at a high rate, and in a direction conducive to rapid economic growth.

4. Capital shortages.

a. Increased demand for replacement capital. As the ratio of capital stock to annual investment increases, a larger and larger share of new investment is required simply to replace worn-out or obsolete capital, and the proportion of net to gross investment as well as the proportion of net investment to total capital stock will probably fall.

b. Capital windfalls from World War II cannot be expected to recur. However, the accelerating effects of war booty have been largely over for several years, whereas the rate of growth of the Soviet economy has continued high.

5. Potential reduction in the productivity of capital investments.

a. Agricultural problem. Since most productive agricultural land in the Soviet Union has already been utilized, the imperative demand for increased agricultural production can be met only by extensive working of marginal lands or by more intensive efforts to improve yields of previously cultivated areas. Both programs would involve heavy agricultural investments—such as machinery, fertilizers, irrigation and even housing and increased consumers' goods for agricultural workers—the return from which would probably be less than if resources were allocated to industry.

b. Pressure for other investments of low productivity. Shortages in housing and other urban facilities are becoming more and more acute. The productivity of investments in these areas, however, is not reflected in the Soviet productivity indexes. Therefore, to the extent that Soviet authorities attempt to remedy these accumulated shortages, the rate of increase of capital productivity, as well as of output, will fall.

c. Diminishing areas where capital of low productivity can be replaced. If Soviet authorities have allocated investments rationally, it could be assumed that they have supplied capital equipment first to those industries where capital would be most productive. This assumption might be true with respect to intra-heavy-industry allocations, but in view of their bias in favor of heavy industry it does not appear to be correct with respect to light vs. heavy industry. Therefore, at least in the short run, capital productivity *could* be increased by increasing investments in the consumers' goods' industries—though this would probably depend in part on prior investments in agriculture, where capital productivity would be low.

6. Resource depletion. Depletion of richer reserves would increase costs by adding to the requirements for both labor and capital in mining, while depletion of the more accessible resources would result in higher transportation and social costs. The extra equipment and manpower needed here would, therefore, not be available for increasing output in other sectors. There are usually possibilities for substitution, however.

Part Two
AMERICAN POLICY REQUIREMENTS

CHAPTER III

MINIMUM REQUIREMENTS

FOR A NUMBER of policy questions, primarily those not involving our immediate dealings with the Soviet bloc, there is a reasonably close correspondence between objectives and methods. We are able to define our goal, to indicate steps which give promise of leading to it, and to have some idea of the effort required. In such cases it is both possible and profitable to arrive at a fairly precise policy statement. Differences, and they may be serious, chiefly concern techniques and costs. By and large, however, such precision is confined to the defense of the vital interests of the United States and the free world and to the averting of certain evils.

In contrast to this area of relative stability and clarity, there are a number of policy questions, primarily those arising from our direct relations with the Soviet bloc, which are not, so far as we can see, amenable to precise or clearcut solution. The ultimate purposes of policy may escape definition. The means of realizing them may be lacking. Or the consequences of the actions which are open to us may currently be unforeseeable. In such cases the formulation and execution of policy must necessarily be tentative. Goals which are set as aspirations may have to wait upon the discovery or arrival of appropriate means. The results of actions must be tested in practice.

This distinction is of real importance if we are to keep the necessary stability of our national policy from degenerating into dogmatism and rigidity and its equally necessary flexibility from degenerating into wobbling and opportunism. In the present section (Part II) we deal with what we take to be the first class of policy questions: those for which the purposes are reasonably clear and for which the requisite means appear to be at hand, if often extremely difficult to apply. In the subsequent section (Part III) we turn to the second class of problems, the area of much of the debate on Soviet-American relations. But at the outset it must be emphasized that they are both parts of a single body of purposes and actions which go to make up United States policy.

* * * *

From our discussion of the potentialities of thermonuclear weapons and the nature of Soviet Communism we conclude that a general war, whether we won it or not, or the world-wide establishment of Communism, whether through general war or by other means, would each constitute a disaster of terrible magnitude. Yet we cannot simply make the avoidance of *both* war and Communist hegemony an absolute policy requirement, since avoiding the one might, under certain circumstances, mean accepting the other. If the choice is put in these narrow terms, the answer has to be that the United States must prevent the world-wide establishment of Soviet Communism—even at the cost of general war. This answer may not be self-evident to all. It would not be acceptable to the Communist, nor to the absolute pacifist, nor even to those who feel that there are limits to frightfulness beyond which no nation can go, even in its own defense, without destroying its own moral being. Debate over the relative inhumanity of labor camp slavery and genocide as against the obliteration of millions through burning and radiation cannot be conclusive, though each person may have no doubt as to his own preference. The reason for the choice must be on other grounds: willingness to accept war is to accept means which may lead to an incalculable disaster as the outcome; willingness to accept the defeat implicit in Communist hegemony is to accept the outcome in advance, with the consequent relinquishment of all means, not merely those of war. That is, the decision to avoid general war at *all* costs simultaneously destroys whatever other means there are, or may be, for averting the disaster of Communist world hegemony. The game is up.

Having said this, however, we must stress the function of our willingness to accept general war as a means of keeping the door open for possibilities *other* than the frightful choice between such a war and the global ascendancy of Communism. Under conditions of thermonuclear conflict a general war as an instrument to advance the national interest, or indeed to achieve any positive objective, is most probably a self-contradiction. A decision for general war is reasonable only as a necessity to avoid our succumbing to the Communist bloc. This also may not seem self-evident to all, particularly to those who believe that a justifiable war is a war in a righteous cause, such as the liberation of enslaved peoples or the vanquishing of the evil of Communist totalitarianism. In circumstances, however, where the liberation of the enslaved is at the cost of their lives, and the vanquishing of evil at the cost of unlimited and indiscriminate suffering by wicked and innocent alike, such justification for general war, as for pacifism, transcends politics and is not a subject for political debate or decision.

Hence we may formulate our limiting requirements as follows: preventing at whatever cost the world-wide imposition of Soviet Communism, and avoiding general war as a means of achieving positive political goals. It is the task, then, of policy not to foreclose on the future either by backing into a total defeat or by pressing forward to a general war.

The state of prolonged and uneasy suspension indicated in these requirements inevitably raises the question whether another requirement is not called for, one that takes account of time. When we consider the prospects for the future, the constantly growing production, stockpiling and development of atomic and thermonuclear weapons; the promised advent of intercontinental ballistic missiles; the likelihood of continuing Communist efforts to undermine other societies, including our own, and to prepare for their absorption into the Communist world; the absence of positive confidence in any self-induced change in the nature and aims of the Soviet regime; the continuing strain upon our own society of meeting, without taking on the attributes of our opponents, a situation that is neither war nor peace—when we consider these prospects, we may be impelled to conclude that such a state of affairs cannot go on indefinitely, that each year our room for maneuver and decision narrows, and hence that within a limited period of time some kind of resolution or showdown is absolutely necessary. Under this view, in which the alternatives of a holocaust or Communist global victory seem increasingly to be the only ones, it is urged that despite present perils an all-out effort to resolve the crisis must be made, since it will be harder to achieve with each year that passes.

Depending upon one's estimate and apprehensions for the future course of events, this demand for a termination of the conflict may take several forms. It may seek a showdown by means of either 1) a sudden preventive atomic strike against the Soviet Union; 2) an ultimatum on such matters as arms control, Soviet domination of other lands and the activities of international Communism, to be followed by war in case of its nonacceptance by the Soviet leaders; or 3) serious efforts for a limited period of time to negotiate a general settlement on these matters, but resort to war if the negotiations fail. In contrast to a showdown, the termination may be sought in transcending the conflict: an effort to establish a world government or some other type of supranational organization possessing the power and authority to compose and settle the conflict.

These views must be taken seriously; the problem they envisage is real and grave. While there is little to be gained from lamenting the past, the experience of the last 30 years does appear to provide a number of examples of situations which might have been saved, catastrophes which might have been avoided, had there been a willingness to deal with a growing menace in its early stages. More vigorous intervention in the Russian Civil War might have kept the Bolsheviks from consolidating their power; universal and full support of the League of Nations in its early stages might have averted some of the disasters of the 1930's; firm dealing with Hitler between 1933 and 1936 might have checked the plunge into war in 1938 and 1939; it is tempting to feel that we would have done well to have had a showdown (which might not have been as violent as now) with the Soviet Union while the Second World War was coming to an end. Certainly our present plight is related to the many things that were not done in the past, though we cannot rewrite history and know how things might have turned out otherwise. (What, for example, would have been the course of

German-Russian relations between 1919 and 1945 had there been no Soviet regime?)

Nevertheless, we cannot accept as a *requirement* this need for an early termination or resolution of the conflict. In the present situation it appears impossible to force a general showdown without bringing about a general war. While it is conceivable that for reasons quite unknown to us the Soviet regime might yield to the demands of an American ultimatum on such critical issues as arms control and international Communism, the chances of such an outcome are exceedingly slight. Given the nature of the antagonism and the nature of the Soviet regime, one's expectation would have to be that such steps, if forced through, could only lead to a general war.

It may, however, be argued that the real choice may be between risking a general war in the near future or facing either sure defeat without a fight or a worse war under even more unfavorable circumstances later on. One cannot deny that this could be the case—that a future generation, if there is one, might heartily regret an American failure to drive for an early showdown. It may be thought that it is a matter of balancing risks and uncertainties. Nonetheless, there is a real and, in our view, decisive difference between the risks and uncertainties involved in pressing for an immediate showdown and those involved in waiting for the future. In the first instance the risks and uncertainties are those of a poker game, but the steps by which this pressing for a showdown could, if the opponent did not yield, lead to a general war are perfectly concrete and apparent. In the second case, the risks and uncertainties are those inherent in any effort to forecast the future; they include not only the unavoidable uncertainties of any effort to derive the future from past and present trends, but also, and most important, the element of real novelty, the things presently unknown and unknowable which might enter the picture and influence it to an entirely unpredictable degree. In other words, while it is not difficult to see precisely how pressure for a showdown could precipitate a war, the same cannot be said for the movement of events into the future. To be sure, in 1936 Churchill was able to state with extraordinary precision the moves by which Hitler, after the reoccupation of the Rhineland, would be able to establish his positions for the events of 1938 and 1939. And we should certainly try to be as foresighted in our estimates of the consequences of particular moves and crises that occur throughout the world. But this is quite different from the much more general and causally imprecise expectation underlying the assertion that a showdown in the near future is a necessary requirement for American policy.

If such a showdown by force or threat of force promises only to engulf us in general war, or presents so great a risk that we could not reasonably embark on such a course, the opposite means of trying to terminate the conflict—by transcending it—carries the other danger of undermining our own security against Communist hegemony. An effort to force the creation of "one world" with the existing radical incompatibility of interests and intentions still festering within it would be disastrous in creating an internecine struggle of an even more desperate and obscure sort. From our previous experience with coalitions of which the Communist party was a member, as well as from our experience in the United Nations, it is not to be believed that the Communist world could be absorbed into a supranational organization without attempting to turn it to its own ends. This is not to argue against international organizations as such but against the effort to place on them the task of bringing off an early termination to the conflict. Even worse than this incompatibility of interests and intentions would be our forgetting or disregarding its existence.

Our requirements, then, with respect to time should be put somewhat differently: we must maintain over time our ability to act appropriately in the event there should develop a real possibility to resolve the conflict without general war or acceptance of Communist hegemony. We must also try to create such a possibility. More concretely, this means maintaining our ability to negotiate, to communicate, to propose. We cannot become so exclusively concerned with checking the expansion of the Communist bloc's power and influence—though we must do that, too—that we are at any time unable to explore and assess in the international scene the prospects, which may remain nonexistent, which may arise suddenly, or which may emerge slowly, for bringing about the termination or radical alteration of the present antagonistic relationship. That we are unable at this point to envisage these prospects or even to define a "resolution" with any precision does not affect the fact that we must be ready to grasp and utilize the new and the unforeseen. Even though we cannot count with any assurance on a more propitious future we must not deny ourselves the potentialities that might reside in it.

On the basis of these very general requirements a number of corollaries may be established:

A. *The maintenance of American strength.* That strength must be both adequate and flexible. Without adequate strength we are inviting defeat. Unless we possess the ability to exert our strength flexibly according to the particular requirements of a situation we may unintentionally precipitate a general war.

American and Soviet strengths take a number of forms, ranging from the brute power of the thermonuclear explosion to the subtler and less tangible but very real manifestations of political and psychological strength. Which of these forms will come into play depends upon the circumstances. Reduction of strength to just one component and reliance upon it alone could force the United States into an extremely rigid position in which it either would fail to have the requisite type of strength to avert a disastrous defeat or would have to rely upon the mutual mauling of a strategic atomic exchange. Consequently, we must accept as a general requirement for policy the building up of all the relevant types of strength to the extent necessary to prevent Communist hegemony.

It follows from this that the United States must develop its own strength along all the lines discussed in the preceding chapter: atomic, military, economic, political. It cannot afford to say that because the issue *may* be settled on one level—nuclear warfare, political warfare, etc.—the other factors of strength can be disregarded. Because of the wide-ranging nature of the conflict, any such simple-minded approach would only lead, through the actions and responses of the Soviet leaders, to a shifting of the contest to a different level of power. It must be said, however, that creating strength is not just a matter of choice; it involves expenditures and allocation of resources. Very real and difficult decisions must be made in determining the best distribution of our energies.[1] The only point to be made here is that such decisions be made within the framework of the need for a balanced and modulated development of our strength, however that may be worked out in actual practice.

B. *Allies.* While strength in a situation of conflict cannot always be measured by simple addition (for example, the importance of United States strength as compared with that of Western Europe is not adequately brought out by a comparison of national incomes or manpower), in the present situation, in which power and strength of all types may, under certain circumstances, play an important role in the defense of the United States, it is indispensable that the United States regard its own strength as a part of the total strength available to defend the non-Soviet world. It is quite true that there might be situations in which, say, Europe's strength could not come into play; but there are others in which it might be decisive (if, for example, both the United States and the Soviet Union were badly disabled after a mutually destructive atomic interchange). Consequently, a requirement of United States policy must be to couple its strength with that of allies. There is ample room for legitimate debate concerning alliance policy, the extent to which allies aid us, the amount of aid which should be granted them, the degree to which a coordination of policies is required (a subject discussed at greater length in Chapter V). But this debate must be within the framework of the general need to make as much of this potentiality as possible.

C. *Territory.* Though it may not be true in every case, in general each time a piece of territory and its inhabitants are brought into the Soviet orbit the free world suffers a loss of strength and the Communists enjoy a corresponding gain. This strength may be primarily in manpower or resources, or it may represent strategic position, or it may comprise a political advantage in terms of prestige and posture. A general requirement of our policy, therefore, must be to oppose

[1] For a further discussion, see Chapters IV and VI below.

any further absorption of territory into the Soviet or Communist system. Here, too, there is legitimate area for debate when it comes to specific policy decisions. It may be that a certain piece of territory is politically important to the United States but a military liability. Such was the case of Berlin; in that instance the political considerations were clearly, and correctly, regarded as the more important: the airlift resulted from the decision to support the city despite the logistic and strategic difficulties. Debates are bound to arise in such cases, and the decisions may reasonably differ under different circumstances. But there must be general recognition that the absorption of territories within the Soviet orbit is far from being a matter of indifference to the security of the United States, since each such loss not only alters the balance of forces but reduces the area of freedom in the world. It is in our interest to have this area as large as possible.

This requirement that we oppose further territorial expansion by the Soviet bloc runs counter, of course, to the view that American interests would best be served by a withdrawal of our forces and commitments from Europe and Asia. This view is worth considering briefly. In so far as it is not just a symptom of impatience or of disinclination to face the problems of the contemporary world, the most persuasive case that can be made for it would probably rest on some such argument as the following:

While advocates of withdrawal must admit the possibility that the entire resources of the Eastern Hemisphere will fall as a consequence to the Soviet bloc, to be developed and disciplined as it sees fit, they might contend that this does not weaken our military position, or does not weaken it more than the costs and risks incurred in attempting to defend overseas areas. If it is conceded that any general war will be won by atomic blows against the heart of the opponent and that the advent within the decade of intercontinental ballistic missiles will have rendered overseas air bases relatively unimportant, then it can be argued that if we maintain and protect a massive retaliatory force in the Western Hemisphere, capable of knocking out any power attempting a knockout blow against us, we shall be as safe as we could be under any other arrangement, and should not be wasting money in more vulnerable areas abroad or getting into foreign crises which might develop into a general war. In any event, as things stand now, we cannot be sure that overseas areas can be defended except by the employment of atomic weapons, and while a conflict might start with their limited tactical employment, a build-up to intercontinental strategic attacks is distinctly possible. The loss of no overseas area, it might be urged, is militarily worth the damage we would suffer through such a chain reaction.

Finally, it could be argued that American morale would be much better with such a withdrawal. We would know where we stood, there would be unanimous agreement that we must defend our homeland, and any attack upon it would be so clear in intent that we would be fully united in resisting it. Any commitment beyond this line, however, threatens to confront us with an endless series of agonizing decisions: shall we hold the Communist powers at this point or shall we make a limited withdrawal. While we may repeatedly declare, "Thus far and no farther," we would never know, under the awful threat of the consequences, whether we, or public opinion, would hold any outlying line. Piecemeal retreats would be altogether demoralizing, and it would be much better to state in advance that it is not our intent to defend overseas areas.

These arguments are not without some weight, nor are they wholly disposed of by counterarguments concerning our commitments to our allies and to the United Nations, or the damaging effect upon American morale at witnessing the destruction of freedom and culture elsewhere in the world. For, it might be maintained, if these are to be defended only at the cost of an atomic holocaust, all values may be reduced to cinders; we would be of greater service to humanity as a free island, no matter how beleaguered.

Even on its own terms, however, this argument for withdrawal has a fatal defect which, in our view, effectively removes it from the range of our policy choices. *It involves an irrevocable loss of the power of decision.* If its worst implications are accepted—i.e., willingness to accede to Soviet domination over the rest of the globe—there is no way to reverse this decision at a later date. We are perforce committed to whatever consequences may ensue. Hence, unless the following questions can be answered categorically in the affirmative, and in the nature of things they cannot, this view must be rejected:

Can we afford to accept as beyond our control or influence whatever may happen (politically, economically, scientifically, militarily and culturally) in the rest of the world over an unlimited period of time, including our encirclement by a more powerful Soviet bloc?

Is the revolution in arms and military strategy such that the coupling of the non-Soviet world's strength with our own will not, under any circumstances, be of decisive significance to our national security?

Is it certain that the American people will in fact acquiesce in the progressive Communization of the rest of the world, were that to take place?

We would answer, no, to each of these questions; in any event they certainly cannot be affirmed without qualification, which they would have to be if a policy of hemispheric withdrawal were to be considered tenable.

Beyond this, however, it is worth observing that this view —and in this respect it bears a close resemblance to advocacy of an early showdown by forceful means or preventive war —demonstrates a complete, and in our view wholly unwarranted, pessimism about even the possibility of managing or mastering the present international crisis by means other than war. The great area of political action, including diplomacy and economic and social measures, is entirely dismissed, and in desperation we either toss in our chips and go home, or start shooting.

* * * *

In the next four chapters we shall develop at greater length the positive implications of these minimum requirements in their application as policy. At this point, though, it may be useful to enumerate in review those positions which, for the reasons indicated in the preceding paragraphs, we reject and which we do *not* intend to discuss further in any detail:

1. A policy of avoiding war at all costs, whether explicitly stated or implicit in a series of actions which deprive the United States of its military capabilities.

2. A policy of preventive general war, whether stated explicitly, or implicit in a set of actions which can only detonate such a war.

3. A policy of territorial retrenchment and withdrawal, which will invite the Soviet Union and Communist China to take over more and more countries and eventually to dominate and exploit all areas outside North America.

4. A policy which disregards or fails to utilize the strengths available in the non-Soviet world.

5. A policy which places exclusive reliance upon any one form of strength—whatever it may be—and is indifferent to the creation of other components of American strength.

In our view each of these policies would, if acted upon consistently, promote either the eventual victory of Soviet Communism or the convulsive catastrophe of a thermonuclear war. We cannot be positive that the policies to be considered later may not do the same. There are no safe bets in these times. But in the above-mentioned policies such disasters seem inherent, and at the very least they reduce our ability to respond with flexible strength to the many forms the challenge to us may take.

CHAPTER IV
DEFENSE POLICY AND ARMS CONTROL

IN THIS chapter we shall confine ourselves to the general outlines of an American defense policy based on the requirements we have established in the preceding chapter. A precise statement of methods, quantities and costs cannot be attempted here, as it would require, among other things, a tremendous amount of technical information, some of it highly classified, which it is beyond the compass of this book to collect or analyze. A false appearance of precision would be a distinct disservice to a study of this nature, since we must above all remain aware that we are in a period of staggering and rapid change in which there are very few military certainties.

Before discussing, even in these broad terms, the components of our military and defense establishment, we must try to clarify its function. What are we trying to achieve through military and defense measures? Inasmuch as we have rejected the idea of initiating a general offensive war against the Soviet Union, or actions provocative of such a war, the principal purpose of our defense efforts is both to deter—to dissuade an opponent from making an attack—and also to deal with an attack should it occur. We must, however, establish the relation between a defense system's value as a deterrent and its value in the event the attack takes place. The two are not identical: a cap pistol may be an excellent deterrent, until it is called upon to perform. In general, a real deterrent, as contrasted with a bluff (which implies ignorance on the part of the opponent, something we cannot count on here) carries one or more of three kinds of threat in case the enemy is not deterred: to *thwart* the attack, to *defeat* the attack, and to *punish* the attacker.

The first—the pure passive defense of the Great Wall of China or the Maginot Line—may be preferable in the abstract, since the creation of the deterrent also creates the defense which can *thwart* the attack. If the enemy is unwise enough to attack, he runs into a stone wall; the defender is not obliged to make a separate decision if the deterrent fails to deter. Unfortunately, in the present and foreseeable state of weaponry pure passive defense cannot do the main job of deterring because it cannot be wholly relied upon if an attack actually comes. While it may be of great value in reducing our losses and increasing the difficulties of the would-be attacker, it cannot be of first priority until certain other requirements have been fulfilled.

The second form of deterrence carries the threat of *defeating* the attack; if the enemy attempts to carry out an attack, his forces, those engaged and those in support, will be subjected to counterattack with the aim of defeating his effort and repelling him from his particular objective. This form of active defense, unlike passive defense, requires a separate decision when the attack is made: we may have created an armed force to dissuade the opponent, but if the attack comes we must decide whether or not to send out the force to try to defeat it. The counterattack is not necessarily directed against the immediate point of aggression; its purpose is to reduce the aggressor's ability to press forward in the area of aggression. During much of the period since 1945 the United States was not in a position, with respect to equipment and manpower, to meet a major attack by the Soviet Union in these terms, though it did, as leader of the UN forces, successfully meet the North Korean-Chinese Communist assault.

Given the difficulty of measuring Soviet land forces against American air and atomic power, the idea of deterrence was geared less to inflicting military defeat than to the third kind of deterrent. The third form carries the threat of *punishing* the attacker, not at the place of the aggression and not necessarily with the result of defeating him militarily. Rather the idea is that, by letting the assailant know that he will be badly hurt if he attacks, we will cause him to decide not to risk it. If the deterrent fails, a separate decision is required: whether to carry out the punishment. This decision is by its nature more difficult to make than that to counterattack, since it really involves setting in train a new pattern of actions which may or may not have a direct effect upon the outcome of the actual attack. As a preventative it has a clear advantage, for, while its intensity may be scaled to "make the punishment fit the crime," it does not have to be tailored to meet the different kinds of attack the opponent may launch in a variety of terrains. But for that reason deterrence through graduated punishment does not provide a particularly flexible instrument if the attack does come.

There is obviously no hard and fast distinction between these forms of deterrence. Defeating an enemy's attack is a form of punishment; conversely, a punitive action may serve a valuable military purpose. Still, the emphasis is significantly different. The purpose of being able to defeat an attack is to keep the opponent from gaining or retaining a territorial or other objective, and if possible to persuade him of this in advance so he will feel it is not worth the effort. The purpose of punishment is essentially preventive; scaling the intensity of the reprisal to match the offense aids in giving credibility to this purpose. The difficulty is that, if the opponent disregards the warning and attacks, there may be no immediate connection between the imposition of the penalty and the outcome of his attack; the forces involved may not be directly engaged and might indeed be operating at a considerable geographic distance from one another. This lack of direct engagement could have the dangerous consequence of depriving the conflict of any limits—the attacker desperately hastening to gain and secure his objective, the attacked progressively increasing the scale of punishments as the aggression continued.

Deterrence by punishment has another shortcoming: it presupposes that the punisher enjoys relative immunity, either because of overwhelming superiority in the means of punishment or because of highly favorable passive defense capabilities. If the punisher is liable to counterpunishment, if his threat of retaliation is met by a threat of corresponding counterretaliation, the value of this form of deterrence is put in serious question. Especially is this true if the fighting is on, or is approaching, the nuclear level of intensity.

Since we must anticipate an approach to atomic parity in the not distant future, and a continuation of the lead that atomic offense holds over atomic defense, we must conclude that deterrence by the particular threat of atomic punishment will be increasingly difficult to maintain or to make persuasive. There seems to be no likelihood of developing our defenses sufficiently to keep us immune from counterattack. We might, for example, be able to reduce our casualties in a counterretaliation from, say, 30,000,000 to 10,000,000 but this is scarcely immunity. In face of such high expectations of losses it would require an extraordinary pitch of national will to be willing to bear 10,000,000 casualties to mete out punishment. Indeed, it seems likely that as time passes there will be only one act which can warrant such retaliation—namely a prior atomic attack involving our survival as a nation; in that case alone there would be no question of risking counterretaliation, since we should already have received the worst the enemy could offer.

Hence we may conclude that, while deterrence by punishment is necessary in the absence of other means, it is a diminishing form of deterrence in the context of American-Soviet relations, especially as it relates to atomic weapons.

If pure passive defense seems out of the question and if punishment by atomic retaliation—not necessarily the same thing as conflict with atomic weapons—is to be applied only in event of a prior atomic attack on us, it would follow that our military and defense policy must be based on deterrence through having the capacity to meet and defeat attacks and that the various defense measures which have been associated with passive defense and with punitive retaliation must increasingly be placed in this setting—which is not to deny their value but to give them a somewhat different function. Passive defense—civil defense measures, etc.—should be thought of primarily as an important aid in carrying on the conflict once it has started. Similarly, our atomic power should also be regarded as a military device, performing, if need be, specific military functions as well as that of ultimate retaliation.

Putting it differently, we may say that we should not let our necessary and wholly justified concern with deterring a general thermonuclear war—both by building up our passive defenses and by possessing a terrible power of punitive retaliation—cause us to overlook the need to deter (or to handle, if need be) other types of conflict, nonatomic aggression, local war, "brushfires." This is neither to say that the thermonuclear bomb is "just another weapon" nor to argue that it serves as a sure deterrent to a general war. The bomb is "different" in its ability to wreak such unlimited, and very possibly mutual, destruction that its use as an instrument for positive objectives is most likely self-defeating, but this very definitely does not mean that a general war is impossible, much less other forms of conflict.

On the contrary, the chances of deterring a general thermonuclear war depend very greatly on our having the capability of deterring all wars, or at least of keeping them in hand, both for the reason that local wars could, under a number of circumstances, become general and get out of control, and because the opponent is less likely to experiment with nonatomic aggression if our power of deterrence is patently capable of defeating such experiments. Finally, and this is of the utmost political importance, while we must have the fundamental resolve to use the full power of thermonuclear destruction if that should be the only way to prevent Communist world conquest, a decision we reached in the preceding chapter, we must also work to keep things from coming to such a pass that we must act on this resolve. This means creating the conditions—and certainly a general ability to deter war is a major condition—which will permit this resolve to stay in the background, not lost from sight, to be sure, but not intruding itself as the sole determinant of all our political and military decisions.

In this light let us examine our defense and military needs. In view of what we have just said, there can be no question of the continuing need to maintain at peak effectiveness our thermonuclear arsenal, our Strategic Air Command, the defense of SAC, and the indispensable research and development in weapons, missiles and planes. The *capacity* for instant and full retaliation against a nuclear attack remains, under existing circumstances, a precondition, though by no means the only condition, for our national survival.

In addition to this retaliatory function, however, our air-atomic force also has its military functions. If a war of sufficient magnitude begins, or develops out of a smaller conflict, SAC has the job of going after the appropriate military targets, enemy bases, etc. Whether these targets will, in fact, tend to become identical with the objects of a retaliatory attack is impossible to say. But it must be clear that the diminishing function of the retaliatory deterrent does not of itself imply the nonuse of atomic weapons for military purposes. They are a part of a military arsenal, and, so far as we can see, they could not be given up *unilaterally in advance* without inviting military defeat.[1] At the same time, there is doubtless a point at which the marginal utility of adding to our strength in this direction, even on the presumption of a general war, is less than that of building up our military and defense strength in other sectors. A general war might conceivably neither begin nor end with an all-out thermonuclear exchange; it might be fought with "tactical" atomic weapons in combination with "conventional" arms.

But we cannot, of course, prepare only for a general war. As we have seen, war or an attack may occur in a variety of ways, may begin as a local engagement with nonatomic weapons and may or may not expand in space or intensity. For these reasons our military force must be a balanced one. Determining the proper weight of its components is a technical question not to be handled in a cursory fashion. The balance is obviously not static but very dynamic, shifting with the progress of new weapons from the drafting board to the field, with changes in the opponent's forces, and with changes in the international strategic picture. The most we can do here is to suggest certain criteria for a proper balance.

The development and introduction of new weapons should be staged so as to cut to a minimum the transitional gaps, in which our striking power is reduced and our vulnerability is increased. The balance of our weaponry should be such as to limit as little as possible the choice of means available to our politically responsible authorities, above all the President. The choice, which is a political one, whether the enemy's aggression should be met by punitive actions or by countermeasures on the spot or in the area, must be

[1] For the possibilities of mutually agreed upon arms control, see p. 101.

left as open as possible. Within the limits imposed by requirements of efficiency and the fact that we cannot have as much of everything as we should like, we should not let the availability of weapons impose answers that should be made on political as well as strategic grounds. In general, of course, the emphasis on development in weapons must be in the direction of greatest military effectiveness; it would be fatal to lag behind the opponent's technological potentialities. But effectiveness means more than getting the "biggest bang for the buck"; it includes such other considerations as flexibility, precision and all the complex factors of adapting weapons to varying types of terrain and enemy action. In particular, we must keep in mind the tremendous developments and improvements in the nonatomic field, in fire power, communications and logistics, which open up quite new avenues, and problems, in strategy and tactics. Unconventional thinking about the use of "conventional" (as well as tactical atomic) weapons may profit us more than conventional thinking about the use of the new thermonuclear weapons.

Manpower requirements must be adjusted to other military requirements. Currently the problem of the number of troops required under conditions of atomic warfare is the object of intensive study. It is by no means clear that requirements will fall off; they may well increase, as the other side's atomic power grows. In any event, this is not a question to be prejudged. While we certainly want to take full advantage of our present but diminishing comparative technological advantage and avoid matching man for man the numerically superior Soviet bloc, we must not let the attractions of limiting our military manpower lead us to the error of relying upon the concept of punitive atomic retaliation in a period when it is almost certainly going to be of diminishing applicability. It might be added that the spirit which is unwilling to meet the manpower requirements is not likely to impress the potential aggressor as one with the hardihood to assume the risks of carrying out a threatened retaliation.

With regard to passive defense measures, the first requirement, as stated above, is the protection of SAC. The next is that of preserving not only our nuclear but also our general military potential. Under certain types of conflict we can count on the tremendous American industrial plant providing the necessary equipment and material, as it did in the last two world wars. The lessons of our past experience can be highly instructive, but need not be gone into here. With the possibility, however, of a thermonuclear war (whether the war starts as such, or develops into such) we have to count on the chance of a very high percentage of our industrial plant being pulverized in a matter of hours or days. Hence we must be assured of stockpiles of finished materials capable of employment in the event our industrial centers are destroyed. Judging from the information in the second chapter, the ratio of our stockpiles to current needs is lower than that of the Soviets and should therefore be increased. Moreover, the stockpiles themselves should be dispersed to avoid destruction. There is no doubt that adequate stockpiling, though costly and subject to obsolescence, is required.

Beyond stockpiling, steps can be taken to reduce in some measure our industrial vulnerability, especially through a dispersal of facilities. Indeed, dispersal—scattering of targets—seems to be the chief defensive answer, in so far as there is any, to the atomic threat. Obviously a sudden and wholesale dispersal of major industries would be fearfully dislocating, and it would be folly to paralyze or weaken our economy over a protracted period of time in the effort to insure against the eventuality of atomic attack. But no responsible person has ever suggested this. A progressive relocation of a number of key industries, however, is probably feasible as well as essential. To take one example, the chairman of the board of the Jones and Laughlin Steel Corporation has estimated that the costs for progressive dispersal of 25 per cent of total American steel-producing facilities, over a period of 8 years, would be about \$9 to \$9½ billion for the productive facilities and \$1 to \$1½ billion for auxiliary facilities. While there are real costs in this transfer, a good part could be absorbed as part of the normal process of replacement and new construction.

A more detailed statement would require extensive study, which would have to take account not only of the time and costs involved but also of the growing destructive power of the Soviet atomic potential. There is, of course, a serious question whether we are in a losing race; whether the power of destruction is expanding faster than our ability to disperse. While this may well be the case, it is not an argument for doing nothing, since at each point in time (up to the theoretical limit when the enemy can blanket all inhabitable areas) a percentage of industry saved is better than none at all.

In addition to defending, through dispersing and stockpiling, as much of our war industry and material as we can, we must also maintain our organization—the chains of essential command, the indispensable minimum of public services and order. The special measures required to assure an organization capable of surviving an atomic attack would have to include the following: certain organizations which require centralized decision and authority would have to be protected by advance planning, which would also include knowledge of the plans by the key personnel concerned. Other organizations may be more satisfactorily protected through decentralization and increased autonomy, through the delegation of responsibility to the state or municipal level. Under conditions of atomic warfare it is important not only that the critical channels of communication and decision be protected but also that lateral channels be developed, so that the destruction of a headquarters or central authority will not isolate from one another all the organs under its responsibility. Finally, there should be, in advance of a crisis, adequate stand-by legislation and skeleton organizations. To create an adequate program to protect our organizational structure is an enormous job. Some serious work has been done; more is required. We are at present more vulnerable than we need to be.

Thus far we have considered the steps to be taken to preserve America's fighting capacity in the event of atomic conflict. An important part of this capacity is the defense of its citizenry. The problem of defending the population, above all the urban population, is a grim one. While valuable measures are being taken in creating a warning system, in developing new interceptors and guided missiles, the pic-

91591

EMORY AND HENRY LIBRARY

ture, as we have seen in an earlier chapter, is not bright at best, and looks very tough indeed when one tries to grapple with the implications of thermonuclear bombs, guided missiles, intercontinental ballistics and fall-out. Indeed, some have been so discouraged by the apparently unequal race between offense and defense as to feel that efforts in civilian defense are a waste of time and energy. Still, we should not identify what *could* happen to us with what *may* happen to us. We are not quite in the ballistic age yet and when, by the exercise of war-gaming, one looks at all the problems confronting a hostile power mounting an atomic offensive against the United States, one realizes what a formidable undertaking it would be and how plans could go astray. Even if we were hit, we might not be hit with all the impact that is theoretically possible.

Furthermore, even if we assume the worst and concede that it may be impossible to achieve any real or permanent defense of our cities or their inhabitants, there is no question that partial protection is better than none. In an earlier paragraph we suggested that reducing casualties from 30,000,000 to 10,000,000 was insufficient to give us a sense of immunity and a willingness to take risks for purposes of punitive atomic deterrence. Nevertheless, that difference of 20,000,000 lives could be of utmost importance in providing the margin enabling us to see the war through, and survive in an organized fashion. Consequently, while it is beyond the scope of this report to discuss civil defense requirements in detail, vigorous efforts are called for, though expenditures on their behalf should not be at the cost of weakening our over-all military capabilities. They must be judged as a component of these capabilities.

The one thing we must not do is "go through the motions" with respect to civilian defense. Making the gestures without seriously grappling with the problems is of doubtful value to our morale, which cannot rest on fictions. The purpose of civilian defense is a severely practical one: to save, in the event of attack, as many lives as possible for the tremendous need there will be for those lives.

We cannot pretend to give an estimate, even in approximate orders of magnitude, of the costs of the above recommendations. A show of precision would be misleading. We can only record a necessarily general impression: that we have not done as much as we should along any of the lines, with the possible exception of the thermonuclear field; that the costs undoubtedly will be very high but that on the whole we have tended to underestimate the economic and defense burden the United States is capable of bearing for a protracted period of time without being undermined in the process. Priorities, based on estimates of the relative marginal returns for different areas of expenditure, would have to be established and some things sacrificed for others. While we have offered certain general criteria for selection and emphasis, it would be preferable first to make a detailed study of our requirements and our capabilities rather than to assume beforehand that certain measures are, or are not, financially possible.

Admittedly, the establishment of a defense budget is at best a matter of approximation. Our conclusion, however, would be that, given the staggering costs of developing and producing the new range of weapons and equipment, and given the imperative need to have as broad and effective a deterrent as we can get, our present appropriations are not as great as they should be, certainly not as much as we are able to stand. If we are uncertain about the correct level of appropriations, the nation should err on the upper side; the budget should not be left within the band of doubt. This recommendation does not reflect a despair of maintaining the peace, much less a desire to exacerbate the world crisis. On the contrary, a flexible power of deterrence is necessary to reduce the chances of war; without it peace is nakedly subject to the vagaries of Soviet intentions.

Control of Arms

The reader may be surprised that immediately after advocating the further strengthening of our military and defense position we should be prepared to consider the question of arms control. Are not the two hopelessly in contradiction? If we proceed with developing our military strength, and if the Soviets, as is only to be expected in such a case, continue to build up theirs, does this not make arms control quite impossible? We would be less than candid if we were to ignore this difficult question or to try to get around it by a verbal formula, of which there have been only too many in the history of arms races.

But before attempting to answer this question, let us briefly examine the subject of arms control to see what the prospects may be in that direction.

It can be argued that, while the discussion in the preceding paragraphs is correct in stressing the need for deterrents and for the United States not to permit itself to become weaker or more vulnerable than the Soviet Union, it neglects the fact that strength is relative. A reduction of the Soviet capacity to attack could be as great a deterrent to war as an increase of our capacity to defend; hence arms control or reduction is not in itself in conflict with our defense requirements.

As a logical proposition this may be acceptable. It does not, however, take account of one feature of arms contests which has made them notoriously difficult to check or control. We may speak of American arms having deterrence as their purpose, since that evidently corresponds with our national policy. We cannot, however, go on to say that deterrence is also the purpose of Soviet arms. Some advocates of disarmament posit this, but we do not know it to be true, and indeed the whole of our discussion of Soviet-American relations indicates that we have good reason to believe that Soviet purposes are not so circumscribed. Armaments, in other words, are an *instrument* for realizing the intentions of a state, and in this respect they are not simply a relative matter. To take the extreme case, for a consciously aggressive power to accept the complete abolition of its military capabilities would be for it to renounce its intentions and to make a radical change in the basic aims of its foreign policy.

Intentions, then, seem to be the key to the question, but in most cases, of course, we do not really *know* the intentions of another nation, and this would include the Soviet Union. We infer them, partly from its ruling ideology and domestic practices, partly from the various territorial, juridical and other particular issues which divide us, and partly, but only partly, from the armaments the other nation is creating.

In some instances the conflicting intentions of two powers are fully expressed by definite, concrete issues. Francis I is reported to have said during a war with Charles V, "My dear cousin and I are in perfect agreement—we both want Milan." When an arms race is a symptom or a by-product of such an issue, settling the "Milan" question is a necessary precondition for any satisfactory discussion of arms control. It may be argued that for an easing of Soviet-American tensions, as distinguished from a resolution of the conflict, it would be more profitable to try first to compose some of the outstanding disputes rather than to seek an agreement on disarmament.

In the case of Soviet-American relations, however, the conflict is more than the sum of the particular issues that have been under dispute in the last decade. From our point of view the nature of Communist totalitarianism is such that it keeps creating issues, and may be expected to do so as long as the outlook which informs it is in command. If this is true, we should not have undue expectations that the resolution of particular issues, while beneficial in itself, would greatly ease the path to arms reductions.

Some would press this point further and maintain that, even were the Soviet Union not a Communist regime, the mere fact of its being a great aggregate of power set apart from another great aggregate, the United States, would work independently of ideological alienation to bring about mutual suspicion, fear and conflicting intentions. This view sees the building up of armaments as an unavoidable product of the existence of independent sovereign powers on the same planet. From this follows the argument that, regardless of issues or ideologies, the international situation will remain precarious and unstable until power—arms—is put under a single planetary control, and that this cannot be achieved within the framework of great power relations.

This argument may be sound, but it would be very hard to prove it from historical experience. We should, however, suggest some doubts as to its adequacy. Before the First World War Great Britain was alarmed by German battleship construction, not primarily because of the existence of the battleships but because of the intentions and ambitions these battleships were presumed—probably correctly—to reflect. There was no equivalent reaction (though some) when the United States navy came to outstrip that of Great Britain. Today, the United States is alarmed by the Soviet possession of the thermonuclear bomb primarily because of its apprehension over Communist intentions; the British decision to develop thermonuclear weapons did not cause alarm, for just the opposite reason. While one could say that *if* Great Britain were the only other great power we would then be equally disturbed, this is an unprovable assertion; in our view such would not be the consequence.

The most striking demonstration of the dubiousness of this argument is the simple but extraordinary fact that in the space of 50 years the United States has moved from being a small factor in the international power picture to being a dominant one *without* producing the consternation, adjustments, diplomatic realignments and opposing coalitions among other states [2] that would necessarily follow if power and capabilities were the only determining factors.

At the risk of promoting self-satisfaction, one may say that the most obvious explanation is that the other nations' reading of American intentions and purposes over the years was such that our tremendous growth in power did not produce corresponding fear and suspicions. To be sure, it might be held that the power of Germany and then of Russia was a distraction, or that the other nations "should" have become alarmed at American might. But the significant fact remains that in the present century American power in itself has not been the source of major conflicts with other nations, except for those whose intentions were demonstrably hostile on quite other grounds.

Admittedly, the instruments of power may on occasion get out of hand and influence nations' intentions and policies. This fear of the instruments becoming masters of the situation has been greatly increased since the advent of thermonuclear weapons and the vision of a "push button" war

[2] It could be argued, of course, that the rise of U.S. power helped to create the Communist bloc. But this is an ideological grouping; other, non-Communist states have not joined this bloc to counterbalance the enormous power of the United States.

with some madman or fanatic at the controls.[3] As we have seen, the new weapons do present formidable problems, not the least of which is the delicate question whether the employment of this power "tactically" and locally can be achieved without leading to an all-out thermonuclear exchange. But while these dangers are real and lead to a conclusion we would support—that a large part of the human race is in peril of being blasted out of existence—armaments are still instruments, however hard to manage, and cannot be considered apart from the will and intentions of their creators.

From the foregoing, three conclusions emerge:

1. In so far as there are concrete issues dividing armed nations, it is probably more useful to tackle them first rather than the arms question.

2. In the case of the Soviet Union we would do well to assume a hostile intent on its part quite independent of specific issues and arms rivalries; any negotiation concerning armaments should proceed on that assumption.

3. The existence of the Soviet-American arms rivalry proves nothing, one way or the other, about the ability of sovereign nations in general to control arms or to disarm without giving up a part of their independent sovereignty.

If the second conclusion is correct we may examine in a little more detail the problems that arise in controlling or reducing arms under conditions of an antagonistic relationship.

In the first place, there must be parity and simultaneity of reduction; neither power dares disarm earlier or to a greater degree than the other. The parity may be defined in proportions or in absolute figures—a matter of much debate—but parity there must be.

In the second place, the reductions and limitations cannot be taken on faith. There would have to be inspection and control. As is well known, this has been a particularly diffi-

[3] One can only speculate whether the United States, in the decade after 1945, would have felt less imperiled had the first atomic bomb been a damp squib; we might have been even unhappier about Russian and Chinese "hordes."

cult feature of atomic arms control. Even if production could be halted, the existing stockpiles are now so large that they alone could cause incalculable damage. Since stockpiles would be easy to conceal, increasing attention has been given recently to controlling the means of delivery: planes, missiles, airfields and launching sites. The purely technical problems, which while enormous might not be insoluble, are greatly augmented by the general implications of control and inspection for the Soviet regime—and also, if to a lesser degree, for any regime. They would involve access to all parts of the Soviet industrial and military establishment, and to all potentially strategic areas, with interrogation of officials and citizens, who would be expected to reveal what normally are the most highly classified state secrets. In short, the necessary inspection and control would be potent levers against any system of society, and especially against a closed system.[4]

In the third place, parity must mean parity for the entire array of military capabilities taken as a whole—not for just one weapons system. A reduction confined to, say, atomic weapons and their means of delivery would probably be to the relative disadvantage of the United States. In most situations it is therefore impossible to make reductions in one branch of armaments without equivalent adjustments in others. This in turn raises all the old issues of the distinction between offensive and defensive weapons and of the qualitative and quantitative "needs" of powers of differing geographic location and size.

Finally, capabilities extend into the area of paramilitary, subversive, political and psychological operations. For example, in Asia real parity could mean balancing troops and police forces against Communist infiltration teams armed with tommy guns and pamphlets. The achievement of parity at this level is probably beyond the power of negotiation. Yet it would be folly to let an understandable desire to achieve control over the more spectacular or tangible weap-

[4] It may be added that, even if a system of control and inspection were agreed upon, this would not insure its enforcement in practice. As happened in the case of Germany during the Stresemann era, there may be political reluctance to disturb a period of international relaxation with bothersome information about arms violations.

ons of destruction lead to a relative weakening of our general defensive position.[5]

There is one further difficulty in achieving arms reduction or control under conditions of hostility. Were it possible to have a mathematically exact measurement of the components of power and of the conditions of parity, then in principle the two sides could, *if* the inspection problem were met, move step by step, stage by stage, down the slope of disarmament, like two Wild West gunmen, first taking their fingers off the triggers, then holstering their revolvers, then putting the holsters on the table. It could be done, or at least it could then be possible to judge whether, behind the surface of mutual mistrust, the opponent's intentions were such as to let him disarm himself in this fashion. But with a problem as complex as national armaments, where real parity would have to cover a large, uncertain and changing range of weapons, such precision of calculation and staging is not possible. Between powers enjoying some degree of mutual trust—say, Great Britain and the United States—each might afford to assume risks and be willing to underestimate its needs with some assurance that the other would not take advantage of this. But in the case of the United States and the Soviet Union we should be impelled to insure ourselves against this area of uncertainty. Presumably the Soviets would do the same. In consequence, there would appear to be no rational way, among all the uncertainties, of assuring to each side what it feels to be its necessary margin of security. It is precisely the element of antagonism that converts what would be a difficult but not theoretically impossible problem into one for which there may be no negotiable solution. It is doubtful that the various disarmament proposals which have been advanced get around this particular difficulty.

[5] Some have suggested that while it is impracticable to encompass the whole range of weaponry it might be possible to prohibit, by mutual agreement, the use of certain weapons, with each side willing to abide the outcome of a conflict fought by other means. At the extreme this is reminiscent of Goliath's call: "Choose you a man for you and let him come down to me. If he be able to fight with me and kill me, then will we be your servants; but if I prevail against him and kill him, then shall ye be our servants." It is to be doubted if modern nations would be willing to accept any such symbolic defeat, and, indeed, after David killed Goliath, the Philistines did not give up but fled, and the fighting was later resumed.

The most interesting are those which envisage transferring arms to a third party, since the possession of power (whether as a monopoly or in decisive preponderance) by some agency outside the antagonistic relationship may be thought to provide that necessary margin of security to permit each state to disarm without fear of being jumped on by the other. But, if this "third party" is another nation or a body with particular interests and intentions of its own, we are only reverting to the classical notion of balance of power, which has never led to disarmament. If, on the other hand, the third party is a supranational agency, such as the United Nations, representing the interests of all nations, we run into a perennial quandary of politics: who is to control the actions of this third party? If the antagonistic states participate in the control, their conflict is only transferred to the agency, as has indeed been a major difficulty with the UN. If the agency becomes autonomous and truly independent of the conflict, we encounter the dangers of Hobbes' Leviathan: an uncontrolled and uncontrollable authority.

Much serious and dedicated thinking has been devoted to trying to meet these quandaries, and we would be quite unfair were we to dismiss these efforts as inadequate without providing a careful analysis of their proposals. Still, we must record our strong impression that there is no device or mechanism that by itself can transcend this element of hostility which, in our view, is not just mutual suspicion, though that is present, but comes from a deeply rooted, hostile intent.

For all these difficulties, which cannot be overlooked, we should not conclude that domestic discussion or foreign negotiations concerning arms control and reduction are ill-advised or a waste of time. Given the intimate linkage between armaments and intentions—especially in the eyes of other nations which tend to infer the latter from the former—the United States must be prepared to relate the level and location of its armaments to its legitimate security needs, partly for reasons of public relations, but more fundamentally to keep the way open, in so far as it can, to any tempering or easing of the conflict which will not run counter to the minimum requirements of American policy. There is a continuing need for the United States to give, in the context of international discussion, a reasoned presentation of its position: the concessions it would make, the types of control it regards as indispensable, the kinds of reduction it thinks feasible. At the same time the presentation should not fail to make the point that the undertaking is of the utmost difficulty and that if the parties fail to reach an agreement the failure really proves nothing: not that the Soviet Union is suddenly any more, or any less, responsible for international tensions than it had been thought to be, nor that the United States is willfully engaging in an arms race, nor that the nation state is obsolete (which may or may not be true, but is certainly not to be demonstrated by the outcome of an arms conference involving the Soviet Union). In other words, we should make the most of the chance that, through mutual fear of thermonuclear disaster, and via the channel of disarmament, we might make headway in overcoming the alienation brought about by Soviet Communism. We should recognize that it is an outside chance and that failure in this endeavor should not disrupt the pattern of actions already envisaged.

In recent months, partly because of the protracted failure to make headway in arms reduction or control, there has been increasing emphasis, especially in the United States, on mutual inspection and exchange of information concerning the disposition, movement and development of military forces and equipment. The aim is to reduce the chances of surprise attack, to achieve in consequence some relaxation of tensions, and to prepare for possible reduction and control of armaments in the more propitious atmosphere that may subsequently result. This line of approach is currently in the process of discussion and clarification, and we can make only a few comments here. The first is the obvious one that bringing data on arms and military establishments into the open, while of potential value in reducing the element of secrecy and uncertainty, does not necessarily pave the way for disarmament or even for reducing international tension. To be sure, in the present situation a Soviet-American agreement to exchange blueprints and have mutual overflights would be rather good evidence that neither side was contemplating a surprise nuclear attack; it could also provide us with advance warning if a change was impending—though this assumes that advance preparations for attack would be observable, or thought to be so. But we should also note that publicity, skillfully used, can be a device of political warfare. The well-publicized flights of new Soviet planes over Moscow have not been without an intended political impact. More dangerous perhaps would be the possibility that overflights would give an aggressor new, or more refined, target data, which he might use later. Beyond that, mutual inspection does not really deal with the problem of local conflicts, peripheral fights, in which the main forces of the great powers, initially at least, are not involved. And yet, as we have seen, wars can start in this way, and they might expand and intensify. It is true, of course, that the American proposals for exchange of information and inspection are not intended as a panacea, but only to deal with one troublesome feature of the arms problem.

The possibility, however, that inspection and publicity might come to be a substitute for, rather than a prologue to, arms reduction and control brings us back to our first question: whether the various proposals for disarmament—even were their formidable difficulties overcome—are in any sense compatible with the maintenance and development of our military capabilities. The question has been raised whether the possession of full capabilities on both sides, plus the knowledge of these capabilities gained through mutual inspection and exchange, may not be more conducive to stability—peace by thermonuclear stalemate—than the effort to reduce capabilities. This is a real issue, and one on which there is disagreement even among those most fully informed of all the technical intricacies.

It is hard to believe that real and lasting stability is to be found in an endless piling up of thermonuclear weapons and means of delivery among an ever-increasing number of nations. One cannot but have the uneasy feeling that sooner or later something may go wrong and lead to the physical destruction of our civilization.

On the other hand, one can equally well feel that a reduction from full capabilities to partial capabilities, to half strength, may only reintroduce a perilously unstable element of uncertainty. It might be that a partial reduction of capabilities would result in removing the admittedly precarious stalemate of a parity based on atomic plenty but without reducing—possibly increasing—the chances of war and aggression on a nonatomic level. But once fighting started there would be tremendous pressure to build up to full capabilities again. We cannot unlearn what we know.

Perhaps the conclusion must be that the situation of full capabilities should be replaced only by a virtual abolition of capabilities and that stopping at half-capabilities in the absence of a political resolution of the international crisis would be the worst of all answers. If so, our objective should be to seek some means of bringing about and securing a reduction of physical capabilities to the level of token forces: forces incapable of overt or "creeping" aggression, forces adequately inspected and controlled to prevent a subsequent build-up. Such an objective might be carried out in stages, but it would be indispensable to avoid the reduction being stalled in mid-course, at a point where the immediate fear of thermonuclear retaliation had been removed but where the possibilities for aggression by other means remained present and tempting.

It is incumbent upon the United States to explore the ways and means of gaining this objective. But we should not forget, when we speak of the mutual reduction of capabilities to token forces, what this would imply for the Soviet Union: giving up the physical means of realizing the goals of Communism. We cannot pretend to be so certain of the absolute correctness of our judgment of Soviet purposes that we would pronounce this an insuperable obstacle. The stakes are too great; we must certainly keep the arms question—and all major questions—open for possible action. But if we cannot make a dogma of Communist aggressiveness, neither can we, because of the size of the stakes, assume that we can disregard this long record of aggressiveness or proceed as if it were not the principal roadblock. The weight of evidence points strongly to the presumption that the key to any significant and safe reduction of arms may be found only in a real change in the aims of Soviet Communism.

CHAPTER V
ALLIES AND NEUTRALS

THE QUESTION to be discussed in this chapter is not *whether* the United States should have allies, but *how* it should conduct its policy so as to increase the benefit of alliances to itself and to its alliance partners. The United States has allies in most areas of the world; since 1949 they have been part of the tissue of American foreign policy.[1] This is as it should be. As was stated earlier, it is indispensable that the United States should link its own strength to the degree possible with the strength available in the non-Soviet parts of the world. Without allies we would lose, at worst, our ability to prevent Communist global hegemony extending even over ourselves; at best, we would have to pitch our exertions to an inhuman level. A policy of nonalliance, of withdrawal of commitments to our own frontiers, would only facilitate the Communist absorption of areas beyond the North American continent and isolate us in a position of increasing inferiority.[2]

Since most gains in this world exact their costs, it is no wonder that the effort to serve American and free-world interests through the medium of alliances has created problems, some of them quite serious. Not only are there the usual difficulties of collective enterprises—the presence of divergent or conflicting views among the allies, the oppor-

[1] It has been suggested that the peoples behind the Iron Curtain should also be considered as allies; they have suffered from the Soviet regime more intimately than the rest of the world, and they constitute a potential source of strength to the free-world cause, though one not easy to measure. This is perfectly true, and important. In the present discussion, however, this extension of the term "ally" could be confusing. After all, even within the allied nations, as well as the neutrals, some individuals and political parties are of far greater value as "allies" than are others. The trouble is that on the level of public policy it is hardly possible to single out and deal separately with such individuals and groups. States, though they are not monoliths, are working units; in this chapter we limit ourselves to states with which the United States is allied—but without forgetting that we may have vigorous supporters elsewhere in the world.

[2] See above, p. 87.

tunities for confused counsel—but the disparity of power between the United States and even the strongest of its allies has given particular poignancy to the task of harmonizing leadership and partnership in a coalition. These difficulties easily lead in turn either to an American mood of impatience and exasperation with allies, or to the elevation of alliances to ends in themselves, to which all other considerations must be subordinated. Both reactions are harmful. Since alliances are a means, an indispensable means, to further ends, they can survive only if they promote the realization of these ends: the independence and security of the alliance partners. It would be as self-defeating to have an alliance adopt, for the purpose of allied unity, policies which weakened the position of the non-Communist world as it would be to reject alliances altogether.

There are several means by which we can work to strengthen the cohesion and purposes of our alliances. First, it is important to promote so far as we can a common *understanding* of the nature of the dangers threatening and of the ways to counter them. Without this our alliances may disintegrate and give way to a sense of futility about any concerted efforts (this is particularly true of military efforts in the face of the expanding Soviet thermonuclear capability). We cannot, of course, be too exacting and expect a degree of political unanimity among different nations that is unlikely to be realized. It is unrealistic to demand, as the condition for an alliance, that our allies have in all respects the same views as the United States of the Communist problem and how to meet it. Indeed, our own views are by no means uniform and firmly fixed. Still, we should, at the very least, strive for mutual comprehension of these views, whether we are presently in full agreement or not. Above all we must work to strengthen the sense of utility in belonging to an alliance. We and our allies have much to learn from one another in this regard. Some of them have had long, intimate and often bitter experience with the habits and practices of the Communist powers; for our part we have been obliged to school ourselves in the requirements, possibilities and limitations of contemporary warfare. Mutual interchange of such experiences and insights will not overcome all differences, but it will aid greatly in removing those that are extraneous.

Second, an alliance may be strengthened if its purposes and procedures can properly be identified with goals which extend beyond the immediate interests of the alliance members and yet are recognized as serving those interests: by establishing, in other words, a broadly accepted *authority,* or *legitimacy,* for the alliance. If such authority can be created, and the terms of its employment defined with some precision, chances are improved of rallying a preponderance of support to the cause of allied action and of being assured of its use in time of need. Such, we feel, is a major advantage of relating our alliances to the provisions of the United Nations Charter and of working, wherever possible, through the UN as one manifestation, perhaps the most important, of the world's general interests and aspirations.

We should stress that the effort must be to make general goals and purposes, such as those of the UN, relevant to the particular interests and needs of our allies and ourselves, rather than the other way around. Ideally there should be complete identity between the two, but this has not always been the case. Just as an alliance cannot survive if it does not serve the real needs of its members, so these general goals and purposes of the UN cannot become operative unless they also serve these needs.

But the UN, of course, includes not just our allies but also neutrals and members of the Soviet bloc. Can the goals of the UN Charter really reinforce those, say, of NATO, and at the same time represent the interests of non-NATO members, including the Soviet Union? Despite the existence of Article 51, which upholds the right of individual and collective self-defense, and despite the rather easy argument that *any* purely defensive arrangement is in harmony with the aims of the UN, this is a real and very difficult issue.

Since its inception, or shortly thereafter, the UN has been the object of a continuing argument as to whether it should be a forum for all nations, a meeting place where differences can be aired and perhaps mediated; or whether it should be an instrument for maintaining peace and security. Both functions were written into the Charter, but with the quickly developing rift between the Soviet Union and the Western powers this ambiguity came at once to the surface and has appeared repeatedly in such debated issues as the "veto," the Uniting-for-Peace Resolution, Chinese representation in the UN and in the Security Council, and the admission of new members.

For this reason some have argued that the very existence of the UN has been a source of friction between the United States and the Soviet Union, since so many of their conflicts have centered in questions affecting the UN. For, were there no UN, there would be no veto question, no quarrel over Chinese representation. But this would be to mistake the form for the substance. In virtually every case the heart of the conflict was the American effort to oppose, through the instrumentality of the UN, further Soviet and Communist expansion (or the consolidation of areas of postwar Communization).

The problem rather has been whether the UN is *an appropriate instrument* for this effort. Individuals, and nations, who have been in full agreement about the nature of the Soviet Communist danger, have differed on this point. This must be emphasized, since it is to the interest of none but the Communist bloc for this divergence regarding the function of the UN to divide us from our allies or separate us from the neutrals. The difference arises from the obvious fact that the UN is not an independent entity speaking with one voice but represents the aggregate of views of its many members. It can achieve no more than its members collectively agree to let it achieve.

Since the members of the Soviet bloc have refused—quite naturally, since they have been in a minority—to let the UN act as an instrument of collective security in the full sense, as an agency whose right to maintain the peace is granted even by those against whom it may take measures, the question then arises whether those members who are so willing should still try to use the UN as a security instrument, or whether the effort should be abandoned in favor of the idea of a universal forum. But even this question cannot be settled by or in the UN; it depends in turn upon the independent decisions of the non-Communist powers. Since a decision to use the UN for the maintenance of security would be taken only against the will of the Communist bloc, pressing for it becomes in effect a political move against that bloc. Hence the decision of each nation regarding the security functions which the UN should have cannot be detached from its foreign policy toward the Soviet Union and Communist China. It is doubtful, therefore, that any of the uncommitted or neutral nations will be willing to increase the security function of the UN unless and until such nations alter correspondingly their policy toward the Soviet bloc. The reverse procedure—building up the security function of the UN with the hope of influencing thereby the foreign policies of the neutral powers—appears to be putting the cart before the horse. They will resist that influence so long as it does not correspond with their interpretation of their own interests.

It is partly for this reason that a number of our allies, and at times the United States itself, have been reluctant to press for what might be called a UN coalition, lest it only alienate a number of nations, especially in Asia and Africa, without substantially increasing the real defensive strength of the non-Communist world.

Hence, when we say that our alliances will be strengthened if we work through the UN wherever possible, we do not mean substituting the UN for the alliances, or trying to have the UN carry a greater security burden than its members can agree upon. We mean rather that only by the act of supporting and working for the objectives of the UN Charter can we make them meaningful to the interests of the nations, and that only in an international atmosphere where these objectives remain alive and relevant can a democratic alliance have much chance of finding a broader sense of purpose and cohesiveness than one of bare expediency. We should recall that when, in the 1930's, the League of Nations was increasingly by-passed in dealing with the crucial issues of the time, the result was not to fortify the existing alliances but to contribute to their worthlessness when they were put to the test.

It is quite likely that the most fruitful area for UN activity will not be that of military power and defense. But this could increase rather than diminish its importance during a time when the Soviet Communist challenge was being met primarily along nonmilitary lines. While we cannot here develop this subject, we should emphasize the practical usefulness to the United States of these other functions of the UN and the specialized agencies, such as the Food and Agriculture Organization, the International Bank and the International Monetary Fund. Although these activities may not be highly publicized, they are of real importance as instruments for cooperation in economics, finance, public health and the like.

A third factor which may strengthen our alliances is the *sense of community* that we have with a number of other nations: the feeling that in sharing so many values they are part of the same family, that their defeat by the Communists would be intolerable, and hence that we must work with them just as we must among ourselves. Britain, Canada, Australia and New Zealand in particular are felt by many Americans to be part of a real community with us. A similar American sentiment, if less deeply rooted in a common cultural heritage, extends to most Western European nations. Among Americans of non-Western European antecedents there is an equivalent sense of community, extending to countries which, like Poland, are currently behind the Iron Curtain. This sense of community may also be attached to more abstract concepts, such as "democracy" or "anti-Communism," though these probably lack the intimate appeal of ethnic, cultural and historical ties.

This sense of community, where it is felt, can be of tremendous significance in holding an alliance together. More than any calculation of interests, it provides the necessary spiritual and emotional energy, the enthusiasm, for a nation to sustain and live with its company of allies. Admittedly, the sense of community cannot be used to prove the value of an alliance to those who do not feel that sense. There is little point in trying to sell an American-British alliance to an American Anglophobe by appealing to sentiment; if he is to be persuaded it will have to be on other grounds, and even then his acceptance may be grudging. But this does not imply that the sense of community is necessarily fixed, or limited to certain countries. A glance at the history of American attitudes toward other nations will show that our sense of community has grown and become more inclusive. This is all to the good, since it is certainly a movement that corresponds with our democratic faith.

The sense of community alone cannot always provide a rational guide to policy. There is weight to the argument that our relatively close emotional and cultural bonds with Europe have at times led to a concern for Europe at the expense of Asia, a concern which went beyond the dictates of political and strategic priorities. The conflicting sense of community and of irritation regarding Spain, both in the United States and in NATO, has not made it easier to devise a coherent policy toward that country. Still, these difficulties are of far less moment than the enormous positive gain of having the capacity to enjoy this sense of shared values with other peoples.

The task of working through alliances can, then, be greatly advanced if we also strive to promote mutual understanding of the dangers to be faced, to relate the alliance to the more universal aspirations of the peoples concerned, and to enrich the sense of community which they may share. In such an atmosphere we shall have the best chance of composing the unavoidable differences and disputes that will arise, since each member can feel that, while some alliance policies are not in accord with its view of its interests, the alliance as a whole is of vital importance to its own survival. Such is the necessary tone of any collaborative enterprise which is to have more than a fleeting existence.

We have still, however, to deal with two features of our present alliances which create rather special problems: 1) the disparity in strength of the different allies, and 2) the presence of possibly incompatible objectives among our allies. As we shall see, these two problems are not unrelated.

When one of a group of allied states is stronger than all the others combined, there is an obvious danger that the alliance, instead of promoting mutuality of interest and responsibility, will become a patron-client relationship. One can argue endlessly, and rather pointlessly, as to whether equality among unequals is really equitable or not, but it is evident that if the relation is one of patron to clients, one does not have a real alliance. The power of decision rests with the patron. The rest are dependent on him; his policy must be accepted by them.

On occasion the relationship of the United States to its allies has been presented in this light, most particularly by the Communists, and the impression of disparity has caused some friction. At times our allies have had the unhappy feeling of being "the tail to the American kite." The American people have shown some impatience with what has been considered our government's quite unnecessary sensitivity to the wishes of allies who were not "pulling their weight" in a presumably common enterprise.

Appearances, it is true, have given some support to this sense of inequality. Enormously powerful industrially and militarily, relatively secure in the Western Hemisphere, protecting the non-Communist world under the shield of its atomic monopoly, the United States seemed cast as patron, and all the others as clients with little to offer and everything to gain from association with us. Even though our treaties of alliance took the form of mutual defense agreements, the historical occasions for their creation were not the direct defense of the United States but the need to prevent the Soviet Union or Communist China from taking over Western Europe, Korea, Formosa or Southeast Asia.

Nevertheless, while it might appear to some that the United States, in its alliances, has not been adding to its own strength but only to its responsibilities, this appearance is quite false. The United States has not been engaging in acts of gratuitous patronage. Preventing such areas from falling to the Soviet bloc is necessary for our own security; a denial of additional strength and resources to the Soviet bloc is equivalent to an increment to our own. The United States shares a profound mutuality of interest with its allies which have been in more immediate peril of succumbing to Communist inroads.

More than that, there is also a mutuality of contribution, though the contributions may be of different sorts: military forces, bases, geographic space, resources, manpower or even such vital intangibles as the will to independence and the passion for freedom. In the case of the British Commonwealth, of course, we profit from a long-established, worldwide network of power, communications and influence that is of the greatest importance.

Further, the double movement in the development of atomic power—toward its accessibility to an increasing number of nations (which will also create its own problems) and toward a parity of utterly devastating potential that may make the threat of atomic retaliatory punishment largely inapplicable in cases of nonatomic aggression—suggests that the military and defense contributions of our allies are likely to be of greater rather than of less importance as time passes. If we are tending away from the pure dependence on the American atomic protective shield and toward a reciprocity of dependence in an international order which, while perhaps remaining divided in two—the Soviet bloc and the rest—demonstrates less polarization of power and decision in Moscow and Washington, we must expect increasing need and scope for alliance diplomacy. Under the peculiar and not fully understood power balances of an age of atomic plenty, the smaller nations may unexpectedly regain a role in international affairs which they had lost in former decades. Hence, while we cannot but feel a certain asymmetry in the relations of the United States and its allies, it does not follow at all that we can be the free agents and that the others must do our bidding because they cannot do otherwise. We are all in the same boat, riding out the same storm.

In actual fact, many of our difficulties have stemmed less from the disparity of power than from the differing ranges of interest and responsibility. Because of its strength and its situation as the chief single obstacle to Soviet hegemony, the United States has been forced to assume responsibilities all over the world, responsibilities reflected in its pattern of alliances. The only parallel is the network of British Commonwealth commitments and even that has engaged Britain far less deeply than the United States in the Far East. In consequence, the full range of American foreign responsibilities extends well beyond the formal scope of any one of the alliances of which the United States is a member. To take the Far Eastern example, in so far as the main burden for the defense of that area rests with the United States and the local forces that can be mustered, it would be difficult to make this a NATO responsibility. While Britain and France have interests in the Far East, NATO as an organization does not.

The United States is not, of course, the only country concerned with, or influenced by, events far removed from its own frontiers. Nearly all critical areas are linked and given general significance by the existence of a common threat, the outthrust of Communist power, and by the possibility that a local crisis anywhere might erupt into a general conflict affecting all nations. Still, beneath this unity of menace and apprehension, there are important differences in perspective. American policy in the Far East cannot be exclusively determined by a NATO point of view, though we cannot act without reference to NATO interests which are affected by events in Asia. The task necessarily falls upon the United States to take the lead in mediating between these divergent perspectives—no other power is in an equally immediate position to do so—and try to find courses of action which can best serve the whole of the non-Communist world.

In face of divergent points of view it is tempting to set up priorities of importance for the various areas for which we have some responsibility. It is doubtful that such a rating can usefully be established. One may argue, for example, that Europe, with its industry, trained manpower and close cultural ties with the United States, is of greater importance to us than the Middle or Far East. But against this it can be argued that Asia is currently the more vulnerable area, more likely to go under, and must therefore be the particular object of our attention, especially since the Communization of Asia would weaken the relative position of Western Europe. Any such rating, however, could be made less than helpful by the fact that the Soviets could take advantage of it and move against those areas to which we had accorded low priority. It is far better to state simply that all free areas are important and that we must do our level best to prevent a clash of interests between them and to cooperate in their defense against Communist expansion.

Admittedly, this is not an ideal solution. In what is essentially a global problem, for which the various alliances are but partial answers, it would be preferable if the United States and all its allies could act in concert on the particular measures to be taken in any given area. We should certainly try to make as much headway in this direction as we can. The European powers, for example, now appear a good deal more prepared to grant the importance of keeping Formosa free of Communist control than they were in the period immediately after the Communists' victory on the mainland.

More serious than differing regional perspectives is the possibility of really incompatible interests among our allies. Some of these may be within the alliance structure itself, such as the British-Greek-Turkish controversy regarding Cyprus, or French-German differences on the Saar. These could be very damaging to the solidarity of an alliance, and we should do our best to compose them, but there is little further we can say about them here without either being platitudinous or moving into a detailed examination which would carry us too far from our subject. Of more immediate relevance to Soviet-American relations are the cases of allies having claims to territory within the Communist orbit: West Germany, South Korea, Vietnam and the Republic of China. The international status of the claims is not the same in the four instances, but they are alike in that the interests of these allies are not fully satisfied by the alliances and could even run counter to them. There have been periodic alarms in the United States, as well as in other allied countries, lest these claims give the alliances an offensive tinge provocative of war. It is feared that, under the cover of American protection, irredentist allies might be tempted to drag the United States into a conflict by starting a military adventure which we would be driven to support because we dared not permit an ally to suffer defeat.

These fears cannot be dismissed as groundless—for one thing, we cannot predict the temper of future leaders of our allies—but some discrimination is called for. In the first place, the alliances are specifically defensive in their provisions. The question whether we would be obliged to support or bail out a rash action would not rest on the fact of the alliance but on our judgment at the time of all the consequences resulting from that action. This judgment would be required of us in any event. Moreover, while an alliance might encourage rash enterprises, it could equally well serve as a device to restrain them; this is a matter for competent diplomacy. The United States, while it must oppose further advances by the Communist bloc, has also shown that it rejects any policy provocative of war. Our position on this must, of course, be made perfectly clear to our allies.

In the preceding paragraphs we have been considering the conduct of alliances under conditions of peace or cold war. In the case of actual hostilities the alliances would then be called upon for a fuller demonstration of their worth, and there is little that we can profitably say about the conduct of such a war or the working out of allied strategy. There is, however, one question which is sometimes raised and which we must try to answer here. We have suggested that the concept of deterrence by atomic retaliatory punishment was likely to play a diminishing role with the advent of Soviet atomic parity, and that such retaliation might therefore eventually be limited to the single case of a prior atomic attack upon the United States. This, however, leaves unanswered the question of an atomic attack upon our allies in advance of an attack upon the United States. This may be considered an unlikely possibility, since the Soviets would regard it as extremely hazardous to initiate atomic fighting (apart, perhaps, from tactical use of atomic weapons) without having first eliminated the American atomic striking force. At the same time the fact remains that, if an initial Soviet atomic attack of a general character occurs anywhere but on the United States, our decision to make an atomic retaliation will be accompanied by the risk of a counterretaliation upon ourselves. Would we be willing to make an all-out atomic response to a general Soviet atomic assault on, say, Greece or Turkey? Would we be willing to accept the sequence, Ankara-Moscow-New York? A fear that we would not may lie behind former Prime Minister Churchill's decision that Britain should build its own thermonuclear bombs, so that the decision for retaliation in the event of an attack on British cities will be securely in British hands and not be solely dependent on United States action. It may be that other nations will increasingly seek to possess their own retaliatory nuclear capabilities (this would not be the same as general military capabilities). It is not impossible to envisage a number of states having at least enough thermonuclear weapons and means of delivery to be able to deliver a damaging retaliation against atomic assault (e.g., Odessa for Ankara). Until that time comes, however, the conclusion seems unavoidable that, despite the increasing difficulty of the decision, the United States must be prepared to assume the responsibility of retaliation for a general atomic attack upon its allies. Otherwise, their independence and morale might easily be undermined by atomic "blackmail."

Neutral and Uncommitted Nations

Among the nations which are neither allies of the United States nor within the Soviet bloc there are marked differences in diplomatic posture. For some, like Switzerland, strict neutrality is a long-established national policy which can be expected to continue even though Swiss political and ideological sympathies are predominantly with the NATO powers. For some, especially in Asia, their lack of commitment reflects a tug of war of conflicting sentiments and passions: concern over possible Communist inroads being balanced by anti-Western and anticolonial feelings and by a desire to concentrate on domestic problems. As a policy, neutrality is variously conceived of as a conscious abstention from external power politics, as an effort to occupy a position midway between contending power groupings, as a way to serve as a "bridge" or mediator between them, or as the basis for an independent third force.

But whatever the form or the motive, the result has been that a considerable number of states, some of them occupying important strategic positions, are not committed to any mutual defense arrangement against the Soviet Communist threat that extends, as we see it, to all non-Communist nations. There have been at least three distinct American attitudes toward these neutral or uncommitted powers. Some have felt that there was no room for neutrality in the present crisis and that, if a nation lacked the will and the wisdom to commit itself to the defense of the free world against the obvious Communist danger, it was not deserving of American support or of economic assistance. Such a view, if carried through vigorously, would cut off our nose to spite our face. While we may not approve of the policies or motives of some of the uncommitted nations, it is obviously not in the American interest to see them undermined or disorganized. In so far as our refusal to extend assistance weakens their internal stability and renders them more susceptible to Communist influence, whether domestically or diplomatically, it is obviously not a profitable line of action.

At the other extreme, some have felt that, since the process of alliance-making may tend to isolate, expose and hence to alienate the uncommitted powers, the United States should place less emphasis upon formal and politically-oriented alliances and should depend rather upon more universal collective security arrangements, principally via the UN, that would afford a greater probability of participation by the uncommitted powers who were signatories to the Charter. This view, however, has been unable to make headway against the realities of the international situation. It has become increasingly evident that a definite organization of effort is required against the activities of the Soviet Union, its satellites and associates. While the Korean war was a UN undertaking, the fact that resistance to the invasion could be organized through the UN was in part due to a fortunate accident—the temporary absence of the Soviet member from the Security Council—and it is by no means certain that this established a precedent which could be repeated. Even in this case a fairly sharp distinction appeared, both in diplomatic position and in the nature of the contributions, between the uncommitted powers and the allies.

The third attitude, which seems to have become the predominant one, and to which we would subscribe, accepts the fact that a number of nations are going to remain uncommitted for the foreseeable future but that this is not altogether a bad thing. We have become increasingly aware that the domestic political and economic situation of a number of countries simply does not permit them to assume the responsibilities of an alliance commitment. Moreover, we have come to recognize that if a nation is willing to maintain its own independence, and may be assisted in doing so with external economic aid, this is definitely to our advantage. In the case of such countries as India, Burma and even Sweden, the most important single fact, from the American point of view, is that they are on the frontiers of the Communist zone but have not allowed themselves to be included within it. So long as they are not, we may be reasonably well satisfied. As with some of our formal allies, while our relationship with them cannot be one of fully reciprocal responsibility it certainly can be one of mutual interest—interest in their independence. It would follow from this that we should not try to *force* the neutrals into alignment, or to press them beyond their conception of their own national interest.

Despite the fact that the neutrality of a number of states is not, then, harmful, there are some real handicaps. In the first place, while a neutral nation may be willing to defend itself, it is quite doubtful that any such nation would be capable of withstanding a serious Communist attack. In such a case it would need our more positive assistance, which it would be in our interest to give. But at that late date, in the absence of any prior military planning or coordination, we should be at a serious disadvantage. Even armed neutrality fails to provide a basis for that planning and coordination which is an important part of setting up the defense of the non-Communist world.

In the second place, and this is often overlooked by the neutrals, the ability of a nation to enjoy what may be considered the luxury of neutrality in the presence of a powerful aggressor is dependent on the fact that some other nations in the world have taken a stand against the potential trouble-maker. Were these committed powers not present, the neutrality of the others would, in such a situation, be short-lived. Admittedly, a neutral power might not accept the American analysis of the international situation and refuse to believe that there are any deliberate trouble-makers abroad in the world. But from our point of view the presence of neutrals in the non-Communist world, while infinitely preferable to the presence of pro-Communist powers, does impose a burden on those nations which have taken on the job of counteracting Soviet pressures. Consequently, though the United States should not try to force neutrally-inclined nations into alliance, it is certainly in its interest, over a period of time, to acquire more allies when these feel capable and ready for such participation.

It will be noted that we have not mentioned "neutralism." This we regard as something quite different from being neutral or uncommitted, and much more dangerous to American interests. By "neutralism" we mean not the decision to refrain from joining one or another power grouping, but the more positive assertion that the power groups, including those with which the United States is associated, are bad, that there is little to choose among them, and that they should be dissolved. Such neutralism, in our view, utterly misinterprets the international situation and is not something to which the United States can accommodate its policies, though we shall have to put up with it. For this very reason, however, we must be careful not to equate neutrality, or the absence of commitment, with neutralism—though there are tinges of neutralism in the position of some of the neutrals—as this would merely alienate a number of nations and political groups who should not and need not lose sight of the common stake which they as well as the committed nations have in the survival of the free world.

CHAPTER VI

ECONOMIC POLICY: THE PROBLEM OF GROWTH

IF ANY single word can summarize the requirements for American economic policy it is "growth," growth of the United States economy and growth of the free-world economies. As we have seen in our discussion of strengths and vulnerabilities, economic strength is not the only basis for comparison, and under contingencies of nuclear warfare it could, in substantial measure, be wiped out. It is nevertheless an indispensable component of American defense and security, not least in affording us flexibility in our choice of policies and actions. It is not difficult to imagine the damaging effect upon morale and political stability, in the United States and abroad, if it became clear that our economy was being overtaken by that of the Soviet bloc. Economic growth is surely one of the prerequisites for avoiding both the erosion of the free world's will and a preventive showdown born of desperation.

Growth can be given two somewhat different meanings: *expansion* and *maturation.* The first meaning, the principal topic of this chapter, stresses increase in quantities and rests on the assumption that the growth of something as complex as an economic system can be measured by some common quantitative standard, such as money, for the purpose of gaining a useful general idea of the strength, dynamism and adaptability of a society. The second meaning, a principal topic of the following chapter, stresses qualitative change and concerns the relation between economic development and the social and cultural milieu of which it is a part.

The Expansion of the United States Economy

Not only is United States economic expansion a necessity for our dealings with the Soviet Union, but it appears to present no significant disadvantages. Alleged disadvantages to our allies and to uncommitted nations would be minimized, if not eliminated, by the concurrent growth of their own economies. The effect of United States growth on Soviet bloc policies would probably not be detrimental to the free world and might be beneficial. These conclusions, however, warrant brief examination.

The principal direct benefit to the United States would be in maintaining the capacity—and confidence in our capacity—to handle the manifold nonmilitary requirements of a cold war while carrying the burden of an adequate and probably increasingly costly military establishment. Chances of keeping up, and increasing, living standards would be improved, though they would also have to depend on the urgency of other demands for the increased output. It would be pleasant if it turned out that we were able to meet the Soviet challenge without a sacrifice in material welfare. But the ability to maintain material welfare cannot be the condition determining our willingness to defend ourselves.

As for benefits to our allies, they could anticipate an expanding market for their exports, on the assumption, of course, that our import restrictions are not so tightened as to preclude this. Moreover, an expanding American economy is better able to provide increased aid abroad, if that is required, regardless of the particular form of the aid or its purpose.

It must be recognized, however, that in other countries some fears have been expressed, especially in diagnoses of the chronic dollar shortage, that American economic expansion might not be an unqualified advantage, and might even be a disadvantage, to them. There is worry lest the prices of raw materials imported by the principal allies of the United States—Great Britain, West Germany, France and Japan—would be raised as the United States gobbled up foreign supplies. There is also apprehension lest the technological advances normally accompanying rapid growth might reduce United States costs or lead to the development of new products, with the result that its allies would be forced to discard usable, but technologically obsolescent, capital equipment and assume very heavy replacement burdens; or would have to reduce living standards at home in order to compete; or would lose "third country" markets; or would become increasingly dependent upon the United States. While it is true that there might be temporary hardships in certain sectors of the economies of our allies, it is very doubtful that these alleged disadvantages would outweigh the advantages or that they would be as serious as some believe—on the condition, of course, that the American economy remains an open one and that our economic policies take due account of the need to temper the impact of our economic expansion upon the vulnerable sectors of other economies.

The uncommitted nations, most of whom are economically "underdeveloped," may be expected to have better prospects for continued or augmented American aid and also to enjoy increased prices for raw materials as the American market for them expands. To be sure, rising prices for raw materials would certainly stimulate research for synthetic substitutes. There is a danger that the underdeveloped countries could end up with expanded production facilities for raw materials in face of a smaller market with falling prices. It must be admitted that, to an even greater extent than the industrial nations, the underdeveloped countries are vulnerable to the changes and dislocations of economic growth. Yet again, on balance, and if we give appropriate recognition to problems of adjustment and if we help nations in solving them, these potential disadvantages are manageable.

In recent years the fear has been expressed that the enormous expansion of economies will lead in time to a "plundering" of the planet, the exhaustion of essential raw materials. In terms of our problem this fear, even if it were justified, could not be decisive. We could not, because of this danger, permit ourselves to be outstripped economically by the Soviet bloc. The issue in this case would be much the same as that foreseen in the atomic race: the prospect of mutual suicide as against allowing the other side to gain dominance. As we have indicated earlier, when the question is posed in this narrow fashion, it permits of only one answer: we must prevent Soviet domination.

This fear of an exhaustion of resources does not, however, appear to be well grounded. While certain resources may be dwindling and may become increasingly costly, the evidence seems reasonably strong that the same advances in technology which create the growing demand for resources are also developing substitutes, synthetics and methods of conservation and of utilizing scrap which appear to be capable of handling the problem. Atomic energy gives promise of providing adequate power for the future requirements of a greatly expanded economy with its attendant problem of costs. We cannot, of course, be cocksure about these prospects. It is obviously important to keep an eye out for likely shortages so that we can take timely action, but the imperative need for continued economic expansion should not be obscured by such fears.

It is evident that growth may vary in the different sectors of the economy and that changes in the pattern could significantly affect the strength of the economy and its capacity to maintain growth. Military and political, as well as economic, considerations enter into the determination of the sectors contributing most to economic strength: the extent to which our defense needs seem reasonably well secured, the willingness of the population to accept cuts in actual or prospective consumption without loss of productivity or morale.

Under present circumstances we would attribute first priority to increasing the production of military supplies as well as the producers' goods, raw materials and human skills necessary for the estimated future requirements of our military establishment. Without these the whole nation and its economy could be imperiled. When production has reached a level adequate to our security—in our view this level has not yet been reached—greater priority should then be accorded to growth in the output of producers' goods for heavy industry. Without that, the rate of over-all economic growth could not be expanded rapidly and sustained for a long period. Consumers' goods and the means of producing them are clearly of lower priority in the present determination of economic strength.

There is little point, however, in talking about the desirability of economic growth and the sectors of greatest utility unless it is possible and feasible for policy to influence growth. Otherwise, to invent an old Russian proverb, it is like telling the lamb it will be safe from the young wolf if it can grow larger faster, especially in the teeth.

Fortunately, the United States economy has been expanding at quite a rapid pace, and perhaps the most important point to make is that the continuing and complex task of keeping this active and dynamic economy in balance and on the track is the primary requirement, to which all specific steps influencing the rate or direction of expansion are secondary. In other words, the proper functioning of our economy is of overwhelming importance, not to the American position alone but to the rest of the world.

In addition to this primary task there appear to be areas of general agreement among political and business leaders and economists about the effect of actions more specifically concerned with growth and its direction. The following measures would seem to promise favorable results:

1. An increase in government orders for military supplies. These increases could contribute to general economic growth, if factories and human resources were not being fully utilized. Once the existing slack was taken up, however, continued use of manpower and resources in defense production and in military services would inhibit the expansion of production in other sectors of the economy. At that time a balance would have to be struck between the costs involved in inhibiting general economic expansion and the value of immediately increased military strength.

2. Substantial incentives to business to encourage production of, and investment in, producers' goods. These incentives could include tax concessions as well as the maintenance of a general climate favorable to private business.

3. Creating conditions favorable to scientific and technological progress.[1]

4. Stimulating the growth of adequate facilities for the production of strategic materials abroad, and also at home. Such an increase might not be too important in stimulating United States economic growth, but it would be very important in maintaining it. The government might also stimulate such adjuncts to growth as road building (e.g., through grants to the states) and construction of power facilities (public and/or private).

[1] See discussion above, pp. 69-70.

Distinct conceptually, but related in practice to the problem of stimulating economic growth, is that of providing incentives to private business to prepare for possible nuclear warfare by constructing stand-by and dispersed facilities. Although such a program is not and probably should not be aimed at stimulating economic growth, it cannot be ignored here, since it could compete with other government actions designed for that purpose, and since its net effect under circumstances of less than full employment would in fact be a stimulating one. Even if its effect were depressing, however, this program would be warranted because it would provide a larger mobilization base and help to reduce United States vulnerabilities to nuclear warfare.[2] Government participation would be called for, since private business, necessarily using investment-decision criteria different from those of the government, could probably not afford to prepare as quickly or as well, without governmental incentives. These incentives, available only for facilities (stand-by or operating) built or installed at "adequate" distances from existing population and industrial concentrations, could include tax concessions; building, transportation and power facilities; or even the subsidizing of stand-by facilities for emergency expansion of output.

It will be observed that the actions suggested above do not question the inherent ability of the American economy to achieve and maintain acceptable rates of growth in the future. They do reflect a concern that spontaneous and wholly undirected growth might not cover short-run requirements, especially in the directions deemed most essential to national survival in the setting of our relations with the Soviet Union. The government incentives contemplated do not represent a radical departure, if any at all, from previous American practices. Since its inception, the United States government has fostered internal economic development in a variety of ways, by granting tracts of land to railroads and homesteaders, by building plants itself during the Second World War, by offering tax incentives to private firms now building defense plants in less vulnerable areas, and by subsidizing as a general practice certain economic activities. As

[2] See also above, p. 98.

a moderate extension of familiar practices, the actions suggested seem justified by the serious demands of our present and future situation.

The question still remains, however, whether natural growth, with some government reinforcement, will suffice to meet the challenge of Soviet economic growth. As we have seen, the Soviet economy has apparently been expanding more rapidly than our own; [3] if it continued to do so despite the measures suggested above, the ultimate prospects for the free world would not be bright. Are we obliged to face the possibility that a controlled and regimented economy of the Soviet type can, over time and in disregard of the human costs, outproduce a decentralized and undirected economy? The first remark to be made is that this obviously controversial question is too important and too complex to be answered off the cuff, on grounds of principle, hunch or wishful thinking, whether optimistic or pessimistic. The second is that, while the question is vitally important, an immediate decision is not required. We do not have to arrive at an answer this year or next. Fortunately, the lead the American economy enjoys is sufficiently great and the growth differential sufficiently small that we can afford to spend some time in a careful examination of the problem. This examination must be made, however, and it requires the attention and efforts of many minds. Among the issues germane to such an examination are the following: the establishment of adequate measurements of economic growth, the obscurities (deliberate and otherwise) of the Soviet data, the comparability of the two economies, the causes for the relatively rapid Soviet rate, the extent to which it may be expected to level off, and the obstacles that may block future Soviet and U.S. expansion. The problem also involves some quite intricate questions: the advantages which may be enjoyed by a free competitive economy in initiating new growth, stimulating and absorbing technological innovation and replacing inefficient methods; the advantages a controlled economy may enjoy in borrowing, adapting and quickly utilizing such innovations; the extent to which our high economic level, in permitting us to apply capital-

[3] See above, p. 54.

saving as well as labor-saving devices, compensates for the high forced capital investment of the Soviet system. We can do no more here than emphasize the importance of inquiry in this direction and indicate our belief that the measures suggested above are adequate for the near and middle future.

Foreign Economic Policy

The United States has a number of reasons for encouraging economic growth in the other nations of the non-Communist world. Faster economic growth would probably contribute to the strength of pro-Western, anti-Communist or non-Communist regimes in giving them stronger and more flexible instruments for averting or coping with unrest—whether or not Communist-inspired—and permitting increased defense establishments without a heavier burden.

As for reducing the appeal of Communism, we recognize that the relationship between economic growth and Communism is a complicated one which is not yet fully understood. We should not make the error of identifying the attraction of Communism with poverty and hunger. On the contrary, economic growth, where it uproots people and leads to social and religious dislocations, may well create an atmosphere more favorable to Communism than a situation of untouched primitiveness and squalor. Still, in the present day of impatience for improved living standards and of increasing expectations that these are achievable, economic stagnation or a slow and faltering growth would seem to invite Communist inroads, especially since the Communists are vigorously selling the idea that they have the only sure cure for economic backwardness. While economic growth alone cannot create that sense of community, of social integrity, which is the basic source of resistance to Communism, its absence in these days could very well undo all other efforts to shore up a society.[4]

In addition, economic growth abroad would, on balance, contribute to further United States economic growth by expanding both supplies and markets. Such expansion in turn would favor greater cohesion in the free-world alliance

[4] For further discussion of these social problems, see Chapter VIII below.

as well as increased mutuality of interests with the politically uncommitted nations.

While all these benefits are of direct relevance to the defense of the United States and the non-Communist world, we should not neglect the improvement of living standards as a good in itself, highly desirable even were there no problem of Communism. To call this materialistic is a quibble. Of course, the improvement of material conditions is not the be-all and end-all of life. At times it must be sacrificed to some greater need. But that mankind should not enjoy what men's minds, imaginations, labor and accumulated knowledge have proved capable of creating seems perverse in the extreme. In any event, economic development will take place, in one form or another, by self-help or with the help of others. We cannot guarantee results if we help, but if we do not we can be quite sure that we are not going to have much influence on many important economic and political trends.

In the case of the industrialized nations there is little we can add to our observations concerning United States economic growth, since the considerations are very much the same. By and large, the presently industrialized nations are in a reasonably good position to help themselves without foreign assistance, though they lack the margin the United States enjoys for taking on large-scale military burdens. The extent of their progress through self-help depends largely on their will to expand production and on the progress of international cooperation; it does not depend—as it did during the period of emergency and recovery after the Second World War—upon the aid of the United States. We should note, though, that the other industrial countries are economically less self-sufficient than the United States and must be assured an increased supply of foodstuffs and industrial raw materials.

When we turn to the economically underdeveloped, nonindustrialized areas, however, we encounter a quite different situation. They do not have an industrial, technological complex to provide the national community with the goods and services of the industrial age: no "heavy industry," little manufacture of consumers' goods and only the beginnings of an intensive agriculture, a banking and credit system and a transportation, communication, utility and distribution network. Awareness of this lack underlies the intense hunger for industrialization which we find expressed with increasing urgency.

The expressions of this desire are often inappropriate: the demand for a quick expansion of heavy industry, the belief that the production and export of primary goods in exchange for manufactured products is demeaning and denudes the underdeveloped country of its wealth. While there is no doubt that the underdeveloped countries could profit economically from an exchange of goods based on their economic complementarity with the industrial nations, there is also no doubt that in the past some of them have been exploited by a combination of foreign and domestic producers and have received, by any standards, an inequitable share of the profits. We cannot write off their mood as simply one of envy, though it frequently fails to take account of the difficult requirements of successful enterprise, nor is it sufficient to point out that exploitative colonialism is largely a thing of the past. What must be stressed is that a moderate rate of industrial growth, paced by the development of agriculture and mining, gives promise of reducing their vulnerable dependence on exports of primary products without subjecting their people to the near-slavery and other sacrifices involved in forced growth effected by Communist methods.

The question is largely one of *timing* and *proportion*. Initially, at least, emphasis on expanding output of primary products of agriculture, fisheries and mining, with concurrent improvements in transportation, utilities and education, would appear to be most rewarding, in improving living standards and in earning foreign exchange. The pattern and rate of industrialization itself should be balanced, so that the expansion in each sector of the economy, including foreign trade, would provide a market and supplies for the other sectors. In most underdeveloped countries this would mean stress in the early stages on processing and light industries rather than on heavy industries, for which both the market and the skilled labor force would be limited.

We recognize, and indeed would underline, that this approach to economic growth in the underdeveloped countries differs markedly from that of the Communists, who see economic expansion proceeding from the nucleus of heavy industry, nurtured by forced savings and tight controls, and by subordination of consumer benefits. We must not, however, overlook the perils of emphasizing consumer benefits and a relatively "natural" progress into industry in countries where the pressure of population and the absence of an entrepreneurial tradition could easily frustrate sustained growth. In many areas an alteration of the prevailing demographic pattern and of social attitudes—and these may be only marginally influenced by economic policy—would have to accompany the economic changes.

It seems evident that, on their own, the present underdeveloped countries are not in a position to bring about economic expansion along the lines envisaged at a rate sufficient to overcome these demographic and social hurdles and to achieve a self-sustaining growth. Self-help, while necessary, must be supplemented by external stimuli.

These may take a number of forms, each of which can make a certain contribution. Private capital flows, long-term loans, short-term credits and technical and organizational assistance, taken in combination with a high and sustained growth of American economic activity, would serve as an important stimulus if the underdeveloped countries were willing initially to concentrate on production in the primary industries and if the terms of trade were favorable and reasonably steady.

While normal economic criteria may provide partial though not complete justification for such measures, the advisability of assistance in the form of grants is, from the point of view of the United States, a question of security rather than of economics. It is best to recognize that investment in the underdeveloped areas is probably not, on the whole, the economically most profitable use of American capital. Assistance in the form of grants is clearly a cost the United States is assuming to improve the security of the non-Communist world.

The extent to which it benefits the United States to make

such grants, as against employing its economic and material resources for other purposes, depends in part upon the amount of such aid which the underdeveloped countries are capable of absorbing with significant benefit to their own economies. (We should make an exception, however, of the particular case of emergency grants to a nation in immediate peril of collapse. In such an instance economic calculations may be out of the question, and the amount of the grant may have to be determined by a rough assessment of the danger and the size of the stakes.) Although some efforts have been made to give a rough order of magnitude to this absorptive capacity [5] it is by no means certain that this question can, in isolation, be given even an approximate answer. Just as the number of pieces that a jigsaw puzzle can "absorb" depends upon putting the pieces in correct relation to one another, so the amount of aid that can be utilized with benefit can be greatly increased by appropriately directed and timed allocations. But quite evidently, if this is the case, absorptive capacity is not like a gallon bucket waiting to be filled, but depends upon the completeness of the knowledge we can have of the whole economic and social pattern, now existing and to be achieved, and upon the instruments—organization, a trained bureaucracy, means of enforcement—which are available to determine and carry out the allocations.[6]

It may of course be argued that the United States can

[5] Ragnar Nurkse remarks that "one might guess that 2 per cent of the national income of the United States, which is equal to about 7 per cent of the present total national income of the low-income countries outside the Soviet orbit, would certainly strain and probably exceed their present capacity to absorb outside aid for productive investment." *Problems of Capital Formation in Underdeveloped Countries* (New York: Oxford University Press, 1953), p. 94, n.2.

W. W. Rostow and R. W. Hatch suggest that South and Southeast Asia are capable of absorbing effectively an extra $2 billion per year over a five-year period. *An American Policy in Asia* (New York: Wiley, 1955), p. 49.

A study group sponsored by the Woodrow Wilson Foundation and the National Planning Association has expressed its belief that "annual expenditures on American economic and technical assistance to the underdeveloped areas could and should be increased to at least double, and probably as much as triple, the present size of such programs without exceeding the existing absorptive capacity of these countries." *The Political Economy of American Foreign Policy* (New York: Holt, 1955), p. 348.

[6] See also below, p. 153.

afford some wastage, that to strengthen the security of the underdeveloped countries it would be worth while to provide more aid than we were certain these countries could usefully absorb. But apart from some danger that deleterious consequences would flow from an excess of aid which could not be digested, it would be difficult to justify this domestically when the total of such aid must be balanced against other pressing requirements for American security.

In general, we can only record our impression that while the amount of world-wide economic aid currently being planned or sought—between one and two billion dollars annually, of which the preponderant part is for the underdeveloped countries—does not appear to be unreasonable, it is probably on the conservative side (especially if one takes into account the emphasis on aid directed to military or strategic objectives, though these are not necessarily a non-economic investment) and could be increased with benefit. The gains to be recorded would probably be as much political and psychological as economic. Any more precise statement would require a breakdown by countries, and by allocations within countries, and the establishment of a time schedule.

With respect to the handling of aid and industrial economic cooperation, a few observations may be worth making. In the first place, it is important that there be mutual understanding of motives and purposes as between the recipient, on the one hand, and the private investor or the public lender or donor, on the other hand, in order to reduce the danger of working at cross-purposes in carrying out the program. Second, the psychological impact is as important as the economic results. The success or failure of a development program in helping shield a nation from Communism might hinge more on the reception it received among the workers in the new undertakings and among local government and other leaders than on the material results which could be achieved. Consequently, the recipient nations must feel that the program is their own. The more the program is able to arouse local enthusiasm, hope and participation, the better. They must feel, too, that the aid is a matter of mutual interest and concern, that our interest, while not charitable or purely altruistic, is concerned primarily with assisting them to create an independent and viable society, and that the aid, in whatever form, will not be chopped off abruptly.

Earlier we observed that the growth of the United States economy, important in itself, must ultimately be set against that of the Soviet Union—that, in the context of our present concerns, comparative economic growth is what counts. This holds true for the growth of the economies in the rest of the non-Communist world. With respect to the growth of industrial countries, most of which are also our allies, the problem is essentially the same as in the case of the United States. Although the growth rates of the Soviet Eastern European satellites have been faster than those in Western Europe, the latter's margin of absolute advantage is still such that the problem, while very important, is not immediate and can allow time for careful scrutiny, measurement, comparison and interpretation. In the case of the underdeveloped countries the problem is more difficult and more pressing. Many of them are politically uncommitted, they are watching carefully to see which way the economic and political winds are blowing, and they are desperately anxious to find some path which promises a way out of their economic backwardness. Consequently, economic development will be measured and evaluated not in terms of local rates of improvement alone; it will probably be compared or contrasted with the achievements of the Soviet Union and especially of Communist China. Moreover, the underdeveloped areas still free of Communist control lack the margin of initial superiority, and hence the margin of time. If in the course of the next five or ten years Communist China's economic progress is not matched by that of the non-Communist Asian nations, a critically serious situation may result. Here above all we must avoid either wishful thinking or premature despair. The Chinese Communist effort may overtax the country and lead to major internal crisis, or it may not. At this point we cannot predict with certainty. But since we cannot advocate the type of measures the Communists employ in whipping their economy up the grade, we must do the most we can with the means that accord with our ethical, political and economic beliefs.

Reduction of Trade Restrictions

The contribution which a reduction of restrictions to multilateral intra-free-world trade might make in promoting general economic growth—the subject of a great deal of debate—is, in our view, moderate but real. The increased trade resulting from a reduction of barriers would not provide all the conditions for a high level of productivity and output, nor would it be without economic costs and dislocations. Nevertheless, the removal of trade restrictions would, over time, significantly stimulate free-world economic growth and bring about a better use of labor and other resources. Even more important, allied cooperation and free-world cohesion would be greatly strengthened by the enhanced opportunities given to the underdeveloped countries and to the industrial nations to expand their economies and improve their living standards by their own efforts.

Because of the economic preponderance of the United States, effective movement toward reducing trade restrictions would have to begin with American actions. The cuts should be large enough, even initially, to stimulate the foreign manufacturer to expand his output. The reductions should be envisaged for a long term, free of invisible barriers and unnecessary administrative procedures. From the point of view of the foreign exporter, the height of the tariff barrier may be less inhibiting than uncertainties as to whether it is reasonably permanent or whether exports to the United States will become entangled in red tape. The American political system makes it particularly hard to guarantee tariff stability. Still, the same could be said about foreign aid, but, on the whole, the United States has succeeded in following a reasonably stable and coherent aid policy. Tariff reductions should be accompanied, however, by negotiations aimed at reducing the trade controls of other free nations or, where advisable, obtaining other economic concessions.

While a persuasive case can be made, and one which we would accept, that in the long run the United States itself would gain economically from an extensive reduction of trade restrictions, in the short run certain adjustments and costs would be involved, principally for the industries, workers, and towns affected by the increased imports. In relative economic terms, the problem of readjustment would not be a serious one. Politically, of course, we encounter an old and familiar debate. We can admit that there are certain commodities (and certain skills) which are urgently needed in wartime and which for that reason may warrant protection or subsidizing, even though the United States does not enjoy a comparative advantage in their production. We may also admit that a gain in international economic cooperation, which also has its political value, might not be worth the cost of a bitter domestic American fight over tariffs. On the other hand, if one is arguing seriously in strategic terms, there is also something to be said for increasing our ratio of imports to home production, for those commodities without strategic implications. With respect to the political controversy, while domestic consensus cannot be sacrificed to international cooperation, neither can the national economic and political interest be sacrificed to particular interests.

Trade with the Soviet Bloc

While the problem of free-world trade with the Soviet bloc is often identified with the issue of economic warfare, such trade may also be seen as a means for reducing tensions between the two groups of powers. It would be evident from our earlier discussion of Soviet Communism that we find little reason to believe that the antagonism which the Communist world feels toward the non-Communist is going to be materially reduced by trade and commerce, any more than it was in the 1930's. Our concern is rather with the effect on comparative economic strength of trade between the Soviet bloc and the non-Communist world.

When one considers the nature of the trade relations between a coordinated bloc of centralized, militarily oriented economies and an uncoordinated or loosely coordinated group of nations with decentralized economies, it is difficult to avoid the conclusion that trade will strengthen the former more than the latter. There is a strong presumption that all trade the Soviet bloc engages in has its strategic function. It is certain that a great deal of non-Communist trade with the Soviet bloc, by the uncommitted nations and by our allies, is not thought of in strategic terms at all. Now if there were no question of a possible war or some other form of power conflict, it might be argued that this would make no difference or even that the relatively free and uncontrolled trade of the non-Communist world would be to its advantage in building healthy and balanced economies. But general economic wellbeing is not the same as effective strength in a situation of conflict, and it would be most unrealistic to disregard this when discussing free-world trade with the Soviet bloc. Consequently, our safest assumption is that, on balance, increases in this trade will be somewhat more to the power advantage of the Soviet bloc than to that of the non-Communist world.

Having said this, however, we should add that the difference in advantage is not likely to affect decisively the balance of the world's forces. To be sure, one can imagine types of trade—selling strategic goods for Soviet gold—where the real disadvantage could become one of major proportions. But, if we except the items of high strategic importance, the advantage is not all one way.

Hence, while there is a good prima facie case for limiting the free world's trade with the Soviet bloc, the case is not so overwhelming that efforts should be made to restrict trade without regard for the costs. Among these we would include the economic losses suffered by some of our allies and the uncommitted nations, to whom East-West trade means much more than it does to the United States, interallied political friction and the costs of establishing and operating the instruments for enforcing trade restrictions.

While our primary concern must be to see that the non-Communist powers do not lose more than they gain by trading with the Communist bloc and that the strength and cohesion of the free world is not sapped by disputes over such trade, it is possible to go beyond this and advocate active economic warfare. The decision to use our foreign economic policy as a sword rather than a shield depends, of course, upon more basic policy decisions which we shall discuss in the next section of this report. We should, however, warn against any undue expectations of the gains to be achieved through economic warfare.

Economic warfare, as a direct form of pressure to weaken the opponent's military power or to oblige him to give up territory, has relatively limited possibilities against an area of continental dimensions, with internal access to nearly all important raw materials, and, in case of need, largely self-sustaining. Nor do there appear to be any really serious bottlenecks which, if exploited, would prove to be very debilitating. To be sure the Soviet bloc allegedly has shortages in nickel, copper and certain electronic equipment, but possibilities of preliminary stockpiling, reduction of civilian consumption and the development of substitute materials are such that economic warfare could probably do no more than raise production costs. Under certain circumstances, this effect might be significant, but the prospects seem very doubtful of greatly altering thereby the balance of economic strength. Consequently, a policy of economic warfare, if it is to be considered a rational course of American action, must avoid certain errors. It must not be advertised as a cheap and easy way to gain *major* political objectives. It would be irresponsible to suggest that blockades, embargoes and other trade restrictions, no matter how drastic—and they would be very difficult to apply effectively—would seriously imperil the Soviet Union or Communist China. Moreover, the United States must not refuse to pick up the check for the costs which may be incurred in the free world by an American decision to press for economic warfare. These costs are both political and economic, and if we failed to meet them, or pretended that they did not exist, we might weaken, not strengthen, our position relative to that of the Soviet bloc.

CHAPTER VII

SOCIAL POLICY: THE PROBLEM OF MODERNIZATION AND REFORM

IN THE three preceding chapters we were concerned with the tasks of increasing the military, political and economic strength of the United States and the rest of the non-Communist world. It is indispensable that we achieve these tasks, but they do not exhaust our requirements. Military capabilities, alliances, economic growth—these cannot permanently defend the non-Communist world unless they are supported by peoples' belief and confidence in their own societies. The security of the non-Communist world is not solely a matter of increments, of adding factors of strength to counterbalance or outweigh those of the Soviet bloc; it depends upon marshalling the inner resources, preserving or creating patterns of social life, homes for the spirit, that can resist the totalitarian erosion of our time.

All would agree that Soviet Communism is not exclusively an external challenge, though it is that, too. The conflict has roots in some very intimate issues: weaknesses, shortcomings and rifts in the non-Communist societies that may dangerously increase their vulnerability. Yet these sources of vulnerability are perhaps the most difficult of all to deal with or even to understand. We may advance theories and achieve partial insights, but we do not really know what makes human societies behave the way they do. We are not sure which are the most significant indices: growth and distribution of per capita income, church attendance, crime rates, health and mortality rates, turnouts for elections, the state of the arts. Much less do we know the "causes" for the movement of these indices. Of course, we are not totally ignorant, and we are making progress in our knowledge, but we have a long way to go. In the meantime we must act as intelligently as we can.

In the present chapter we shall deal only with the problems of the so-called underdeveloped countries. We are not suggesting that the industrial countries are so immune to social crisis or Communist inroads that they can be disregarded. Such is obviously not the case. The size and endurance of the Communist parties in a number of Western European states are but one symptom of a continuing crisis of serious proportions.[1] Nor dare we be so complacent about our own American society as to think it without social vulnerabilities. We are all aware of weaknesses, though we might not agree on their relative importance or their source.

But precisely because American society, and those of Western Europe, are "mature" industrial democracies, any discussion of their internal social policy which is to go beyond generalities and exhortations would necessarily lead us to a detailed study of domestic conditions and policies. This would have to be the subject of another book. If, as we believe, the democratic philosophy, as it has evolved in the course of much experience, can still promote a cohesive society able to correct its own shortcomings, our message here while urgent is simple (though its application is difficult): we must make our social, economic and political practices conform to our democratic principles. But this is something we should do in any event, not just in response to Communism. To say, for example, that racial discrimination increases our vulnerability in face of the Communist danger is true enough, but such discrimination damages us even more by making us false to our own principles. In other words, the enormously complex job of democratically arriving at a more perfect union must be worked out on its own grounds, not as an adjunct to Soviet-American relations. Otherwise we would be introducing a most undesirable note of contingency to our democratic principles.

Some, to be sure, may feel that the principles themselves have become threadbare, or at least do not give us the guid-

[1] There are a number of features of Western European society which, from the American point of view, seem to call for reform: class stratification, the political party system, entrepreneurial lassitude, etc. Still, the problem of reform in Western Europe is fundamentally the same as in the United States: adaptation and correction within a social order which itself has been one of the creators of modern industrial democracy. This is quite different from the problem of the underdeveloped areas, though parts of Western Europe may more nearly resemble the latter.

ance we need in meeting the fantastic changes of recent decades, and hence that we must rethink, reformulate or "update" our national philosophy. Such an excursion into philosophical construction is beyond the scope of this report, and we can only observe that, while political philosophies have occasionally been drawn up on order, the spirit which gives them life is not thus evoked.

It may be thought that we have run our argument into a corner: if we feel we cannot undertake here a discussion of social policy within the United States, the country we know most intimately, how can we say anything useful about social policy toward the underdeveloped countries, which we understand far less well and which may or may not be progressing in the direction of democracy? This point would be well taken if it were a matter of our trying to create new societies or remodel old ones in the American image. But this is not and cannot be our goal. Such a goal would drive us into a most extreme kind of imperialism in basic conflict with our own democratic premises.

There is, however, a vitally important contribution that we can make to the social problems of the underdeveloped areas: not to create the good society—that only its members can do—but to assist in avoiding pitfalls, in removing certain evils which may prevent these areas from having even the opportunity to develop as free nations. Just because we have a mature industrial society (non-European societies may be equally or more mature than we in their spiritual and cultural achievements, but not as industrial societies) we are in a position, which they are not, to know what is happening to them, what forces are at work. We may not be sure just what their impact may be on any particular country, but we do possess many valuable clues from our own and the Western European experience, as well as from that of other relatively lately developed nations. It is with an eye to this contribution that we consider the problem of reform and modernization.

We should start from the enormous impact of modern industrial society, an impact that has become the more jarring in each successive decade as it has spread out from its North

Atlantic-Western European center to all other cultures and societies. Some of them are primitive, others are of ancient refinement, but nearly all have proved relatively helpless against this massive force. This impact has been a bewildering mixture of industries, technologies, ideas and political and economic methods, which developed more or less together in Western Europe but which now impinge on underdeveloped areas unevenly, at differing tempos and with differing force. We cannot sharply distinguish between ideas and machines, economic and political effects. It is remarkable what a cargo of machine guns can do to the political ethics of a nation which had not known them; it is equally remarkable what ideas—about democracy, about medicine, about economic betterment—can do in unsettling a preindustrial economy or technology.

This tremendous impact has had a number of consequences that must be borne in mind:

1. The effects of this tidal wave, which has washed over virtually the whole globe, cannot be undone or eradicated. No Chinese Walls can check its influence. We must accept it as something given and make the best of it. Nothing is to be gained in bewailing the loss of untouched, primitive Edens; they are going or already gone, and the values they represent can only be preserved, or recaptured, within a new setting.

2. The impact in the non-European areas frequently leads to results that are disconcertingly different from those in Europe and the United States. A trade union in Pakistan is not the same thing as a trade union in Great Britain; a political constitution based on the Belgian or the American model may function very curiously when superimposed on a tribal society. Just as deep ploughing in arid regions can produce, not the abundance of a temperate climate, but galloping soil erosion, so the techniques and methods developed in and devised for Western society may lead to untoward results when uncritically applied elsewhere.

3. The results are not only different but also, as in all ecological change, multiple and complex. Introducing penicillin and better diets affects the birth and death rates; these in turn affect employment, land relations, party programs

and so on, until the whole structure of the society is altered, and not always for the better.

4. Because of this, the combination of relative equilibrium and self-generating advance which is to be found in Western economies is peculiarly difficult to achieve, a point noted above in the discussion of economic growth. Growth is not just the increase of this or that output; it is dependent, if it is not to be monstrous, on a harmony and proportion in which noneconomic elements are of major importance.

5. Consequently, economic expansion, in the absence of corresponding social and political adaptations, may produce dislocation, uprooting, and even intensify tension and domestic conflict. Economic expansion alone is not sufficient to create that sense of political community and cohesiveness which is the sign of a healthy society.

6. There is no question that all these tendencies offer a most fertile field for the Communists. Their temper, doctrine and propaganda are geared to these or similar irritations and dislocations. Their experience with Russia as a relatively underdeveloped area—a valuable propaganda point—has given them much useful practice in exploiting, controlling and manipulating such anomalies. The totalitarian controls which they have created are also brutally effective devices to this end.

Any social policy that the United States may pursue with respect to the underdeveloped countries must take account of these consequences. We should be prepared to accept the risk that actions we take, influences we exert, can be double-edged, at the same time constructive and destructive, promoting organization or leading to disorganization. A great deal depends, of course, upon the particular country with which we are dealing; measures that "take" and are highly beneficial in one may be wholly unsuitable for another. Still, in the present report we must limit ourselves to some general recommendations, while emphasizing the great importance of flexibility and close acquaintance for their local application.

First, inasmuch as the underdeveloped countries are in the trying process of change and development, there is no question that they do require what has come to be called "technical assistance." This we would interpret in the very broadest sense: not simply information and guidance on how to build a dam, set up a clinic, practice contour ploughing, but an understanding of the social function of innovations, the manner in which they can best be adapted to local needs, how they can be used and the consequences of misusing them. The real problem is not to teach people the way to use new tools, but to discover the appropriate tools for a particular society. Should peasant cultivators, for example, be encouraged to come into factories and then given the social amenities and benefits to replace the rural community they have left, or would decentralization and movement of the industries to the villages be preferable? This involves some extremely intricate questions to which there is no pat answer, and it is not our job to try to make another people decide whether they want to become urbanized or not. But certainly technical assistance would fall short of its goal if it did not encompass these broader considerations.

Second, there is the question of social and political reform, a particularly touchy issue since it concerns the most sensitive part of another society: the quality and competence of those who wield power and authority. From our perspective it may seem that in many countries a drastic overhauling is called for. But we must be cautious in our ambitions to tinker with something as complexly unfamiliar as an alien society. There is the danger that precipitate reforms directed against traditional relationships and privileges may weaken, without providing an adequate substitute, the only groups capable, no matter how inefficiently perhaps, of organizing the society and its defense. We must repeat that we do not know what kinds of societies are emerging. They are certain not to be replicas of the United States, they will bear some relationship to the traditional culture, and they will continue to be grounded in patterns of organization, loyalty and behavior, the functions of which we may not easily grasp. It would be an error for us to consider ourselves social engineers; at most we are consulting gardeners forced by circumstances to try our hand at espaliering and grafting, but with a still rudimentary knowledge of social horticulture.

We may take the example of land reform. There is a great deal of historical experience to indicate that precommercial land tenure relations—especially those between peasant cultivators, who may or may not own the land they till, and large landowners, who may or may not be absentees—are almost predictably a locus of social tension in times of change and modernization. Old, possibly benevolently patriarchal, relations dissolve and are replaced by a bitter competition for land and labor. This source of tension is, of course, one that the Communists are particularly interested in exploiting, and they have a long record in this regard. In a number of areas "land reform" may be the indispensable prerequisite for social stability. At the same time "land reform" is a notoriously difficult and delicate undertaking, which, if not handled wisely, may have such untoward effects as a falling off of output, a retrogression in productive methods or the spread of dwarf holdings incapable of improvement. These pitfalls are known to competent specialists, and it is not necessary that a country fall into them. But whatever the difficulties, a blind solution in the form of a murderous struggle between frightened landowners and frantic peasants and tenants is no solution and may be avoided if steps can be taken in time.

Similar problems arise in connection with reforms of the legal code, police forces, education, etc. In no case is the answer simple, and to the degree that the United States is involved, whether as an adviser or in providing technicians, we should avoid the temptation of thinking that the mere transfer of a successful American practice to another land constitutes a reform.

Third, there is the task of easing or moderating the dislocations created by modernization. Here again our advice may profit from a number of long-familiar but perpetually recurring experiences: the plight of the individual craftsman when hit by the competition of machine-made goods, whether domestically produced or imported; the uneasy relations between employer and employees in new factories where the working force is fresh from the village and the managers lack the experience of Western entrepreneurs in bargaining with labor.

Particularly elusive is the role of the new intelligentsia, which has such tremendous potentialities, for good and evil, as the principal agency by which external influences are transmitted and interpreted locally. The members of this group are the most self-conscious section of the community, susceptible to manipulation and perversion because their place in the evolving social order is uncertain and their role ill-defined. It is not the function of the United States, whatever the Communists may do, to indoctrinate or manipulate these intellectuals, but we can try to see that they have access, through travel and exchange, to the best and most honest thinking our age can provide rather than to the second-best or, even worse, to Communist nostrums. If our confidence in the sustaining power of democratic ideals is real, so also must be our trust that exposure to these ideals, in their practice and in their philosophical and spiritual foundations, will, in time, prove to be the best assistance we can give in helping the intellectuals create a place and role for themselves in their own society. This will not happen overnight.

Finally, there is our general contribution in training. Our major hope must be that these areas of belated access to the twentieth century can eventually become full participants and contributors on their own. It is of the utmost importance that these peoples share in developments and feel themselves to be creators rather than victims of change. This means a bias in favor of activities on the local level, of promoting wherever possible local initiative in rural and urban areas, of social and political evolution proceeding from within and moving out.

Our assistance in training should be directed to that end. We must not, however, slight the formidable difficulties of this approach. We may favor "grass roots" over "enlightened despotism" as the source of growth and improvement (partly because an enlightened despot is so easily followed by an unenlightened or corrupted one), but this aim of building from the bottom up is in sharp contrast to the usual movement of events and influences, which has been from the outside in and from the top down. The task of mediating between these contradictory impulses, of avoiding getting tangled and immobilized in the roots, is perhaps the most difficult challenge confronting any social policy. It cannot be solved in the abstract but only on the terrain of a particular country.

Such, in necessarily general terms, appear to be the principal elements of a social policy that the United States should develop for the so-called underdeveloped countries of the non-Communist world. In concluding we might turn briefly to ways and means. While these nations might welcome increased American emphasis on economic and social betterment, especially an emphasis which gives due recognition to local needs other than those of a military or strategic nature, neither we nor they should overlook the central fact that in the last few years this has necessarily become an especial concern of United States foreign policy because of its bearing on American and free-world security. We believe, of course, that the economic and social improvement of these and of all nations is a good in itself independent of the course of Soviet-American relations. But we should not pretend, and no one would believe us if we did, that the United States does not have a very real national stake in the successful future of non-Communist nations. The need for an active American policy in this field of social affairs is as urgent as the requirements we have set forth in previous chapters. Nevertheless, while we do not want to exude an aura of disinterested benevolence, we emphatically do not believe that there is a conflict between our national interest and the interests of the underdeveloped countries. The interests are both compatible and complementary.

This is not to disparage the importance of spontaneous, disinterested, nongovernmental assistance, which is one of the best features of the American tradition. Much of the relatively good opinion the United States has enjoyed in Asia and Africa can be attributed to the activities over many years of American individuals, philanthropic organizations and religious and educational bodies, which have devoted themselves to the health and welfare of nations all over the globe.

But it is precisely because these humanitarian activities have been unofficial and not directed that they have been so valuable. There is a real danger that if we here extended our discussion to such private activities, and brought them within the scope of public policy, we should not augment the advantages they have afforded the United States but would cast over them the shadow of power politics. Obviously, private activities will be particularly helpful if they are in harmony with the broad purposes of American policy, but an overzealous effort to coordinate them would run the risk of making them quasi-official agencies.

Nevertheless, even within the range of public policy, it is not necessary that we always work directly. The United Nations and its specialized agencies can be an extremely practical instrument for formulating and executing social policy. Not only do UN actions avoid the possible imputation of U.S. control, and U.S. "imperialism," but they can make use of the varied and important talents of many nations. A non-European technician may, by training or by cultural background, be more useful in many underdeveloped areas than an American or a European. After all, what we are trying to achieve by social policy is not gratitude to the United States for its assistance, but the social cohesion and independence of these countries, many of which are in a very difficult state.

In the end, however, we must recall the necessary limits of our aims. We are not here drawing up plans for Utopia, nor are we trying to create new Americas. What we want to do is to help clear channels and remove impediments so that the people of a very large part of the world will have some chance of becoming autonomous, self-reliant and free to develop their own culture, after they have been blasted by the modern age from the protective shelter of their earlier communities. It is a limited goal, but a great and necessary one.

Part Three
AREAS OF CONFLICT

CHAPTER VIII

DIRECT RELATIONS: THE PROBLEM OF POSITIVE OBJECTIVES

IN THE preceding section we were concerned with the indispensable requirements of American policy for meeting a threefold task: 1) preventing the establishment of Communist global hegemony; 2) reducing, so far as it is within the power of the United States, the chances of general war; and 3) keeping the door open for future developments which may alter the international situation in the direction of American and free-world interests. These requirements call for strenuous endeavor and the exercise of imagination. At the same time they do provide for some relatively clear-cut and unambiguous policy goals and for corresponding courses of action. They do not, however, take care of all the areas of American policy with which we must deal. The goals in question are largely *negative* in their ultimate intent: to avert certain possible disasters. The supporting actions are largely confined to the non-Communist world: the United States, its allies and the uncommitted nations.

When we turn to our direct relations with the Soviet Union and to the areas of conflict marking that relationship, we are on less certain ground. This is not surprising. It is easier to say what should *not* be the outcome of the course of Soviet-American relations—Communist hegemony or general war—than to define or agree upon *positive* goals. It is easier, too, to estimate the results of a course of American action in areas beyond Communist control than to devise policies which depend for their success upon gaining Soviet acceptance or beating down Soviet resistance.

Indeed, we face the very serious question whether we can in fact derive from any general positive objective the particular policies the United States should follow in the various areas of controversy. This is not to suggest that we cannot develop policies to meet problems such as those presented by a divided Germany, the Eastern European satellites or

Communist China, or that we should rely only upon *ad hoc* measures taken on the spur of the moment. But we must ask whether we can hope to devise a blueprint, or even offer a choice of alternative blueprints, which can serve with any precision as a positive guide to our direct relations with the Soviet Union and the Communist bloc. In our view we cannot. This conclusion, however, requires justification.

What do we mean by positive objectives? In 1947, the late Henry L. Stimson wrote that he had been forced to conclude that the Russians could not choose to be our friends because those who determined Soviet policy had chosen otherwise. Hence the aim of American policy should be, he said, to create conditions under which "the Russian leaders may either *change their minds* or *lose their jobs.*" (Italics added). While it could be worded differently, we may accept this shorthand statement of positive objectives as representing a conclusion most Americans have also reached in the decade since 1945.

The desire to make it possible for the Russian people to be our friends correctly indicates that we do not see the conflict as one between the two peoples. It also suggests, and appropriately, that our ultimate hopes are for something more than just the achievement of formally "correct" relations with the Soviet government. But, while this sense of friendship, existing or potential, is vital to the spirit of a democratic foreign policy, it informs rather than guides that policy. The usual difficulty of knowing just what is meant by "friendly relations," especially when speaking of the future, is here compounded by the possibility that friendly relations with the Russian people and correct, or normal, relations with the Soviet regime are not complementary objectives, but distinct or even incompatible ones. It is not likely, of course, that American-Russian friendship can develop and thrive so long as the relations between the two states are antagonistic and their citizens face the prospect of battling one another. On the other hand, the Soviet leaders' view of "normalizing" relations has excluded any real freedom of communications between us and the Russian people, who, to the present at least, have been carefully insulated from direct knowledge of a purportedly hostile "capitalist" world.

If our general goal is imprecise, so, too, are the nature and extent of the changes required. By a "change of mind" we presumably mean an alteration in that ideology and outlook which have kept the Communists playing the *enfant terrible* on into a sinister and menacing adulthood. But this change could be very difficult to detect. The Soviet leaders might, in time, privately shelve their ideology but maintain lip service to it, becoming, as it were, nonpracticing world revolutionists. Or Marxism-Leninism itself might undergo further evolution, leading to a change but in a direction we cannot anticipate. Or, the Kremlin might, for an indefinite period, make any number of gestures intended to suggest a change of attitude, while holding fast to the goal of world Communism. The demand for "deeds not words" may miss the mark in establishing evidence of intentions; as has been evident in Western efforts to assess recent Soviet moves, nearly any Soviet act may be variously interpreted as a harbinger of a new temper, as a means to gain time, or as a tactic of "reculer pour mieux sauter."

Similarly, when we speak of causing the Soviet leaders to "lose their job," do we mean a shift of personnel within the ruling group, or the dissolution of the Communist party, or the breakup of the Soviet state and its instruments? Further, the relationship between a change in outlook and an alteration of the regime is exceedingly ambiguous. The first suggests a solution within the existing Soviet order, an evolutionary outcome; the second suggests an alteration of the order itself, a revolutionary outcome. It is doubtful that American actions taken to unseat the Communists would lead them to change their views about the implacable hostility of the capitalist world. While either a significant change in the Soviet outlook or a significant change in the regime would greatly promote peace of mind in the rest of the world, it is not certain that American policy can work for both at once.

Numerous efforts have been made to reformulate these objectives, make them more precise and rid them of their possible inconsistency. Yet these refinements tend to force us to conclusions beyond the limits of our present knowledge. Some argue, for example, that a meaningful change of purpose and outlook in the Soviet Union is impossible so long as the Communist party, its ideology and its instrumentalities remain in power. The hope of normal relations is a chimera; the only feasible goal is to bring about a change of regime sufficiently complete to dislodge the present holders of power and discredit their ideology. Against this it can be argued that all revolutionary movements lose their enthusiasm in time, that this erosion of zeal will come to affect both the Communist party and the Soviet state apparatus. Hence, opportunities for a real change in outlook, without an overthrow of the system and its masters, do exist and can be increased by the right actions on our part.

The trouble is not that these, or other, efforts to make American objectives more precise are wrong (we cannot know in advance whether they are wrong or right, or even irrelevant) but that the ambiguities which they try to cut across are the product of our necessary uncertainty about the future course of Soviet developments and our ability to influence it. To disregard this uncertainty, to try to give an impression of clarity where things are not clear, does not help the making of realistic policies. We are not here dealing with remediable ignorance; the future course of such a complex and unprecedented entity as the Soviet system is not something to be demonstrated, even in terms of probabilities, and the policy maker would be most unwise to act on faith in such a demonstration, no matter how cogently or persuasively argued.

Our positive aims must be tentative for another reason. Even were they capable of more precise definition, they still could not serve as a guide to policy unless we were able to establish some correspondence between them and the available courses of action, a connection between ends and means. But, when we look at the means open to United States policy, the most striking fact is that there are *no* sure ways to bring about either a significant change in the Soviet outlook or an alteration in the regime. The one exception might be our initiation of a general war, but this we definitely exclude. The task is not necessarily impossible, and we shall consider a number of proposals presently, but no line of action we have encountered offers any guarantee of success with respect to the results to be achieved, the costs and effort demanded or the time needed. There is no self-evident way to realize our aims; there are a variety of possibilities, the odds for which cannot be calculated.

More than that, the United States is frequently obliged to act for reasons not related to these positive goals. Measures, for example, to maintain our military capability or to support our allies—actions necessary for the negative purpose of checking Communist expansion—may not work to bring about a change in the Soviet regime or its outlook and may indeed (as in the case of our overseas bases) strongly reinforce the Communists' fear of "capitalist encirclement." Yet we cannot sacrifice such pressing current needs in the interest of long-run and somewhat uncertain objectives. In all likelihood it will be impossible for the United States fully to harmonize the multitude of actions it must take in matters relating, directly or indirectly, to the Soviet Union. There will be conflicts and cross-purposes which must be dealt with as they arise.

All of which leads to the conclusion that we cannot provide a blueprint, or even a choice of blueprints, for our positive goals. While a plan for a factory may have to be modified and corrected during construction, the architect and engineers have at least a pretty good idea—from a vast accumulation of previous experience with buildings, tools and materials—what the completed factory will look like and what will support it. In the present case that fund of guiding experience is lacking, and the field of our endeavor, as in Alice's croquet game, constantly changes its configuration.

But if a blueprint is beyond our powers, it does not follow that American policy must proceed at random, piecemeal, and without guidance. Ambiguous and general though it is, we have some notion of what we are working for—the opportunity for normally friendly relations with the Russian people as an outcome of a change in the Soviet outlook or a change in the regime—even though the exact physiognomy of the goal and the means by which we can reach it are not clear and will probably alter with the passage of time.

Beyond this, however, we do have a number of clusters, or congeries, of related actions and purposes which, if they cannot be elevated to the status of a blueprint, can provide us with a partial organization of the problem, a guide to analysis, a clue to the consequences of actions and a sense of the important political impulses. The debate on "containment vs. liberation," for all the oversimplifications and partisanship which accompanied it, was an attempt to explore the prospects of significantly different approaches. The same may be said for the debates on German reunification and rearmament, and on the recognition of Communist China. These have been inconclusive and have neither "solved" the particular issues nor fixed our general stance, but they are valuable for the policy maker, if also a headache. They cannot make his actual decisions for him, but they can help to reveal the meaning of his decisions, the goals they imply, the consequences they entail. This is a great deal.

Among these congeries of actions and purposes, which we will term *perspectives,* three appear most fruitful as means of suggesting the various avenues of American action in our direct relations with the Soviet Union. They can be labeled, respectively, (A) Defense of the present line dividing the Communist and non-Communist worlds, but no attempt to reduce the area held by the Soviet bloc; (B) Defense of the present line but also an attempt to induce the Communist powers, through negotiation and diplomacy, to reach agreement on international wartime and postwar commitments, especially those affecting the nations and peoples forcibly incorporated in the Communist bloc; (C) Advance and pressure against the Soviet bloc by means short of war or the calculated risk of war.

All three, in opposing further Communist expansion and in not initiating war, comply with the requirements laid down in the preceding section. We exclude from our discussion those perspectives envisaging either a withdrawal of American commitments to the Western Hemisphere or the advocacy of preventive war or war-provoking advance.[1] Even with this limitation the range of purposes and actions here

[1] See above, p. 81 and p. 87.

contemplated is sufficiently extensive and covers most elements which must go into the determination of policy.

In the first place, the perspectives represent important *political facts* which cannot be neglected in arriving at policies. In the American domestic scene they correspond roughly to positions which have been advocated under the somewhat stereotyped labels of "containment," "negotiation from positions of strength" and "liberation." In the world at large they echo divergent interests and goals among our European allies, our Asian allies and the United Nations.

They also reflect three fairly distinct but familiar *responses* to confrontation by a hostile force: live and let live, seeking an arrangement, and counterpressure. These psychological roots doubtless influence people's inclination toward one or another perspective and account for much of the vigor with which they are upheld.

They are, however, more than psychological reflexes; they also suggest differing *expectations*. The hope of the first (A) would be a gradual diminution of the dynamism and hostility of the Soviet regime, brought about in time by a firm but nonprovocative and noninterventionist attitude on the part of the United States. The second (B) would look to a diplomatic stabilization of Soviet-American relations. The third (C) would look ultimately to a change in regime, either its moderation under pressure or its replacement. Thus each emphasizes one facet of the positive goals which were rather ambiguously formulated in the preceding paragraphs.

Finally, these perspectives warn us of *consequences* which may flow from American actions, regardless of the intentions behind them. Thus the first (A) warns against the deleterious effects of stimulating Soviet belligerence and aggressiveness by our seeking to detach areas from Soviet control. The second (B) warns against the danger of losing all communication with the Soviet regime: the inability to use diplomacy to extract limited gains or to cover possible losses. The third (C) warns against the debilitating effects on the strength and morale of the free world in accommodating itself to the indefinitely protracted presence of Soviet Communism, as an inflated power and as an ideology.

This is all too neat, of course; the world does not fall into such tidy categories. Yet this organization of perspectives may serve the purpose of exposition and analysis. We may now develop these perspectives at somewhat greater length, to give some idea of their meaning and flavor.

A. Acquiescence in the present territorial frontiers of the Communist bloc proceeds from the premise that the division of the world, as it was brought about by the Second World War and its aftermath, in Europe and the Far East, constitutes the most realistic and promising basis for a Soviet-American relationship that may avoid deteriorating into a further expansion of Communist power, or a general war. The potential strength of the non-Communist world is deemed great enough, if (but only if) it is developed and organized, to maintain a successful defense against Communist inroads. As things stand, of course, many non-Communist areas are not in a healthy condition and are susceptible to being drawn or dragged into the Soviet orbit. Consequently, our primary and overriding task must be to support the free world, an area to which we have relatively direct access, and to root out as vigorously as need be the Communist danger in it. We should stress full vigor of defense, the strengthening of ties among the countries organized against Communism by developing their military power and by vitalizing their domestic life, and the promotion of anti-Communist trends and forces within countries now uncommitted, with the purpose of preventing such countries from falling under Communist control and of attracting them, instead, into associations and alliances organized against Communism.

In contrast, this perspective finds little opportunity, under present circumstances, for profitable action within the orbit of Soviet control. Trying to detach countries from the Communist bloc by force or threat of force promises either to be fruitless or to introduce an unwarranted risk of general war. While the Soviet Union may possibly consider some of its outlying satellites not worth a war for their retention, it has an extremely important ideological and prestige stake in those areas which it has taken over and remodeled in its own image, and it is likely to react very strongly to any effort to detach them. A move at detachment which was shown up as a bluff would be altogether a disadvantage.

Moreover, according to this perspective, pressures short of war (including even propaganda to the satellites) would have little of the desired effect—especially if the Soviet leaders knew we had no intention of risking war—and would continually serve as a stimulus to the regime to maintain and intensify its ideological vigor, its disciplined control over its subjects and its economic and military preparations for the defense of the Soviet zone and for its future expansion.

Admittedly, Soviet hostility toward the outside world, the sense of facing an implacable external enemy, is largely self-induced and derives from the Leninist origins of the regime and the basic concern with maintaining, preserving and advancing its own power at home and abroad. Because it is largely self-induced, there is probably very little we can do directly to change that attitude; no statement of pacific intent, no declarations concerning the will to coexist are likely to have a significant effect.

Nevertheless, according to this perspective, our demonstration over a long period of time, in actions more than in words, that the creation of a strong and viable non-Communist world is exclusively for purposes of defense, and does not mean an attack upon the Soviet homeland or upon the Communist zone, might have the effect, quite independent of any confessed change in the ideology of world revolution held by the Communist leaders, of dampening the aggressive impetus of the regime, of slackening the rate of development of Communist military capabilities, of making it increasingly difficult for the leaders to create on the minds of their subjects a plausible image of a menacing world, and thus lead to a diminution of the peculiar dynamics of the regime. It is to be observed that this view does not question, but even emphasizes, the inherently hostile and aggressive nature of the Soviet regime, nor does it acknowledge or uphold the "legitimacy" of the present Soviet imperium or the right of the Soviet Union to dominate non-Russian lands; it accepts this domination as a tragic reality. It affirms, however, as a reasonable possibility and an ultimate hope, that some relaxation of internal controls and outward thrust of the Communist world may eventually follow from a consistent adherence by the United States to this position.

Fundamental to this perspective is the belief that in undertaking any kind of direct attack on the Communist regimes, and especially in attempting directly to detach and de-Communize any of their territory, we should be following exactly the pattern their ideology prescribes for us, and should thus confirm and strengthen the belief of the leaders in that ideology and their zeal to promote its application at home and abroad. Obviously any hope that this perspective may offer of moderating the zeal of the Communist leaders must depend upon its consistent application for a period of some years.

In terms of policy, the principal objective in our direct relations with the Soviet Union would be to achieve a mutually acceptable arrangement for defining and maintaining the territorial *status quo,* to keep the frontiers of the two worlds as clear-cut as possible and to disengage, so far as can be done, the pressure exerted by the two blocs upon these frontiers. Perhaps the chief use of negotiations would be the creation of neutral border zones at various danger points along the frontier. These zones—conceived of primarily as military no man's lands of limited depth rather than as politically neutral states or areas—would have to be based on the existing power relations and include equivalent territory on both sides of the present frontier between the Communist and non-Communist worlds.

B. The second perspective differs from the first primarily on the position to be taken toward areas of Communist postwar expansion. Instead of accepting the present territorial division as the most realistic and promising basis for our policy, it would maintain, and be willing to press, the legal and political claims arising out of wartime and postwar agreements affecting non-Russians now behind the Iron and Bamboo curtains (e.g., East Central Europe, East Germany, North Korea).

This perspective, with its political interest in the state of affairs within the Communist bloc, entails a more active policy with regard to the Soviet Union. Moreover, in rejecting the use of military or provocative means to advance this interest, it must envisage a considerably more extensive role for negotiations. Because there are areas behind the Iron Curtain which we should like to have freed by peaceful means, we must be prepared to negotiate, or seek an arrangement, on a number of issues which would remain dormant were we prepared to tolerate, however reluctantly, the territorial *status quo*.

The second perspective, too, would be more disposed than the first to welcome into the free world such segments of the Communist empire as are able to free themselves. The difference may be one of degree. Any reasonable American would, of course, be happy to see major detachments from the Soviet bloc if the result were both to liberate people and to weaken the Communist core so that it would be less likely, or less able, to set off an atomic war. The first perspective, however, would be more skeptical of the advantages of minor defections since these might serve only to tighten the hold of the Soviet regime over its remaining territories. In particular, it would be doubtful of the value of United States initiative in fostering or supporting such possible defections. The notion of active diplomacy to seek an arrangement more in line with American and free-world interests implies, in contrast, a freer hand: we should not commit ourselves in advance to a position of nonintervention and noninvolvement in the Communist zone.

The eventual hope of this perspective would be that by skillful policies within the non-Communist world, by taking advantage of Soviet bloc defections, should they occur, and by pursuing an active but not provocative diplomatic course, we could, at the least, so build the strength and cohesion of the free world and so confine the Communist bloc that it would cease to be a major peril, and, at the most, arrive at a more satisfactory territorial and diplomatic arrangement than is possible under the present division of the world.

C. Despite their differences, the first two perspectives are alike in giving much the greatest emphasis in American policy to developments within the free world. Activities in the Soviet orbit are at best marginal to the main effort. The third perspective represents a somewhat different weighting in this respect. While recognizing the requirement that we should not initiate policies that carry with them the clear risk of general war, it is not prepared either to renounce direct pressure against the Soviet bloc or to limit it to the level of diplomatic claims and agenda for negotiations. In this perspective, the only basis for a Soviet-American relationship which would not play into the Communists' hands or tempt them into war-inciting ventures is the exertion of pressure against the Soviet bloc sufficient to counterbalance the pressure it exerts against the non-Communist world.

Several considerations enter here. While the strength of the free world relative to that of the Soviet bloc must be built up, it may be argued that a reduction of Soviet power is equally significant in determining the ratio of strengths, and possibly less costly. The energy and resources spent in exerting pressure against the Soviet Union might produce a more advantageous shift in the balance of forces than the equivalent exerted exclusively in the non-Communist world. It is extremely difficult, of course, to establish any basis for measurement. The Soviet leaders, to judge from the attention and energy they have devoted to external propaganda and the work of the foreign Communist parties, attach great importance to softening up the opponent as well as to strengthening themselves.

A second consideration is the disadvantage which the party of static defense suffers in the face of an active and aggressive opponent who is able to select the time, the place and the occasion for his offensive actions. It may be that, to maintain the balance, it is necessary for us to keep the opponent guessing, to oblige him to divert part of his time and attention to preparing for a variety of actions against him.

A third consideration is that in the experience of recent years a nonprovocative policy seems to prompt the Communists to try to make cheap gains; the resulting American reaction to such attempts has served to produce a situation even more tense than before. From this experience it may be surmised that the constant exertion of pressure against the Communists may have a sobering and stabilizing effect in checking this propensity for probing and penetration.

Finally, and in sharp distinction to the first perspective, it can be contended that as far as hopes for the future are concerned the best chance of the Soviet regime's moderating or breaking down from within lies in our making things as difficult for it as possible. Doubtful that the absence of pressure will lead to a diminution of will and determination —since this has been so successfully maintained over four decades, chiefly by internal stimulation—this perspective would hold that if we do what is possible, short of war, to prevent the Soviet regime from consolidating its gains, from realizing its economic plans and from gaining the passive support of its subjects, there is a chance—not a certainty—of an eventual alteration. While our efforts would probably not disrupt or dissolve the regime, they could well have a debilitating effect upon a totalitarian order with its compulsive desire to manage society and manipulate human beings. If, by our pressure, we can frustrate these pretensions, we may reveal a vulnerability peculiar to such a regime. The continuance, say, of a spirit of unrest and disaffection in the satellites may not directly imperil the physical or even the political security of the Soviet empire, but it is a constant reminder of limitation and fallibility.

There appears to be no sure way of judging which of these divergent surmises about the future is the more likely, whether a hands-off policy or one of pressure is more conducive to changes in the Soviet order which would be to the benefit of the United States and the non-Communist world. Without opposition the Soviet leaders are free to develop their order as they see fit, including the continued building up of the revolutionary bastion. The absence of pressures against or within the Communist zone might utterly fail to induce any diminution of their zeal.

On the other hand, under pressure the Soviet leaders may respond with renewed vigor and aggressiveness. It may be that without the threat of war in the background, as the ultimate form of pressure, efforts short of war are more likely to stimulate than to impede the progress, consolidation and expansion of the Soviet regime. For this reason some have argued that, in giving up the threat of possible military pressure against the Soviet bloc, the United States would put itself at a serious disadvantage; the Communists would know the limits of our actions—that we would not use force except in meeting attack—whereas we would not know the limits of theirs. This is a disadvantage, but it is, in our view, unavoidable. We cannot make this threat without creating the risk that it will lead to war. But any rationally calculated risk must take account of the stakes as well as the odds; the outbreak of war would lead to quite incalculable consequences. We will fight aggression if it occurs, not because of any calculation of risks, but because, as free men, we must. Nor is it feasible to suggest publicly that we may exert military pressure, while resolving privately not to do so. This would create an intolerable gap between the public and its leaders, as would the contrary course of privately deciding to exert military pressure while giving public assurances to the contrary. Both are incompatible with a democratic foreign policy.

What use can we make of these perspectives? None is demonstrably fallacious; none is able to promise the realization of its goals. Each is designed to meet certain problems arising out of Soviet-American relations, but they are so different in intent, method and style (especially the first and third—A and C) that the effort to combine them may lead to utter confusion. We cannot simultaneously try to promote disaffection within the Soviet orbit *and* induce the Communists to relax their zeal and hostility. Because of this, it might be argued that even though these perspectives afford no sure success we must at least opt for one or another, especially if we are to have any hope that our policies may exert a cumulative effect over a period of time.

This problem of decision is not to be sidestepped, and we shall give in the following chapters a number of examples where a choice between opposing lines of action is required. But on what level, in what context should the United States make these decisions? In our view, these decisions should be made in association with, though not as a by-product of, concrete actions to meet specific problems. For it is only in this setting, when choice crystallizes into action, that we can apprehend the meaning and burden of our decisions.

In the first place, our aims regarding the outcome of Soviet-American relations form only a *part* of American foreign policy interests. The need to shore up the defenses of the free world and to reduce the chances of a general war erupting, not to speak of all the foreign policy questions only indirectly connected with Soviet-American problems—these must also be taken into account whenever we embark on a particular course of action, and they may well have greater claims to our attention.

In the second place, the significance of the decision also depends greatly on the level of action contemplated. If it is a question of determining whether or not to try to wrest a piece of territory from Soviet control, a clear-cut choice is required. If it is a question of devising a directive for radio broadcasts behind the Iron Curtain, the contrast of perspectives is less sharp and the need for decision somewhat less pressing, though by no means absent.

Hence the isolated act of opting for one or another perspective does not free us of the necessity of thinking out decisions in each new situation; policies will not flow automatically from such general choices. Nor does it eliminate the possibility that, for any number of reasons, we may frequently have to pursue a line of action which is not in accord with the perspective of our preference. Conversely, it is perfectly possible to take actions, such as supporting the economic growth of the free world, which are in harmony with all these perspectives. If we become so preoccupied with establishing our stance that we lose our sensitivity of touch, timing and balance in political decisions, we do ourselves more harm than good.

For these reasons the primary function of these perspectives is not to make decisions for us in advance but to give us, in making concrete decisions, the greatest possible awareness of their overtones and implications. This point will perhaps emerge more clearly after we have grappled with some of the particular areas of Soviet-American conflict, for these offer precisely the type of testing ground where actions and purposes must be reconciled.

CHAPTER IX
GERMANY

A NUMBER of the principal objects of Soviet-American conflict have been territorial issues, disputes concerning the defense of, or control over, certain geographic areas. While these areas extend like an earthquake fault along the zone dividing the Communist from the non-Communist world, we may distinguish two subregions: a) where the outthrust of Soviet power is the immediate problem, the subject of this and the following chapter; and b) where Chinese Communist power is the immediate problem, the subject of a later chapter.

Any point in this zone may become a critical area, depending on the shifts and turns of Communist tactics. The Near and Middle East, for example, was in 1945 and 1946 an area of intense Soviet pressure, especially against Iran, and has recently become so again with the shipment of Soviet-bloc arms to Egypt, Soviet diplomatic support of the Arab states and the travels of Khrushchev and Bulganin. We cannot, within the limits of this report, analyze all the problems. We have limited ourselves to a few selected areas of special and continuing importance. In the regions peripheral to the Soviet Union we shall discuss Germany and the Eastern European satellites. This selection does not mean that other areas are less important; all are important and many quite vulnerable, including some not immediately bordering Communist territory.

Before grappling with the crucial German question, we should try to place it in its general European setting. Between the end of the Second World War and 1948, Europe came to be divided sharply by the Iron Curtain. Although one Communist-ruled country, Yugoslavia, broke with Moscow, and although Finland, which had been defeated by the Red Army, has not been Communized, by and large the dividing line has been a constant one, in marked contrast, say, to the confused and much more fluid state of affairs in

Southeast Asia. In Europe, on both sides of the Iron Curtain, there seemingly is recognition that the European area does not lend itself to probing military operations; the lines are drawn, and a major explosion would almost certainly result from any armed excursions in either direction.

The minimum requirements of American policy in Europe are reasonably clear. In an earlier chapter we concluded that the United States must resist the absorption of any more territory within the Communist orbit. We also concluded that we must couple our own strength with that of other nations outside the Communist orbit. This twofold requirement has been given appropriate though incomplete expression in the North Atlantic Treaty Organization. The United States is obligated morally, by express agreement and in its own self-interest to defend against attack the area covered by NATO. We should go even further and say that outside the area of our existing commitments in Europe any major trespass by Soviet-Communist military forces across their present line of "farthest advance" would probably have to be interpreted by us as a movement of the Soviet trigger finger, indicating more far-reaching designs. In other words, any further advance of Soviet or satellite military forces in a westerly direction carries the heavy risk of hostilities involving United States forces.

Athwart this line of demarcation lies Germany, the most important area of political and diplomatic fluidity in Europe. With its manpower, industrial potential, skills and talents, and its location in the heart of Europe, it is only natural that Germany should be of critical importance. Nor is it surprising that the problems it presents—to the Germans themselves, to the Russians and their satellites, to the Western Europeans and to us—should be peculiarly baffling and intractable.

Both the Soviet Union and the Western powers must exert utmost efforts to see that the whole of Germany does not align itself with, or fall under the control of, the other. The Soviet Union hopes to have all of Germany in the Communist bloc; American policy would like to see a reunited Germany in NATO. The resulting tug of war has perpetuated the division of Germany and led to the separate creation of the

German Federal Republic and the German Democratic Republic (the former Soviet zone). This division, by being at odds with the wish of the Germans themselves to be reunited, has caused both sides to declare it a temporary and undesirable state of affairs. Yet a unification which resulted in the effective diplomatic and military neutralization of all of Germany would represent a much larger loss of capabilities to the Western alliance than to the Soviet bloc. It is, moreover, a serious question whether real neutrality or neutralization could be realized, even were all concerned to make an agreement to that effect. It is doubtful that a self-imposed neutrality, determined and decided upon by the Germans themselves, could possibly be enduring even if the Germans so wished. Every economic, political or military decision of a country of Germany's size, location and potential strength would necessarily affect the European balance. On the other hand, neutralization imposed from without implies, if it is to have any meaning, effective cooperation and agreement between the United States and the Soviet Union regarding not only Germany but the over-all equilibrium of forces in Europe. But this is to posit the disappearance, or the very great reduction, of the general hostility between the Communist bloc and the free world. It is difficult to imagine that, if at any time in the foreseeable future a neutralized united Germany showed signs of favoring either the United States or the Soviet Union, the country so favored would consult with the other about the means to bring Germany back to the middle of the road.

When one adds to this major problem the internal difficulties of creating a unified Germany from the two existing regimes, the anomalous position of West Berlin which prevents a clear-cut division between East and West Germany, the problem of the areas beyond the Oder-Neisse line and the memories in Western Europe and Eastern Europe of Nazi Germany, one is able to understand why the German question has been a diplomatic squirrel cage, spinning without stopping but without getting anywhere.

Before turning to the policies the United States might pursue regarding Germany, we should establish some conditions based upon our earlier discussion. First of all, we cannot adopt a policy which would promote a chain of events leading to the voluntary or involuntary transfer of West Germany to the Soviet bloc. This would exclude policies toward West Germany which would cause it to seek close and therefore dependent relations with the Soviet Union. It would also exclude formulas for German unification which would permit the Communists to infiltrate or gain control over an all-German regime or a vital sector thereof.

Second, we cannot adopt a policy of military or other advance against the Soviet positions in Germany which accepts the risk of general war. This would exclude an armed effort to liberate East Germany.

Third, we must recognize the limits of American policy with respect to West Germany. If Germany was not to be a controlled power—and that, whether or not it was ever desirable, became impossible with the breakdown of the wartime alliance—it was inevitable that it become an independent power. This West Germany now is. While it is in increasingly close working association with the United States and with the other Western European powers, it has again become master of its own decisions. The United States can influence German decisions; it cannot make them nor can it prevent them from being changed by shifts in German policy or by new political alignments within West Germany. To take an example, a defeat of the present government, like any political change in any of the free nations with which the United States is associated, is not under the control of American policy, though our policies may influence the chances of such a defeat. While it would be unrealistic to suppose that our policies do not or should not have some bearing on domestic politics abroad, it would be equally unrealistic to adopt a policy which ignored the chance of political changes and was unprepared to cope with them when and if they occurred.

Fourth, in so far as West Germany is considered to be not merely an important part of the non-Communist world, which must not fall to the Communists, but also a participant in the Western mutual defense coalition—and such is the import of Germany's admission to NATO—it is necessary that United States policy in matters concerning Germany be coalition policy, that is, a policy worked out in concert with Germany and the Western European states which have assumed reciprocal responsibilities for the defense of the NATO area. This means, as was pointed out in an earlier chapter on allies, that on such a subject as German reunification, German, Western European and American policies must be in reasonable accord. If they are not, the differences could undermine the whole structure of the alliance. An agreement to disagree will not suffice in a situation where the subject of disagreement is vital to reciprocally assumed responsibilities. The same, of course, applies to Franco-German relations and to Franco-American relations affecting France's role in NATO.

It is within the severe limitations imposed by these conditions that American policy regarding Germany must proceed. Several lines of approach have been proposed to deal with this intractable issue. Each contains serious difficulties; none affords a sure way of securing its own goal. Indeed, Germany provides a striking example of a problem for which there may be no pat solution. In dealing with a problem shaped by so many incompatible elements, policy cannot be a matter of deciding to select a certain set of means to reach a particular end, but must rather be a constant adaptation of actions and purposes. In this it resembles the game of musical chairs for which there is no seating arrangement to satisfy all players; policy is necessarily fluid. We shall consider this point again after looking at some of the proposed courses of action.

A Divided Germany

We may start with the policy which would make do with the present division of Germany and limit its range of activity to the Federal Republic. The major aim in this case would be to have West Germany firmly associated with the West, assure its defense against Communist inroads and support its military participation in Western defense.

There has been, of course, a protracted debate on the importance of the German military potential to Western European defense. Because of the revolution in military concepts which the recent innovations in weaponry are causing, this question cannot be answered with any precision. It is probably more misleading than helpful to conceive of the necessary German contribution in terms of a particular number of divisions or so many thousand men. Nevertheless, when we take a broader look at the power conflict between the Soviet Union and the West, the combined human, economic, political and military assets of West Germany can obviously augment greatly Western Europe's capacity to defend itself, especially when we consider the doubtful future of the so-called atomic shield which was once but is no longer an American monopoly. Consequently, we can conclude that German participation in Western defense is of great importance and must be supported, though it is much less certain that this participation is to be expressed purely, or even primarily, in strictly military terms.

The great obstacle, however, to such a policy of working on the basis of the territorial *status quo* is, of course, the matter of German reunification. It may be admitted that the Russians have shown no sign of relinquishing their hold on East Germany. It is also highly questionable whether they could be forcibly dislodged without the near-certainty of general war. At the same time one cannot but feel that a divided Germany is hardly the prescription for a stable Europe. A great deal, to be sure, depends on the attitude of the Germans themselves. If the German people, on both sides of the dividing line, were quite without interest in reunification, there would be no particular reason for the United States to make an issue of it; it is possible for people speaking the same language to form separate political entities if they so will. But this is not the case in either West or East Germany today.

There has been a good deal of controversy about the real intensity of the German desire for reunification. We shall not try to assess that sentiment here; various observers and experts have come to quite different conclusions. From all the evidence, however, it does appear to be politically impossible for any German party or spokesman to renounce the goal of reunification. The debate between the German government and the opposition has centered rather on whether an attempt to achieve reunification via negotiation with the Soviet Union should take precedence over Germany's consolidating its position in the Western alliance, or whether German partnership with the West improves, and is indeed a precondition for bettering, the chances for reunification later on. Thus far the government has been able to sustain the second view. So far as can be seen, however, reunification will continue to be an important factor in German domestic and foreign politics and could, if exacerbated, be disruptive to the new fabric of German political life.

To what extent is accommodation possible between a policy which accepts the present division of Germany and the German impulse to unification? Toleration of the territorial *status quo* incurs no obligation to concede the legitimacy of the German Democratic Republic; it is acquiescence in a matter of fact, not of right. For its part the West German government has renounced any intention of resorting to force to recover East Germany. To this extent there is mutual recognition that we are dealing with a *de facto* situation, the alteration of which must not provoke a war.

Efforts at Reunification

In contrast to this approach, American policy in the last few years has put a good deal of emphasis on reunification, as something which both the Soviet Union and the United States have publicly advocated, as a right of the German people and as a necessary step to remove a source of trouble. Although this policy has had the advantage of corresponding more closely with German public sentiment, it has encountered the as yet unsurmounted difficulty of combining the claim for a reunified Germany with the need to have the Federal Republic within the Western alliance. The Soviet leaders, naturally enough, have not welcomed proposals to detach East Germany from the Soviet orbit and place a united Germany in NATO; as Molotov said flatly in November 1955, "The Soviet Union cannot sympathize with such an aim and by no means can it facilitate its attainment."

Several formulas have been suggested to get around this obstacle:

The first is that once West Germany is firmly a part of

NATO, and NATO itself has become a fully effective defense organization, the Russians, seeing that there is no longer any opportunity for exploiting weaknesses in Western Europe, will become more accommodating and may be willing to relinquish their unpopular hold on East Germany. This seems a very unlikely outcome. While it is true that the Russians have on occasion backed down and retreated in the face of firm resistance, it has been a case of retracting tentative forward moves of their own—as in Iran or Berlin. There appears to be, from their point of view, no good reason why they should pull out of East Germany under the circumstances envisaged, and many good reasons why they should stay on and tie East Germany even more tightly to their satellite empire. It would violate one of the most fundamental principles of their system of theory and practice if they were to release to the non-Communist world a significant area that has once been Communized. Any immediate hopes resting on this doubtful release of East Germany by the U.S.S.R. are almost certain to be blighted, and if much faith is placed in them the results, especially in Germany, are likely to be very unsettling.

A second formula has been to press for reunification concurrently with furthering the Federal Republic's participation in the Western defense system, but to recognize the great urgency and importance of the latter; we will do what we can to promote reunification and keep the issue alive, but not to the extent of jeopardizing the primary job. This formula, which broadly corresponds with the actual course of American policy, is satisfactory so long as the Germans are willing to accept the same order of priorities. In terms of timing, the Adenauer regime has been willing. But the ability of a German government to stand by this order of priorities depends, however, upon a prevailing belief that the need of protecting West Germany against the advance of Communism is more urgent and pressing than the desirability of trying to unite all Germany. Over time, and with the disappearance of an immediate threat, this belief might falter.

A third formula, one which has in fact been attempted in negotiations with the Soviets, could be put in Sir Anthony

Eden's phrase: "That if a new united German State were to take the place of the German Republic, she would have the right either to assume, or not to assume, the previous obligations of the Federal Republic." Under this formula a free and united Germany must enjoy all the attributes of sovereignty, including that of determining its foreign commitments. The presumption, of course, is that a freely united Germany—and this presupposes free elections—would in fact maintain the Western orientation of the Federal Republic and would elect to reaffirm German membership in NATO. There are some advantages to this formula. It recognizes that the decision on this matter must, in the last analysis, be Germany's. As a diplomatic device it forces the Soviets to accept the onus of infringing on the sovereignty of a united Germany. But while skillfully conceived, it has not gained Soviet acceptance, since Moscow probably makes the same assumptions we do respecting the Westward orientation of a really free Germany. Nor is it by any means certain that those Germans who are looking for the reality of reunification rather than the scoring of diplomatic points against the Soviet Union can be won over by this line of approach.

All these formulas suffer from the same difficulty: they are striving simultaneously to avoid any diminution of Western strength, to acquire the increment of East German power and also to persuade the Russians to agree to it. Put in these terms, it is impossible for the Russians to accede to any such unrewarding arrangement unless forced to do so, and the force required would certainly involve the serious risk of war. We may conclude, then, that the effort to combine a German-Western alliance with reunification, via an agreement with the Russians (who are physically capable of preventing reunification), is unlikely to succeed within the German framework alone. It may be worth trying in a larger European setting, and we shall return to this possibility somewhat later.[1]

Reunification without Alliance

If accepting Germany's division leaves a source of tension in Europe which could damage the political stability of

[1] See below, p. 191 and p. 202.

West Germany and our relations with it, and if combining a West German alliance with reunification can be blocked by the Russians, one is led to consider a third line of policy: German reunification without alliance with the West. Such a policy could press for German reunification while accepting Germany's withdrawal from NATO and the withdrawal of all foreign troops from German soil. The core of this policy has been the argument that the West's greatest trump in Germany is the strong anti-Communist feelings of the great majority of inhabitants, in both West and East Germany. If German reunification could be achieved through a free expression of the feelings of the German peoples—an indispensable condition—the regime based on such feelings would be anti-Communist and anti-Soviet regardless of any restrictions on its alliance-making capacity.

According to this line of approach the United States would stand to gain whether negotiations with the Russians on reunification succeeded or failed. If they succeeded, the major gain, of course, would be the retraction of the Communist sphere to the Oder-Neisse line. Moreover, though the resulting German regime would not be an alliance partner and would be barred from participating in Western defense, its political orientation would be pro-Western, in that its concern for its own security and independence would place it in the ranks of the free nations.

It is, of course, precisely these possible advantages that make it doubtful whether the Soviet Union would in fact be willing to accept such an outcome. Still, some have argued, there is a gain even if the effort failed. The blame for blocking German unity would once again rest clearly with the Soviet leaders. Their refusal to accept such an offer would demonstrate that even within the limits of some formula for German nonalignment, they could not afford to permit the sentiments of the East Germans to be freely expressed. Moreover, it might be salutary for those segments of German and Western opinion which have been stressing reunification above all else to be given a chance to recognize the ultimate impediment to German unity. Unless they are presented with such clear-cut evidence they will continue to think, or to persuade themselves, that United States policy, by clinging rigidly to an insistence on German participation in Western defense, is the stumbling block.

Briefly, then, this approach envisages either a territorial gain—not to the NATO alliance but to the non-Communist world—or the scoring of a major political and diplomatic gain.

There are, however, formidable drawbacks to this proposal. In the first place, were such negotiations to succeed, we should lose the accretion of the German contribution to a Western European alliance. The Soviet loss of East German strength and territory would not be an adequate compensation. In other words, by any quantitative measurement of strength the West would lose more than the Soviet bloc by having the whole of Germany taken out of the equation. We should warn again, however, against putting too much stress on purely military considerations. Moreover, if Germany were to some degree armed in its own self-defense, even though it were politically unaffiliated, it would not represent a complete power vacuum.

But perhaps more important than the military considerations is the argument that politically it is of the utmost importance for Germany to be, and feel itself to be, a member of the Western community and that such a feeling of community is best nourished by Germany's assuming its share of the responsibility for maintaining the defenses of the West. In this, of course, there are unavoidable echoes of Germany's past behavior, the fear that a Germany left to itself, unattached by any formal bonds to the Western European nations, might be tempted to fish in troubled waters, to play off East against West or even to set off an expansionist course once more.

If negotiations with the Soviets on the terms suggested did not lead to a free and united Germany, the diplomatic gains envisaged might prove illusory. Even though the Soviet leaders were shown unmistakably to be the obstructionists, would we profit greatly from this demonstration? That the Soviet leaders are fearful of the free expression of public opinion, that they cling tightly to areas they have taken over and organized—these are not novel discoveries waiting to be revealed to the world for the first time. Indeed, in the Geneva meeting of the foreign ministers in October-November 1955, Mr. Molotov, while directing the weight of his attack against the Eden plan, made it perfectly clear that the Soviet Union had no intention in any event of permitting a reunification of Germany through free elections. "The formation of the German Democratic Republic," he said, "was a turning point in German history and in that of Europe as a whole. The working masses in Germany have for the first time found in the German Democratic Republic their real fatherland. . . . The German Democratic Republic, being a state of German workers and peasants, has a great future since it follows the main road of the development of the whole of humanity and has strong and true friends." Consequently, any "mechanical merger," i.e., free elections, would be an infringement on the interests of the working masses. Those not persuaded by such blunt remarks would probably not change their minds with reiterated evidence, but would seek some other explanation for Soviet obduracy and intransigence.

To reduce this very involved question of unification vs. Western alignment to its simplest terms, three interrelated issues may be posed:

1. The preferability to the free world of maintaining West Germany within the Western alliance, as against achieving the detachment of East Germany from the Soviet bloc at the cost of this connection;

2. The preferability of a West Germany whose policies could be coordinated with our own, as against an uncommitted Germany which might be expected to display, within the limits of an international agreement, an informal orientation toward the West, but which was under no commitment to do so;

3. The preferability of a definite line of demarcation between the Soviet and Western spheres, behind which we could organize Western defense; as against a large uncommitted area, which might not be a power vacuum if an independent neutral Germany were permitted to arm, but which would not be part of a Western defense system.

When these issues are looked at purely from the point of view of Western defense, the conclusion seems inescapable that our preference in each case would be for the first alternative, in maintaining German strength committed to the Western alliance, and in giving it a voice in determining the course of events in a highly strategic area. Hence we may conclude that there is necessarily a strong impulse for American policy to support, as it has over the last five years, a West Germany in NATO rather than to favor a united but uncommitted and uncommittable Germany. Still, as we have stressed above, the choice is not ours alone. German actions could quite effectively block our preference. We should not deceive ourselves into believing that West Germany can be so tightly tied to the Western alliance, by pacts, treaties or any other device, that it would be unable to negotiate alone with the Soviet Union concerning the conditions for unification, if that were felt to be the only avenue to German unity. We may do all we can to keep the Germans from *wanting* to do this; less and less will we be able to prevent them.

Forward Pressure

Finally, a fourth policy might seek to press forward, by measures short of war or the provocation of war, and break the Soviet hold on East Germany. There is no question of the desirability, on both humanitarian and political grounds, of detaching some 18 million people from the Communist orbit. It has also been argued that, of the areas of recent Communist expansion, East Germany is perhaps the most vulnerable to external pressure. It is relatively accessible, it has been somewhat less thoroughly integrated into the satellite network than the other Eastern European nations, its status has been more fluid and many of its inhabitants have demonstrated, by the events of June 1953, their vigorous antipathy to the existing regime.

All this is to the good. But how is such pressure to be applied? Several lines of action have been proposed. Some have suggested a strengthening of Western and West German forces to the degree that the Soviet leaders would feel obliged to surrender the area for fear of worse consequences.

This suggestion, which obviously rests on the threat of war, is unacceptable in the terms of the basic requirements of this report.

Less risky, but probably for that reason correspondingly less promising of success, is a buildup of West German strength, which is then to be used as a trading point for the reunification of East Germany under free elections. German rearmament, under this proposal, is considered less a measure of defense than a means of bargaining from strength, with the idea that German *dis*armament would be exchanged for reunification. This could be difficult to apply in practice. If the German people were unaware of its purpose as a bargaining point, the policy would encounter the same difficulties that might be met by any policy pressing for rearmament in advance of reunification. If, on the other hand, the Russians were aware of the purpose of this gambit—as they probably would be—some of its bargaining value would be lost.

Another possibility is that of vigorously exploiting and supporting such events as the June 1953 uprising. It has been urged by some that the United States "missed the boat" on that occasion, that the Soviet regime in the immediate aftermath of Stalin's death was beset by internal strains and uncertainties and was not in a position to engage in foreign skirmishes. Hence, it is argued, had the United States openly and vigorously aided the uprising, it is quite possible that the Soviet leaders would have felt obliged to give way. It is possible this would have been the outcome; it is also possible that the threat of such a foreign reversal would have driven the Soviet Communist hierarchy together. We cannot debate the question here. But it must be noted that this possibility in the past does not help us very much for the future. It is impossible to tell in advance whether the Soviets will or will not react violently to United States support for an uprising in their sphere; they would react if they could, and if they could react we would be running high risks of a general war. It is hard to see, therefore, how one can prepare in advance much of a policy along these lines, since its feasibility would depend entirely upon an on-the-spot assessment of the risks inhering in a specific set of circumstances.

In addition to waiting for a German uprising, it can also be argued, the United States should work to promote disaffection and resistance in East Germany, through political, psychological and economic warfare, less with a view to creating a particular crisis, which we might or might not feel able to exploit, than to debilitating the Eastern regime, reducing its strength and effectiveness, and keeping the Communists preoccupied with maintaining order in their own zone. This line of approach will have to be considered in more detail when we discuss the Eastern European satellites, where many of the same considerations apply. At this point we will only say that if this policy is to avoid certain impermissible results—precipitating a war, provoking premature uprisings which result only in reprisals and disillusionment, or stimulating the Soviet regime—it would have to be considered as a long-run undertaking seeking to affect the general political and moral balance of forces. It would not resolve the German issues which we are here discussing.

Requirements for a German Policy

As must be evident from our review of these various lines of policy, the German problem appears to be incapable of resolution on its own terms. Any specific line of action that we can envisage either promises to run into a blind alley or points to the need for a solution extending beyond Germany itself, encompassing the European power balance and even the underlying hostility between the Communist bloc and all who would oppose it.

At the same time, the German problem puts in doubt the feasibility of the efforts, discussed in the preceding chapter, of deriving a particular policy for a given area from any general premise or perspective concerning Soviet-American relations as a whole. Indeed, one of the most striking features of American efforts to deal with Germany in the last decade has been the practical impossibility of setting up any such general guide to action for a problem so complex and refractory. The policy maker has had to feel his way, sometimes with relative success, sometimes not so successfully. The reason is clear from the four lines of approach we have been discussing. Of these the first and the last—accepting the territorial division of Germany and pressing forward—are only applications to the German case of two more general perspectives (A and C in the preceding chapter [2]): acquiescing in the present territorial division between the Communist and non-Communist worlds and advancing by means short of war to reduce the area of Communist dominion. But it is to be observed that neither has in fact played an important role in the actual formulation and expression of American policy in Germany, for the reason that the main practical issue which the statesman must deal with—how to support, without disrupting the NATO alliance, a Western-oriented German regime that is necessarily intensely preoccupied with overcoming the division of its own country—is not answered by either policy.

The policy maker must proceed from the concrete problems confronting him, and in Germany the first need is obviously to take all steps necessary to try to keep West Germany independent and associated with the West rather than with the Soviet bloc. From this need has followed the decision to have Germany participate in Western defense. From this need, too, follows the decision to support German unification lest the abandonment of that aspiration lead either to uncontrollable tensions or to the collapse of any pro-Western regime and West Germany's turning to the East as the only way to realize its goal.

Since these two aims, stressing the Western alliance and achieving reunification, appear blocked by the Soviets, two divergent approaches have emerged (the second and the third above), the one hoping that somehow reunification can follow a Germany firmly established in NATO and Western European Union, the other hoping that a formally neutralized but independent, unified Germany would not shift the power balance away from West to East. We have already given our estimate of these hopes; neither is likely in the present international setting. But the point here is that these approaches have not derived from any general perspectives regarding Soviet-American relations but from definite requirements of the German situation itself.

Nevertheless, policies resulting from the necessary con-

[2] See above, p. 166 and p. 169.

cern the United States has with the status and orientation of West Germany do have implications extending well beyond the German question. Whether they are intended or not, they affect the general posture of American foreign policy. Several examples may be given.

First, while it may be accepted that the leading purpose of an American effort to have a reunited Germany free to participate in NATO is to prevent a weakening of Western defense, the achievement of this purpose would in fact constitute a major roll-back of the area of Soviet domination. The Soviet leaders obviously regard our policy in that light, reject it, and will probably continue to do so despite all assurances that our German policy is not directed against the Soviet bloc. This does not mean that the United States, to be consistent, must adopt a perspective of forward advance for the whole of its relations with the Soviet bloc. It does mean that a decision to support German unification in the manner we have entails the cost of its being a continuing challenge to the integrity of the Soviet-controlled bloc.

Second, our interest in West Germany has implications for our attitude toward Western European cooperation and integration, a most important subject which cannot be discussed in any detail here. There is little doubt that the United States should support efforts to increase the extent and effectiveness of Western European cooperation, as a positive contribution to European security, prosperity and political harmony. Certainly the strength and cohesion of the NATO structure is vital to American security. At the same time, because of the sense that, in the absence of any immediate prospects for German reunification, the German people must be provided with some other goal to which they can attach their hopes, there is the chance that the United States might come to view Western European union as a sort of lightning rod for German frustrations in the East. This does not necessarily contradict our other reasons for favoring Western European cooperation. But it would be unfortunate to forget that Western European cooperation also concerns allies other than Germany, and that the problem of unity and integration is highly complex and delicate. If we let our preoccupation with Germany exclusively determine our position on the form, extent and tempo of progress toward European cooperation, we might well create serious trouble.

Third, there is the problem of creating neutral, neutralized or disarmed areas between the Soviet bloc and the free world. If an effective neutralization of the whole of a united Germany would result in a greater loss of capabilities and strength for the West than for the Soviet bloc, the answer may appear to be to create an equivalent neutralized area to the east of a united Germany, in, say, Czechoslovakia and Poland. This may be a possibility worth exploring, but it raises important questions relating to other territories. The neutralization of the Eastern European satellites is hardly a feasible project so long as Communist regimes are in control and not disarmed. Hence a change of regimes, or their effective disarming, would be indicated, in effect a radical roll-back of Soviet power. This may be a desirable objective, but it should not be introduced through the back door, as a device to prevent a diminution of Western power under one possible formula for German reunification. German criteria alone should not guide us on a decision involving the whole question of the postwar expansion of the Soviet imperium.

Fourth, there is the problem of a general European security pact. A general Soviet-Western agreement on mutual security as a means of achieving a *modus vivendi* is, of course, something much broader and more far-reaching than the German question. But it is evident that the principal practical incentive which has led to Western proposals for a security arrangement has been the stalemate on the German problem. If the Western powers feel that a united Germany must be in NATO and if the Soviet Union regards this as a threat to itself, then it is quite natural that, in order to gain Soviet approval of our German proposals, the Western powers should devise some way to reassure the Soviet Union. But there is the danger that our concern for Germany may lead us to overlook other important considerations: whether a mutual agreement with a regime such as the Soviet Union can add anything to the provisions already existing in the United Nations Charter, to which the Soviet Union and the United States are signatories; whether we wish to commit ourselves to the security of the present Communist regimes in Eastern Europe; or whether a security pact for the Communist bloc's western flank may not increase the possibility of Communist aggression in Asia. The answers to these questions may not be self-evident, but at least they must be faced on their own terms and not slighted because of preoccupation with our German policy.

In brief, precisely because Germany is such an important and difficult problem we must guard against the temptation to disregard or underplay other equally important and equally concrete requirements of American policy. While we cannot deduce our German policy from any over-all guiding perspective, neither can we let our day-by-day efforts to deal with the German question warp our judgment on general issues or those vitally concerning other areas.

Having dwelt rather heavily on the difficulties of working out an appropriate German policy, we may now, in concluding this chapter, try to list the positive elements it should comprise.

1. The United States must act vigorously to persuade West Germany, now an independent state, of the desirability of continued and close cooperation with the West and of participation in its defense through whatever institutions (and these must be flexibly conceived) give best promise of promoting European cooperation.

2. The division of Germany is, whether we think it should be or not, a source of friction and tension in the heart of Europe. So long as this is the case, the unification of Germany, on the basis of free elections, appears to be the only way of removing that tension. It is not the function of American policy to stimulate the German desire for reunification or to disregard it, but to recognize it as an important fact in the situation, a fact over which we have relatively little control, though we may have a share in determining whether the desire for unification is to find constructive or destructive expression.

3. Consequently, the double aim of reunification and the participation of Germany in Western defense is a necessary element of American policy. It is to be regarded neither as a pious hope nor as a public relations measure to satisfy German

nationalism. We cannot neglect the fact that this aim is altogether unacceptable to the Russians and for very important reasons. It is, nevertheless, an accurate reflection of the German situation, and within that situation we can find no acceptable substitute to serve as a basis for policy. We can, as we have for the last several years, carry on a meaningful foreign policy even though Germany is divided, and there is no necessary time limit to our ability to do so. Still, the fact remains that the continuation of a divided Germany could, under certain circumstances, be disastrous to American and Western European interests.

4. The principal alternative approach to German unification—by way of some form of neutralization or nonalignment—holds no greater promise, for the reason that the Soviet Union has made it clear that it would not accept the reunification of Germany under any conditions which did not preserve the Communist hold on East Germany.

It has been suggested that even without free or reasonably free elections the strength of West Germany is such that it could successfully handle a coalition, or other form of joint administration, with the Communists. It is within the power of the West Germans to come to such a conclusion and it might, conceivably, be successful. It should not be the function of the United States, however, to support or advocate this kind of solution. Our presumption should be that the Soviets would not permit the formation of such a coalition unless they were sure of being in a position to preserve the "gains of the working masses" in the East zone.

5. Whether it is desirable to underline and publicize this basic Soviet intention is largely a tactical decision. In our view the effort required to make the Soviet leaders openly admit that they intend to maintain the Communist order in East Germany under all circumstances may not be very rewarding. Apart from the Soviet skill in keeping the public appearance of issues obscure and confused, American energies may be expended more profitably in supporting the positive goal of developing Western European strength and cooperation than in trying to prove for the nth time the unhelpful and unyielding aims of Communism.

6. As far as the Germans themselves are concerned the

United States should aim more at developing the practical values to them of working with the West than at stressing the futility and peril of toying with the Soviet bloc. A drift to the East cannot be checked by arguments or warnings alone.

7. American support of Western European endeavors in cooperation should not, however, be regarded as an adjunct to our German policy or judged solely in terms of its effects in Germany. If a pattern of Western European cooperation can evolve that is both useful to the nations concerned and expresses in some measure the values of Western European culture which must be preserved, it will have all the attractions that are possible. These attractions cannot be conjured up as a way of distracting the Germans from their present division.

CHAPTER X
THE EASTERN EUROPEAN SATELLITES

THE FORCIBLE installation of Communist-controlled regimes in the states on Russia's western borders marks the origins of the postwar Soviet-American conflict. Before the Chinese problem became acute, and while Germany was still an area of reasonably satisfactory allied cooperation, the Cold War had set in for Rumania, Poland, Yugoslavia, Albania and Bulgaria, to spread later to Hungary and Czechoslovakia. With the possible exception of the West's increasing awareness of the world of concentration camps within the Soviet Union, nothing has been so responsible for the revulsion of feelings regarding the Soviet regime as the Kremlin's actions in the smaller countries of East Central Europe.

In most tangible respects the creation of the satellite empire is a great triumph for the Soviet Union. It has pushed the frontiers of Communism far to the west and has provided the Soviet Union with a greatly expanded area for defense and offense, as well as control over many strategic points and passages into Central Europe. The resources, economic output, population and military potential of the satellites have increased Soviet strength in these categories by between one-third and one-half. The expansion of the "Socialist camp" is of enormous prestige value in supporting Soviet boasts of the eventual triumph of Communism throughout the world.

The United States and Western Europe have suffered corresponding losses: a narrowing of the strategic space for the defense of Europe, an unfavorable shift in the balance of European manpower and resources. Above all, and especially to the United States, the Communization of Eastern Europe represents a grievous and galling political loss. Though victorious in the war against Hitler, the United States was unable to prevent 100 million Europeans from falling under a domination that was alien and unwanted, and which represented a negation of the values for which the United States stands.

A great proportion of America's diplomatic energy in the early postwar years was spent in a fruitless attempt to check or reverse the course of Soviet actions in East Central Europe. While the United States in some measure swallowed its losses—in signing peace treaties with the former Nazi satellites and assuming diplomatic relations with the Communist regimes—it has never, officially or in public sentiment, reconciled itself to the outcome.

It may be, of course, that all the advantages will not prove to be on the Soviet side. It may turn out in the long run that the disillusionment and shock created by the brutal Sovietization of Eastern Europe will have done the Communist cause irreparable damage, in the hatreds aroused, in the loss of the good will which the Russian people and the Red Army had amassed in the Second World War, and in giving the lie to propaganda about achieving Communism through persuasion and self-determination.

Nevertheless, virtually no American would regard the present state of affairs in East Central Europe as anything but malignant. There is no doubt but that a change would be almost universally welcomed in the United States even though there might be a great deal of disagreement concerning the desired lineaments of a post-Communist East Central Europe. But the unpleasant question raises itself, as it has again and again since 1945, what is to be done about it? For it must be admitted that there is little prospect of the Eastern European situation curing itself in the foreseeable future.

Although the Soviet Union has not been able to impose its control without economic costs and political strain—and these may have been even greater than the information available to us would indicate—the satellites are and promise to remain net assets of considerable magnitude. Nor is there much reason to believe that the Soviets could enjoy these assets without most of the controls they have instituted. There is nothing natural about the present political and economic organization of Eastern Europe. It is a thoroughly artificial creation. Consequently, there are very definite limits to the changes which can be inaugurated, or tolerated, by the Communist leaders, as seems to have been demonstrated by the very uncertain and faltering efforts to embark upon the "new course" after Stalin's death. Any steps which increase real autonomy of decision in the satellites would promote forces that could threaten to get out of hand. It can be argued, to be sure, that were the satellite regimes to be permitted a fair amount of relaxation, in the direction of economic easement or reduced political controls, or even of granting greater independence to the local Communist regimes, the peoples of Eastern Europe would be sufficiently gratified by this alleviation to suffer the absence of complete freedom and independence. This could be, yet there is a great deal of historical experience to suggest that few things are more difficult than keeping in control a real relaxation of a dictatorial system. "The appetite comes with eating," and no one is more likely than the Communists to be aware of this adage.

If there is little prospect—certainly nothing we should count on—for a voluntary improvement of the situation by the U.S.S.R., neither do chances seem bright that the captive nations themselves can, in the absence of a mortal crisis in the Soviet Union, extricate themselves from their alien domination. As one anti-Communist Eastern European exile has observed: "Western statesmen must accept the axiom that the nations behind the Iron Curtain will not cast off the Soviet yoke by themselves." Again we may be painting too pessimistic a picture; the human spirit is capable of quite unpredictable achievements. The system of totalitarian controls may have deep flaws that are not yet visible. Though it has shown remarkable ability in smelling out, checking and liquidating most traditional nuclei of revolt and resistance, it may be creating in the process new types of opposition and opponents to which it is peculiarly vulnerable. It is tempting to speculate on such possibilities; yet we cannot base a policy on the likelihood of their occurrence, even though we should not dismiss them or fail to be on the lookout for them.

The chances of a schism in the Communist leadership of the satellites, in the form of a "nationalist" revolt against control by Moscow, are not much greater. The other Communist parties of the area lack the independent power that Tito possessed, and there has been, in the years since 1948, an apparently thorough purging of nationalist deviators. It is, of course, quite likely that continuing Soviet demands upon the satellites will create tensions conducive to such a schism, but the Russians have evidently learned a good deal from the Yugoslav case and should be in a position to keep discontent within the party from becoming effectively organized.

Though we cannot count on a basic alteration of the Eastern European regimes taking place from above or below or at the hands of "national" Communists, there probably will be, as there have been in the past, significant fluctuations and changes, as the Communists shift from one line to another, tightening or loosening political and economic controls, raising or lowering the Iron Curtain in some measure. We must be prepared to take account of these changes, which may be only marginal and designed for any number of purposes we can only guess at, but which may be of much importance politically and diplomatically, not least in the manner they are interpreted abroad.

If the United States is to take account of these changes it must relate them to its own policy. In sharp contrast to West Germany, where American policy must meet immediate and continuing responsibilities in an area to which it has direct access, American policy toward the Eastern European satellites operates in something of a vacuum. Perhaps for this reason debate on United States policy in East Central Europe has been in somewhat abstract terms. Here more than anywhere else has been the conflict of general perspectives, the familiar battleground between the oversimplified formulations, "liberation" and "containment." The debate has tended to become one of formulas precisely because the concrete possibilities have been so unpromising.

Acquiescence in the Status Quo

A perspective of acquiescing in the territorial *status quo* in East Central Europe is a logical deduction from a few premises.[1] It assumes first that the satellite area, which the Soviet Union has taken over and remodeled in its own image, is of such importance to it, ideologically, militarily and economically, that it would defend its position there by all means up to and including general war. At the very least, it would be most risky to assume that it would not. The perspective assumes further that the totalitarian controls exerted are of such effectiveness that means short of war would have little or no chance of detaching significant portions of the area (with the possible exception of Albania). Finally, it would assume that pressures short of war exerted against the satellites would have as their main, and undesirable, effect an invigoration of the Soviet regime, an extension of the controls and a renewal of ideological zeal to counteract the real evidence of "capitalist encirclement." From these assumptions it is concluded that forward pressures lose more than they gain, and that even nibbling efforts or the willingness to pick up windfalls would probably be disadvantageous.

It is to be stressed that this perspective in no way grants the legitimacy of postwar events in the satellites, nor does it suggest that the United States make any formal guarantees to the Russians that we have no interests in the area—such formal guarantees by us would have no more meaning to the Russians than did their own formal dissolution of the Comintern in 1943. Rather, it is held, in line with the general tenor of this approach, it is in the interest of the United States to devote its energies to the free world and not to dissipate them in random efforts behind the Iron Curtain.

This perspective also points, though with no sort of certainty, to the hope that a long-term relaxation of tensions between Communist states and the West may promote the supposed tendency of zealotry to relax and may thus contribute indirectly to some gradual moderation of Communist controls over the Eastern European satellites.

As applied to this region, the perspective that acquiesces in the *status quo* has little positive appeal. Indeed, it offers no direct outlet for the sense of chagrin one must feel not only that the Soviets took over these states by exceptionally nasty

[1] See above, p. 166.

methods but that, for all we can do, they may get away with it for an indefinite period. It is distinctly a policy of the lesser evil, forced upon us by the perilous times in which we live.

There are, moreover, two points at which the adequacy of this perspective may be questioned. In the first place, a policy based upon it would be dispiriting to the Eastern Europeans themselves. Feeling written off by the West, their will to independence would lack any outside reinforcement, and they would have to rely solely on their sorely tried inner resources. This, in the eventuality of some major crisis in the satellite empire, might mean the difference between a kindling of active resistance and sodden apathy.

It may be argued that the Eastern Europeans already feel abandoned, that after a whole decade of Soviet domination they have by now discounted any Western intention to liberate or have come to comprehend our difficulties in offering them any tangible expectations. The peoples of East Central Europe are not unfamiliar with the ways of the world, and it does them an injustice to impute to them a mood of simple trust disillusioned, in place of their deep-abiding, slightly bitter and ironic toughness. They are too wise to hang on words and they have a shrewd sense of what is possible and what is not. Even with this qualification, however, it is scarcely to be expected that they would be heartened by such a policy.

In the second place, while we may admit that exerting pressure against the satellites will probably have the immediate effect of reinforcing the regimes and sharpening their vigilance, the question may be raised whether the proper conclusion has been drawn. By tightening the screws the Communist leaders may strengthen their regimes, but this may also increase certain long-run vulnerabilities, a point to be considered presently. Moreover, as we have observed earlier, it is by no means sure that refraining from pressure will in any way reduce the regimes' vigor or their capacity to make increasing demands on their subjects. A striking feature of our experience with totalitarianism so far has been that the harsh and repressive features seem to increase rather than diminish as the regimes' apparent security improves. Admittedly we cannot establish this as a general rule. The time period covered by our experience with the new totalitarianisms is pretty short. But it is a moot point whether our non-involvement in East Central Europe would have, even in the long run, a soothing effect.

A Policy of the Free Hand

A second perspective differs from the first both in continuing to voice the political claims arising out of wartime and postwar agreements affecting the nations of East Central Europe and in reserving a free hand as regards our position and actions concerning the satellites.[2] In this perspective, we should not discontinue our declarations that the U.S.S.R. and the satellites should fulfill the commitments they made either at Yalta, or as members of the United Nations or as signatories of the peace treaties of 1947. These commitments include the holding of free elections, respect for human rights and, in the case of the former allies of Germany, not rearming beyond treaty limits.

As a practical matter this perspective would find no gain in discontinuing the use of what are, at the least, diplomatic counters, useful in refuting Soviet pretensions of being anti-colonialist, law-abiding and in favor of independence and self-determination. Nevertheless, voicing our claims for this reason alone does not really constitute a policy for East Central Europe. Stipulating what *should* be without indicating *how* the claims may be realized does not take us very far. We have encountered a similar difficulty in our advocacy of German reunification, which also concerns the plight of people currently caught in the Soviet orbit, but, in the German instance at least, reunification is tied to an intricate complex of issues in which the United States can and does play an active role; reunification, as we have seen, has been a necessary part of our policy respecting West Germany. In the case of the Eastern European satellites, however, this linkage is absent, with the result that the reiteration of our claims could easily be an empty gesture, requiring neither effort nor imagination—a salve for inaction.

What use might be made of these claims in influencing the

[2] See above, p. 168.

international situation? One use would be to advance our claims regarding East Central Europe as active counterdemands to Soviet pressures concerning Western Europe. It might be feasible for us to agree to certain concessions in Western Europe in return for a removal of Communist controls over some or all of the Eastern European satellites. One such possibility, which has been touched on already, would be the creation of a neutral and/or disarmed area covering a united Germany and a number of states bordering Germany and Austria on the east. In principle, this arrangement could take the form of a general arms reduction within the area to a level sufficient only for internal security, while continuing the present political and diplomatic orientation of the states concerned. Or it could go beyond this to the creation of a politically neutral or unaffiliated Central and East Central Europe, which would entail the disappearance of the present Communist regimes in the satellites.

Any such exchange of concessions would be extremely difficult to work out in practice. Exchanges are likely to work the other way, to strengthen rather than weaken the power positions of the two blocs. Given the West's primary concern with bolstering Western Europe—a concern the Soviet Union probably shares for its area of control—any East-West bargaining may well have the effect of reinforcing the *status quo* rather than altering it. This is evident in at least two recent developments: a) the admission of 16 new members to the UN—accepting Rumania, Hungary, Bulgaria and Albania, in return for such Western European states as Ireland, Italy, Portugal and Spain,[3] and b) the negotiations for a European security agreement which, apparently, would include guarantees for at least Communist Poland and Czechoslovakia as well as for a united Germany. Such arrangements have the effect, perhaps only a marginal one, of reinforcing the present line-up of powers and ideologies. The advantages gained might be worth it, though this is by no means sure, but it is evident that such arrangements would not advance our claims regarding the status of the areas behind

[3] The other states admitted are Jordan, Austria, Finland, Ceylon, Nepal, Libya, Cambodia and Laos.

the Iron Curtain and might in effect weaken them or render them inoperative.

Pressures Short of War

A third perspective, that of exerting pressures short of war, or the provocation of war, against the satellites would aim explicitly at the withdrawal of Soviet Communist power to the Soviet frontiers in order to permit the people of the area to decide freely what type of regimes they want.[4] It is necessary to make a significant distinction, however, one that is often overlooked in the debates on "liberation." Some people, in advocating a policy of pressures short of war against the satellites, have been inclined to regard it as a substitute for military operations but producing the same results. This is a fallacy. If you wish, in the short run at least, to achieve the kind of results which naked power produces, you must be prepared to use naked power; there are no cheap substitutes. To count on political, psychological or economic warfare without military backing to produce results as tangible as the liberation of one or another East Central European country within a determinable period of time is to court serious disappointment and frustration. Critics of a policy of pressure are justifiably alarmed by the probable consequences of this point of view: political warfare being built up to armed conflict, or the exposure of the Eastern Europeans to fearful reprisals with consequent disillusionment and defeatism.

It may be argued, however, that it is incorrect to put a policy of forward pressure on such a footing. Rather than aiming at specific and concrete results the purpose must be much more general: to frustrate the rulers' attempts to win over support from important segments of the community, to inhibit their efforts to consolidate and normalize their regimes, to keep alive a spirit of independence, to create fissures wherever possible between the rulers and the ruled, and between the local rulers and Moscow, to attempt to improve the day-to-day existence of the captive peoples by forms of pressure on the regimes. Such measures, when taken together, do not add up to an overthrow of the regimes, to-

[4] See above, p. 169.

day, tomorrow or in any certain period of time. But they do, it may be held, affect the conditions for future developments, work in our favor and against the Soviet bloc and could, in a real if currently unpredictable fashion, make a difference in the prospects for the eventual freedom for the area. Under this approach, one would avoid quixotic or premature adventures and would not try to evaluate results in terms of the number of street fights or strikes instigated.

A major problem for this perspective is whether a Communist regime is likely to be weakened or strengthened by outside pressures short of the amount required to overthrow it. According to this view, forward pressure against the Communist satellites, while it might not directly sap their strength and might indeed stimulate their fanaticism and provoke them to more strenuous efforts, could, nevertheless, be damaging in depriving them of their ability to be flexible, to shift the balance of their policies, to manipulate "hard" and "soft" lines—devices which appear to be an important factor in maintaining the uneasy equilibrium of a totalitarian regime. The application of these pressures, constantly and over an extended period of time, might reduce the Communists' adaptability and their capacity to organize a society and keep it running.

Whether the dynamism of Communist regimes is more likely to be reduced by the presence or the absence of external pressure does not permit of a sure answer, though it is reasonable to suppose that pressure against the satellites promises to be somewhat more effective in this regard than that exerted directly against the Soviet Union itself. Because power and authority in the satellites are largely derivative, the local leadership is less capable, on its own, of deciding upon and carrying through vigorous countermeasures. But for the same reason the greater the pressure from abroad, the more the local leadership may be driven to depend upon support and direction from Moscow.

The perspective envisaging pressure against East Central Europe raises another problem, one of territorial definition. In most of the debates concerning "liberation" the captive states have been considered as a unit and as distinct from the

Soviet Union itself. Is it possible a) to limit the withdrawal of Communist power to a selected zone within the larger satellite area and b) to limit the aim of withdrawal to the satellite area alone without extending it to the whole of the Soviet system?

As for the first question, some have argued that the United States would err in regarding the satellite area as an indivisible unit, to be liberated or not as a whole. Such an all-or-nothing attitude may fail to exploit opportunities for a partial territorial retraction of Communist control. Perhaps, it is argued, a combination of pressure and negotiation might induce the Soviet Union to relinquish at least the westernmost satellites.

The persuasiveness of this argument depends largely upon the assessment of the reasons which have impelled the Soviet Union to impose Communist regimes since the Second World War. If the purpose has been purely, or predominantly, power-political, to defend the western approaches to the Soviet Union, then it might be possible to achieve a retraction of the area the Russians deem it necessary to control. There is some evidence that during the war the Soviet Union did have differing degrees of interest in the countries to its west. It was clearly determined to secure control of certain bordering areas; for others its interest seemed more tentative and exploratory. But whatever distinctions there may have been then, the whole area has now been taken over and thoroughly Communized. The Soviet Union itself has given no evidence that it considers Hungary and Czechoslovakia to be more expendable, say, than Rumania or Poland—they are all part of the camp of "peoples democracies." That the Soviet leaders would willingly accept the detachment of a single Communist state seems very doubtful, indeed.

This, however, leads to the second question, whether the whole of the satellite area can be considered separately from the U.S.S.R., or whether an effort to detach it would amount to a challenge to the Soviet system itself. It might be said that, were the area of Communist domination to be reduced to the Soviet frontiers of 1939, the mission of forward pressure in Eastern Europe would be accomplished. But the problem is not that simple.[5] If one's primary concern is with the fate of peoples who have fallen under Soviet domination, there is no evident reason for favoring the Hungarians or the Bulgarians over the Ukrainians, the Byelorussians or even the Russians themselves: all have come under a regime not of their choosing and concerning which they have never been permitted a free expression of opinion. From a military point of view a retraction of Soviet power would be of benefit to the West, but it would not render Europe secure in an atomic age. Moreover, Moscow would still remain the ideological headquarters of Communist totalitarianism and world revolution.

Even, however, were *we* to limit our efforts to the regions Communized since 1939 or to the areas covered by obligations assumed in the Yalta Agreement, the Soviet leaders would almost certainly respond to these efforts as they would to actions against the entire Soviet system. The fault lies not with the desire to rectify the injustice of Soviet aggression—this is an altogether proper desire—but with the nature of the Soviet regime; against such an opponent it is extremely difficult to apply distinctions and limitations.

* * *

When we turn to appraise these various perspectives concerning the Eastern European satellites, we would conclude that, notwithstanding all the difficulties and the absence of any immediate prospect for a successful outcome, an approach which works for a withdrawal of Soviet-Communist power from the area best indicates the objective of American policy, though primarily for reasons other than those of strategy or power politics. There is no question but that this approach will be strenuously resisted by the Soviet regime and the local Communist authorities. It is more than doubtful that it is, in any foreseeable circumstance, a position which the United States can advance by negotiation or mu-

[5] Even the definition of frontiers presents some difficulties. Under this definition the Baltic states would be included in the area to be detached, even though they have been incorporated within the U.S.S.R. (an act which the United States has not recognized, though a number of its allies have). But what of eastern Poland, Bessarabia and Northern Bucovina, areas conceded to the Soviet Union by the United States at Yalta or in the Rumanian peace treaty?

tual agreement; the conflict of interests is too radical, the Soviet stake too great. For all that, however, we believe that the attitude of the American people toward the plight of this region is most suitably expressed in such statements as President Eisenhower's Christmas message in 1955 or former President Truman's declaration in 1952 to one of the captive nations: "You are going to survive as a free country. You are going to have our whole-hearted cooperation in trying to survive."

We should, however, be clear as to the meaning of this purpose, which is not "liberation" for the sake of gaining positions, acquiring resources or altering the "balance of power," though Moscow may take it to be such. We could not pretend to calculate the strategic importance, or unimportance, of East Central Europe in a general war. Nor, conversely, can our purpose mean initiating a war for the sake of liberation. More generally, it cannot mean that we impose immediate hardships and sufferings on the people of East Central Europe for the sake of their eventual benefit. While the security of the West may at times require us to take actions against their regimes—trade restrictions, for instance, which fall upon the people—it would be of very dubious morality for any country to try to increase the misery of these hard-pressed people in the hope of producing an uprising of desperation or the paralysis of exhaustion.

In the range of possible actions designed to maintain and increase contact between the West and the nations (not regimes) of East Central Europe, the idea of psychological or political warfare—war by proxy—is misleading if it suggests that Czechs, Rumanians and Poles are to be objects, pawns in military or quasi-military plans. News rather than propaganda, support rather than prodding, the preservation of cultures rather than the sabotage of regimes—these should represent the main direction of our efforts. Our goal, then, is to keep faith with them as fellow men, to keep hope alive, and a sense of community.

A Note on Yugoslavia

Yugoslavia has occupied a unique position in Europe in having a Communist regime and yet being, after 1948, outside the Soviet bloc and, during much of the time, at serious odds with it. To find Communists taking a stand against the Soviet Union has been troubling to orderly minds, who have sought to warp this odd fact to some simple conclusion. Some have argued that the issue dividing the United States and the U.S.S.R. has, therefore, not been Communism but Soviet aggressiveness. Others have maintained that the Tito-Stalin break was an elaborate deception, or that sooner or later Communist Yugoslavia must return to the fold or undergo a counterrevolution. Titoism has been variously interpreted as indicating a structural fault in Communism that would spread to other Communist regimes, or as a viable "third way" between Communism and democratic Socialism.

None of these conclusions is really substantiated by the available evidence. They show the mark of preconception or wishful thinking and an unwillingness to accept the Yugoslav case as an anomaly presenting unexpected, though not necessarily unanswerable, questions to the Yugoslavs and the Russians as well as to the non-Communist powers.

While the Soviet-Yugoslav rift in 1948 was a real one, it was not the prior intention of either party to cause a schism in the Communist bloc. Tito did not try to break away; he merely refused to lose control over an independent power position he had created in the course of the war. Stalin was not trying to isolate Yugoslavia, but only to get rid of a group of individuals who refused to submit to the discipline and controls he had developed over the international Communist movement. The fact that the rupture occurred, and that Tito was able to survive it, depended on a very special set of circumstances, including the independent military and police power possessed by the Yugoslav Communists and the personalities and loyalties of the party leaders (who were also South Slavs). It depended also on Stalin's mishandling of the issue; a mishandling that need not be repeated in subsequent cases of disagreement between Moscow and a national Communist party.

Once the break had occurred it developed a momentum of its own; the rift broadened, and step by step Tito was forced from a wholehearted support of Soviet foreign policy to a necessary reliance upon the Western powers against the threat of Cominform attack. The United States and Great Britain extended military and economic aid; Yugoslavia joined in a defensive alliance with Greece and Turkey. Simultaneously, the Yugoslav Communists undertook to give an ideological content to the rift. Making a virtue of necessity, they sought to establish a distinction between true Communism and its Soviet distortion and to modify a number of economic and political practices—generally in the direction of somewhat greater freedom and relaxation of controls.

On neither the domestic nor the foreign front, however, did these developments follow through to their ultimate consequences. Tito has not asked or been invited to enter NATO. Instead, he has announced his independence from and disapproval of blocs. More recently there has been, at the least, a very considerable "normalization" of Soviet-Yugoslav relations. Domestically the Djilas affair showed that the regime had no intention of making a full retreat from Communism and dictatorship. At the present moment, then, Yugoslavia's position is not only anomalous but tentative. Yugoslav domestic and foreign policy could shift in either direction, or it could remain as it is for an indefinite period.

Although American policy toward Yugoslavia after 1948 has been criticized by some for not being sufficiently cordial and by others for failing to insist upon democratic reforms before providing any assistance, its cautious, pragmatic approach seems to have been appropriate to the situation. The principal gain for the United States from the Tito-Stalin rupture was simply that in the balance of political and military forces an independent Communist Yugoslavia was preferable to a Yugoslavia which was an integral part of the Soviet bloc. To try to press this advantage, to seek out Yugoslavia as an alliance partner would probably have incurred more costs than benefits, even had Tito been able and willing—which is doubtful—to join the Western alliance. On the other hand, however much Americans may regret the continued Communist hold over Yugoslavia, it is doubtful that our own interests or those of the Yugoslav people would have been served at any time after 1948 by making the removal of the dictatorship the key to our Yugoslav policy. To have taken such a position while Yugoslavia was threatened with Cominform attack would have been a dubious gamble, more likely to have brought Yugoslavia back under Soviet control than to have created an independent non-Communist Yugoslavia. With the relaxation of Soviet-Yugoslav tension we lacked the leverage to realize such a policy.

With respect to the future it is very difficult to make any useful predictions or prescriptions, partly because Yugoslavia's position is so tentative. Were Yugoslavia to return to the Soviet bloc the answer would be simple: our policy should correspond to that adopted toward the Soviet Union and its Eastern European satellites. It can be argued, of course, that Yugoslavia, having once achieved its independent status, is unlikely to become a mere satellite or dependency. This may be true but irrelevant. The Soviet leaders, who have evidently adapted themselves to Communist China's status as an ally rather than a subordinate, also seem, from their actions in recent months, to be willing to accept Yugoslavia on equal terms. In other words, the resumption of a Yugoslav-Soviet connection need not imply a reversion to the situation prior to 1948.

On the other hand, there is the possibility that, from the post-Stalin point of view of Soviet interests, Yugoslavia can serve a useful function in developing, along with such uncommitted countries as India and Burma, a position of active nonalignment. Such a demonstration of the possibilities of "peaceful coexistence" in the area between the Soviet bloc and the Western alliance may be thought to promote divisive trends in the non-Communist world.

Consequently, the problem of dealing with Yugoslavia is now more subtle and complex than in the years shortly after 1948. So long as the Soviet bloc was actively pressing outward and harassing the nations on its periphery, the logic of the American decision to aid the nations so threatened—even a Communist state such as Yugoslavia—was evident. It may be less easy to devise an appropriate policy under recent circumstances, with Moscow patching up relations with Yugoslavia, with Khrushchev, Tito and Nehru visiting one another's capitals and signing lengthy statements of common interests and aspirations.

The most likely motive for the Soviet support of nonalignment and neutralism is the old Leninist effort to neutralize one set of potential opponents while isolating the major adversary. Although Yugoslav policy may, either consciously or unconsciously, support that motive, we should not for that reason alone reverse our policy and take a hostile stand against Yugoslavia. Indeed, to do so would be to play the Soviet game. It is necessary to remember that Leninism's divisive tactics are not political magic. Their success, even in their own terms, depends upon a favorable "objective situation." The effort to "neutralize" also has serious risks for the Communist position, in blurring the party line and in setting forces in action that may be difficult to control. Consequently, while we must keep alert to developments in Yugoslavia's orientation, we would do best to hold to a cautious, pragmatic approach.

CHAPTER XI
COMMUNIST CHINA AND ASIAN SECURITY

It is necessary to state at the outset that in this report on Soviet-American relations we cannot give the question of Asian security the detailed examination it warrants as a major preoccupation and concern of American foreign policy. While the world faces in Asia the same danger as elsewhere—the outward thrust of Communist power—the principal instrument of that power in this area is Communist China rather than the Soviet Union. Moreover, many lands on China's periphery, extending from Japan through Southeast Asia to Afghanistan, face not only a military and ideological threat but a bewildering variety of domestic problems which seriously weaken the ability of these nations to withstand this threat. Some of these problems have been discussed in our chapters on Economic Policy and Social Policy.[1] A further regional analysis would require close study of each of the Asian countries. Finally, this report has tried, so far as possible, to look at middle- and long-term issues. In Asia it is very difficult to speak of long-run prospects when so much may hang upon the outcome of several intense, if local, crises. What occurs, say, on Quemoy and Matsu or in South Vietnam, possibly in the very near future, could profoundly affect the whole future of Asia. Yet we cannot try here to resolve such intricate and shifting issues.

Still, we obviously must give some consideration to these Asian problems, if only because of their bearing on the American position toward the Soviet Union and the Communist bloc. Our treatment, however, is general and confined to two principal questions: American policy in supporting and strengthening non-Communist Asia, and American policy regarding Communist China.

Communism in China

Most of the features of Communist totalitarianism which were outlined in the first chapter apply to Communist China

[1] See above, p. 128, and p. 146.

as much as to the Soviet Union, though they are not so fully developed. Students of the subject have debated whether Maoism is a tactical and organizational variant of "normative" Marxism-Leninism—especially in regard to the role of the countryside as a revolutionary base—but they appear to be in increasing agreement that the observable variations are a response, a successful one, to local circumstances rather than the sign of a heretical bent which might lead Chinese Communism down a significantly different path. Both the Chinese and the Russian Communists have been at pains in recent years to deny that Maoism represents a deviation. Since the Communist victory in 1949 these differences seem to be of decreasing rather than of increasing significance in the over-all picture of the two regimes.

To be sure, the fact that Chinese Communism was imposed on a culture and an economy quite different from that of Russia, by different means, and a generation later, has had its effects. Just as the behavior of the Yugoslav Communist party frequently displays the temper of the South Slavs, so the style of the Chinese Communists has been influenced by history and environment. These effects should not be exaggerated. The observer who has been trained to think in terms of national characteristics and interests may not realize the extent to which Communism, when in power, is able to take over these characteristics and interests without losing sight of its own goals.

It is true that Marxism is not historically rooted in Chinese culture, but it is a recent graft on Russian history, too. One may regard its Leninist and Maoist versions as progressively greater distortions of a philosophy born of Western European industrialism, but there is no reason to believe that Maoism may not thrive as well as Leninism. Indeed, it has been argued that the traditional structure of Chinese society and government lends itself to submission to the Communist ideology and governing apparatus. Communism is not yet as thoroughly anchored in China as it is in the Soviet Union, and the administrative cadres are still in process of formation, but, barring external disruption, there appears to be no insurmountable political or social impediment to the consolidation of the regime's authority and organization.

Economically, of course, China starts from a considerably lower level than did Russia, and it can be persuasively argued that a Chinese attempt to reproduce the methods, and the rate, of Soviet industrialization and collectivization—which put terrible strains on the Soviet economy in the hectic first five-year plan—might well create such hardships and tensions in China as to lead to a breakdown. This is probably the most vulnerable feature of the Chinese regime, though we really do not know the limit to the burdens a Communist-controlled society can bear without collapsing. We must remember, however, that the Chinese are in a position to profit from the Soviet experience and should be able to avoid unnecessary blunders in means and timing. Moreover, unlike the Soviet Union of the early 1930's, China does not stand alone in making its transformation; it can get material, technical and organizational assistance from the U.S.S.R., though certainly less than would be needed to keep the transition from being a very painful one. It is possible—some observers think it likely—that China's serious economic problems will force its Communist leaders to direct their attentions and energies internally for many years. On the other hand, serious economic crisis, were it to occur, might lead instead to a desperate expansion outward to take over the raw materials and food of Southeast Asia.

In some contrast to the Russian Communists, who came to power through revolution, which they subsequently consolidated through civil war and the repulse of foreign intervention, the Chinese Communists came to power through military success in a civil war following the defeat of Japanese intervention. In consequence, perhaps, the major and immediate Chinese threat to other Asian areas—Korea, Formosa, Southeast Asia—has been from the beginning military as well as revolutionary. In Asian eyes, however, China, as well as Russia, is not just a military or revolutionary power but also the testing ground for a massive political and economic experiment, the results of which may markedly influence the ability of other Asian powers to withstand Communist propaganda, infiltration and frontal attack. As with the

Soviet Union, the Chinese impact abroad is a mingling of ideology, practice and power.

Because the Chinese Communists have only recently come to power, some have felt that their actions in Asia display a rashness and a belligerence which are in contrast to the presumed cautious maturity of the Soviet Union. The conclusion is even drawn that the Soviet leadership may be dismayed by the impulsiveness of its allies and is trying to restrain them. This may be, but we have little reliable evidence to support it. In the last decade the Soviet Union has entered upon, or instigated, a number of incautious enterprises, such as the Berlin blockade and the Korean invasion. For their part the Chinese have by no means shown themselves to be heedlessly reckless. Mao and Chou En-Lai, who are no tyros, have repeatedly demonstrated their ability to proceed warily when "objective conditions" required it. The difference between Chinese and Russian actions is probably to be explained less by the contrast between youth and maturity than by the differences in immediate interests and the condition of neighboring territories. The situation on China's frontiers has been very fluid; the opponent in the Chinese civil war has not been eliminated.

There is perhaps one respect in which the passage of time between the Russian Revolution and the Chinese Communist seizure of power has created a significant difference in outlook. Although the Chinese have shared with all Communists the defensive-minded axiom of "capitalist encirclement," they came to power with the advantage of seeing the Soviet system as a going and expanding concern of some 30 years' standing. Moreover, they were in an area where the European world—seen by them as the forces of "colonialism" and "imperialism"—was already in retreat. Perhaps, as a consequence, the Chinese Communist regime starts from a mood of greater confidence of riding the wave of the future, not merely because of Marxist faith but because the course of recent history provides seeming corroboration. It may be, then, that Chinese Communism has somewhat less of that fear of backsliding, of being unable to make the revolution stick, that one finds in Soviet history and that has had, in the past at least, a marked influence on Soviet attitudes and practices.

In general, though, we may conclude that the Chinese Communist regime is essentially similar to the Soviet, though not a replica and not as fully developed. What of the relations between these two centers of Communist power? One of the fundamental characteristics of Communism has been its centralization of power and control, a characteristic antedating the Stalin era and evident in Lenin's disruption of European Social Democracy. Hence, the appearance of a second, coordinate rather than subordinate center of power would seem to present the Communists with a serious problem.

Unfortunately, this problem has been viewed largely as a debate over the prospects of Chinese "Titoism," a debate that has frequently missed the point. In so far as Titoism is taken to describe a maverick who willfully and intentionally bolts from the herd, the term is misleading. Tito was ousted from the Cominform; it was not the initial intent of Stalin to oust him, nor was it Tito's intent, before the break, to lead a schismatic party.

It seems safe to say that should there be a rupture between the Soviet and Chinese centers of Communist power it would be against the intentions and conscious interests of both parties. First of all there is the powerful ideological bond. The Soviet system remains the model for the Chinese Communists, whatever local variations they may have introduced. The Russians for their part, very possibly profiting from the experience with Tito, have done their best to recognize Mao as an important contributor to Marxism-Leninism.

In the second place, given their ideology, both regimes derive advantages from their close relationship that would be absent were they operating independently or at odds with one another. In terms of pure power interests, without Communist ideological considerations, the value of the connection is not altogether self-evident: as the weaker state, with a long and exposed frontier, China might well look to another great power to balance Russia. But if the Communist view of the world as divided into two opposing camps is accepted, the practical advantages to the partners on the Communist side are obvious: the rear of each is secure, the "imperialist camp" is forced to divide its energies. Moreover, China's opportunities for expansion lie in parts of Asia that are now defended by Western powers. It has a much better prospect of increasing its power territorially if it sides with the Soviet Union against the West than if it did the opposite.

Economically, the advantages are less obvious, and, as we have remarked above, the economic sector is perhaps the weakest feature of the Chinese Communist regime. While the Soviet Union has given assistance, and has exported experts and technicians, China could, in theory, gain much from closer ties with the non-Communist countries. From the Russian point of view the task of modernizing and industrializing China may necessitate a lengthy and considerable drain on Soviet resources. In the light of long-run Communist expectations, however, there is the vision of a vast two-continent Socialist economy, which, once the transition is made, will be a tremendous asset.

Finally, if we ask what could be the advantage, from the Communist perspective, of a voluntary rupture, there appears to be no positive answer. It could only give aid and comfort to the "imperialist enemy," who would certainly not then be more inclined to satisfy China's claim to its "lost" territories or to tolerate revolutions elsewhere in Asia. For the Russians such a rupture would be an incalculable setback in prestige and potential strength.

To say that we cannot anticipate a voluntary rupture between China and Russia does not, however, dispose of the possibility of differences. Certain issues conceivably could separate the two Communist partners, in a sense against their wishes:

First, past relations between China and the Soviet Union have not been smooth, especially in the vital border areas of Manchuria, Mongolia and Sinkiang. These areas remain a potential source of friction.

Second, if China is obliged to rely exclusively upon the Soviet Union for economic assistance, the probable insufficiency of Soviet aid may ultimately cause serious dissatisfaction, if not an open break. Under domestic pressure Mao could well be driven to demand more assistance than the Russians were able or willing to give.

Third, it may prove that the Soviet approach to the agrarian question, which has not been an unqualified success in Russia, may prove so unsuccessful in China as to lead to a major policy crisis.

Fourth, since China is an independent Communist power of considerable magnitude there is the possibility, which some observers have stressed, that Moscow and Peiping might come into conflict over their respective influence in the Communist movements elsewhere in Asia.

Finally, is the fact that from its prerevolutionary inception under Lenin the Soviet-Communist system has never been organized to handle cooperative relations between equals; the world has been made up of enemies to be defeated or handled with cold power politics, masses to be manipulated and subordinates to be directed and controlled. The practice of give-and-take among equals has been conspicuously absent in both domestic and foreign policy. With such a system represented by two independent powers, there is little precedent to rely on for working out differences, for preventing disagreements from degenerating into schisms, for keeping the possessor of relatively superior power from trying to exploit it to the full. Hence there is the possibility that virtually any major issue *could* get out of hand and lead —as it did in the case of Tito—to a break.

Still, we must avoid the fallacy of counting upon deductive argument. In actual fact, the Chinese and the Russians have been remarkably successful, so far as we can tell from very little detailed evidence, in working out agreements on some potentially dangerous issues, such as the Manchurian question, cooperation in the Korean war, the Russian withdrawal from Port Arthur and the granting of credits. While the Communist system may contain its own nemesis when it spreads to more than one controlling authority, we cannot say that it must, or that the very considerable intelligence and insight of the Chinese and Soviet leaders cannot find satisfactory ways of settling their differences or meeting the above-mentioned problems, when the penalty for failure is so great and self-evident.

The question arises whether there is anything the United States might do to increase the chances of a Chinese-Soviet rift. Some have urged that, by adopting a relaxed and unhostile attitude toward the Chinese Communists and by offering them participation in international economic and cultural activities, we might enable them to see the rest of the world in a better light and might even promote an independent Chinese policy. In our view this is a misreading of the Communist outlook. A United States offer, for example, of massive aid to Communist China in expectation of a loosening of Soviet-Chinese ties, would probably be written off simply as "capitalist bribery" and, if the aid were accepted, it might merely reduce the austerity but not the firmness of Soviet-Chinese ties.

It has been suggested, in contrast, that the best way to promote a split is to increase the political and economic isolation of the Chinese Communists as a means to drive them as closely as possible into the Russian embrace, from which in time they may heartily wish to emerge. But how much more closely can they be driven? If such mutual repulsion occurs, it will in all likelihood be for reasons quite beyond our control.

It has also been suggested that the United States might seek actively to exacerbate the areas of potential friction outlined above. But, when we examine them, it does not appear that we are in a position to exert much leverage in promoting territorial disputes, aggravating economic tensions or fostering intraparty rivalry. Moreover, being on the outside and relatively uninformed, we would have little idea whether our endeavors were producing results or were a waste of time and energy.

In brief, there seems to be no particular line of action the United States should follow with the *principal* aim of creating a Chinese-Soviet rift. Our policies may of course have some effect in this direction, but such effects are likely to be marginal, and our policies cannot be embarked upon for this reason alone. Hence we may conclude that for working purposes we should assume that the Chinese Communist regime is internally viable, that it will probably maintain close ties with the Soviet Union and that the Communist bloc will remain a fixture for an indefinite period.

Asian Defense and Construction

With this assumption, what are the requirements for American policy? The primary and indispensable one is that any further expansion of the Communist bloc be resisted. We have discussed the reasons for this requirement in an earlier chapter [2] and need not repeat them for Asia. Whether the expansion is directed against territories to which the Chinese Communists lay claim, whether it takes the form of military or paramilitary action against bordering lands, whether it appears as open or covert assistance to local Communist parties and military formations, whether it is an ideological campaign directed against the many weak social and political sectors of South and Southeast Asia, or whether, finally, it is an ostensibly pacific extension of economic and political influence—the United States must work to check any further encroachments upon the non-Communist world. This is a terribly difficult and complex task involving many kinds of action in many lands, steps to counter sudden emergencies, programs to strengthen and encourage the Asian nations. There is no single solution to the problem of helping non-Communist Asia to defend itself. A brief review of the possible avenues of Communist expansion may give some idea of the scope and seriousness of the job.

With regard to territory claimed by the Chinese Communists, there is by now little debate, in the United States at least, about the need to defend Formosa. The United States is formally committed to it, and the independence of Formosa certainly corresponds with our requirement to resist the further expansion of Communist control over peoples and territories. The military importance of the island has been debated at considerable length, in part because of the rapid changes in weaponry, but on balance it is a significant military asset for the defense of Japan and the Pacific.

It is a moot point whether the Chinese Communist attitude toward the United States would be changed by the gain

[2] See above, p. 86.

of Formosa; they would still be a Communist regime and we the "capitalist encirclers" who somehow had failed to maintain one link in the encirclement. While some of the non-Communist Asian nations have a low regard for the regime on Formosa, it is not to be expected that their will to independence and their resistance to Communist inroads would be heightened by the Communization of Formosa, which could only be interpreted as a strong indication that the Communists were now on the winning side. Our unwillingness to meet this challenge, if it is offered, could undermine the whole structure of our overseas commitments. Finally, and perhaps most significantly, the existence of an independent Formosa presents, if only as a symbol and an aspiration, an alternative to the Chinese Communist regime. It is in the American interest that this symbol be as firm and attractive as possible, both to the Chinese in China and to those scattered through southeastern Asia.

The much debated question whether the defense of Formosa ought to include the defense of the small offshore islands, Quemoy and Matsu, is exactly the type of intricate, potentially explosive local issue which cannot be profitably discussed in a general study. We will only remark that, in the argument between letting the islands go to Communist China and, if necessary, fighting for them, we should not permit ourselves to disregard the fate of the local inhabitants who have been placed in this perilous situation. If it is at all possible, they should neither fall under Communist rule nor be wiped out by bombing, from whatever side.

The defense of Formosa is not solely a military question. The capacity of the island to survive and present itself as an alternative way of Chinese life depends equally on its success in organizing a free society and a viable economy. The issue, nevertheless, has been marked by a clear-cut and easily defined power conflict, resulting from the trial by arms during the civil war, by the fact that both the Communist regime and the Nationalist regime are fully aware of the meaning and intentions of the other, and by the relatively clear territorial demarcation between the two.

In a few other Asian countries the issue is equally sharply drawn, notably in Korea, another area of previous fighting and of territorial demarcation resulting from that fighting. In such areas the initial function of defense is to secure them from further overt military aggression and to build up the necessary economic and administrative backing. This is a very difficult job but an obvious one.

On the whole, however, the problem of Asian defense is much less simply described, and because of this there has been a tendency to present it in the form of a debate between military aid and economic aid, between defense and construction. This is unfortunate if it suggests that these are alternatives. Certainly from the point of view of Communism, with its peculiar unitary approach to philosophy and politics, ideological, economic and military expansion are but differing modes of the same impulse, which is to transform the world.

The danger is a double one. It would be a fruitless undertaking to work to create a democratic society with a vigorous economy if it could not then be defended militarily; it is even doubtful that such a society could be created under the shadow of an impending invasion which it felt powerless to resist. On the other hand, stress upon creating areas of military strength, to the exclusion of all other considerations, would inhibit a society's ability to develop a sound economic and political structure (or even to support its own military establishment). But, while it is easy enough to conclude that both military strength and nonmilitary development are required, we are faced with the task of establishing priorities for the allocation of attention, resources and energy. What should be the proportions of military, economic and other assistance? Which should come first, and at what rate?

It is impossible to arrive at any definite or fixed answer to these questions. We are dealing with an opponent who may revise and alter his tactics in order to strike at the weakest point. There is the distinct possibility, for example, that, were we to devote our efforts solely to building up military strongpoints in Asia, our endeavors would never be put to the test. The opponent might then rely on ideological infiltration and subversion; he might even bide his time, waiting until domestic crises undermined the will to resist. Had this military strength not been created, however, an overt attack might, in the meantime, have forced the victim into the Communist camp. As in any competitive situation, the problem of allocating resources is constantly changing, depending in part upon relative local needs and in part on the opponent's immediate intentions and tactics.

It is said, not only in the countries of Asia but also in the United States, that American aid in the last few years has overemphasized military assistance, that in our preoccupation with a defense line we have lost sight of the urgent and continuing need for economic, social and political construction. In so far as this criticism points up a tendency to take an exclusively military view, it is probably justified. That some of the Asian countries have this belief is itself a political fact we must take into account. Nevertheless, one can hardly say that the military efforts are adequate or sufficient, that Asia is overinsured against military invasion. In terms of relative capabilities, the non-Communist countries of Asia, which extend along a vast arc, are still at a great disadvantage against the military strength of Communist China backed by its Soviet ally. We should not have the delusion that a switch in emphasis to economic and social betterment would somehow serve to *complete* the shoring up of these areas.

The independent existence of the nations of Asia, especially those of Southeast Asia, is at stake; unless that is preserved, the very opportunity to improve the social and economic situation will be lost. In this sense, power—power of immediate survival—has a necessary priority over health. To take the case of South Vietnam, efforts to assist in its economic and political reconstruction could easily be negated unless the United States were willing to support the new regime, diplomatically and militarily, in the pressing and immediate task of preventing its being engulfed by Vietminh, whether by military invasion or by elections (scheduled for the whole of Vietnam in 1956) in which rigged and unfree balloting in the north would give a preponderance to the Communists. Unless we give assistance in both directions—immediate support and long-run aid—we may witness a disaster which would extend far beyond the boundaries of Vietnam itself.

To turn to the question of military power. Since the defeat of Japan in 1945 no concentration of Asian strength has been nearly equivalent to that of China. The United States has been obliged to try to make up the difference and has in fact become a major military power in Asia. But given the distance of the Far East from the United States, and the global extent of American commitments, it would be highly desirable if there were centers of greater strength closer to the scene. This is particularly true when we consider recent and probable developments in weaponry. So long as the United States was in exclusive possession of the atomic bomb and of long-range means of its delivery, it was possible in theory to use the threat of this power rather than the build-up of local Asian strength as the means of checking Communist aggression. Politically, of course, this could be a difficult method, since it might involve the employment of nuclear power against nonmilitary targets in some very ambiguous situations. As we have argued in an earlier chapter, however, with the advent of nuclear parity this response will be less feasible. Instead, we must develop the ability to meet and defeat attacks by methods appropriate to the form and intensity of attack. The aim, of course, is not to invite the Communists to engage in hit-and-run local conflicts, which they can initiate or drop at their pleasure, without great cost or risk, but rather to make such enterprises so costly to them that they will see no opportunities for advances on the cheap. To what extent can Asian governments achieve this aim and to what extent must it remain an American responsibility?

It is scarcely to be expected that the United States should assume the burden singlehanded. Local strength is also necessary. It may be that in time Japan and India, the two major non-Communist Asian powers, will be in a position not only to defend themselves but to contribute to the security of the arc of lands between them. It seems unlikely, however, that either can assume a role of leadership for the non-Communist powers in the area. Japan, because of its war record, is viewed with considerable mistrust by a number of countries, and India, so far, has shown little inclination to assume the burden of such responsibility. The most we can hope for in the near future is that India and Japan will be largely able to defend themselves. In the short run, therefore, it is indispensable that the Southeast Asian countries be militarily strengthened as much as possible. A step in this direction has been made with the creation of SEATO, but SEATO does not include all the nations in the area and it is still largely dependent on the power of non-Asian states, a political as well as a military disadvantage of considerable importance.

Southeast Asia is also exposed to the tactics of subversion and guerrilla warfare, which the Communists have employed in preference to, or as a preparation for, overt military assault. The United States alone cannot meet such tactics. While it can provide assistance, this type of attack must be met by local police and military forces, enjoying the cooperation and confidence of the inhabitants.

Meeting subversion and guerrilla warfare involves a series of measures greatly increasing the instruments of power in the hands of those in command of the local Asian forces. This power could, of course, be misused for self-seeking purposes, especially in countries where the relationship between power, authority and responsibility is in the process of rapid change and reformulation. Since the beginning of American assistance to Greece and Turkey in 1947, however, there has been perhaps an excessive tendency to argue that regimes which, from one point of view or another, appeared unrepresentative or in need of reforming could not be expected to survive. But the experience of the last decade would appear to show that these regimes, unless they have had their backs broken by war or invasion, have much greater vitality than certain features of their domestic performance might suggest. The relationship between reform and power of survival is not one of simple correlation. The stronger case for reform proceeds from the fact that the conflict between the Communist and non-Communist worlds is ideological and moral as well as military. The progress of mutual support and mutual respect within what we commonly call the free world depends on the extent to which the area of freedom among the non-Communist nations can be expanded. For this reason primarily the United States has a real stake in the advance of democracy in Asia.

Although the job of countering subversion and guerrilla warfare is a difficult one, there may be some compensations should the Communists increase these activities. By and large the Asians, and this seems to be particularly true of India and Burma, have not been impressed by the American concern about overt military conflict with the Communists. Despite the Korean war, they are not inclined to accept our view of the Communists as militarily expansive. Because of their own experience, however, they may come to be more sensitive to the problem of local subversion and infiltration, at least in areas where Communist activities can no longer be excused as an expression of anticolonialism or pent-up nationalism. Burma, for example, is quite sensitive to events in Laos and Cambodia; aggressive Communist movements in these areas might create a strong Burmese reaction.

As for the equally important, but more protracted, task of assisting in promoting the health and well-being of the non-Communist Asian countries, the general purposes which should inform American policy have been outlined in Chapters VI and VII dealing with Economic Policy and Social Policy. In no place in the world are these policies more indispensable for the maintenance of lasting independence. Without attempting detailed recommendations, we would emphasize the following considerations for American social and economic policy in Asia.

First, it is necessary to grasp the enormous differences of conditions and problems in the various countries of that continent. Japan, for example, is an industrial power of major importance, as its performance in the Second World War indicated only too clearly. Its economic problems are, in the main, those of an advanced economy: access to markets and raw materials, terms of trade, economic relations with other nations. Only by maintaining its progress as an industrial power can Japan have any hope of coping with a dense population on its small island territory. At the same time the Japanese social and political structure is an altogether unique mingling of the indigenous and the Western, including the Western features introduced in a rush during the Occupation. It would be hard to predict Japan's social and political evolution or to prescribe actions the United States should take in assisting Japan so that its very considerable capabilities and talents may strengthen the freedom and independence of Japan itself and of eastern Asia. The general direction of our efforts, however, is clear. If Japan is not to lapse into uneasy neutralism, or seek a unilateral solution of its problems, as it did in the 1930's, or gravitate toward the Communist bloc for want of an alternative, the United States must do all it can to establish conditions under which Japan sees promise of a reasonable future in the free world, a free world in which it has an important part to play and in which it can hope to surmount its very serious economic difficulties.

India, with its tremendous manpower, its resources and its location is of equally great importance for the future of Asia. But its problems are quite different from those of Japan. Economically it is far less advanced; its great domestic challenge is to gather sufficient economic momentum to achieve a self-sustaining growth that can take care of its enormous and very poor population. It is often said, but is no less true for that, that the eyes of a great part of the world are on China and India and on the relative success these two vast nations have in meeting the demands of the industrial age. While India, like Japan, also has a confused mingling of Western and native elements in its social and political organization, it may also have, in the Gandhian heritage, a spiritual dynamism of its own, neither Western nor Communist, but of great creativity. Some indeed feel that this could be India's great contribution to the contemporary world. We are too close to tell, but it is evident that it is a force that may be of great value in sustaining and fortifying India —if it is able to meet the formidable demands of the times.

Then, there are the many smaller states lying between Japan and India, on China's periphery. Formerly colonies (except for Thailand), they were the object of Japanese expansion in the Second World War and have (except for Malaya) achieved independence only in the last decade. Possessed of important raw materials, and of areas with food surpluses, they offer a valuable prize to an aggressive power.

They are economically underdeveloped and largely lacking in internal or external unity. Non-Communist Southeast Asia, together with areas in the Middle East, is the most acutely vulnerable and hard-pressed sector of the free world. Here, perhaps more than anywhere else, social and economic assistance may spell the difference between disintegration and independence.

In an area of such weakness, where there is very little established strength to be relied upon, where the foundations of the new national structures have not yet hardened and where disaster may strike in any number of ways, there is no substitute in American policy for agility and flexibility. At one point we may confront the problem of helping to deal with a Burmese rice surplus, at another of deciding how best to carry on relations with a government in peril of being taken over by the local Communists, at a third of helping to stabilize rubber prices, at a fourth of trying to suggest a rational program for agricultural development. Some of the problems require steady attention over a long time. With others we may appear like a person rushing about setting pails under a leaky roof. While the pails are necessary to prevent flooding, we should also try to help patch the roof.

The dual task of assisting to create a minimum of military security in Asia and of promoting economic and social well-being would be difficult under the best of circumstances and even if the states of the area and the United States were in general agreement on the nature of the threat. Unhappily, that basic agreement is not present in all cases. In our policies we face a strong current of neutralism, which is closely related to the colonial background in Asia.

The strongest emotional and political force in Asia is anticolonialism, which encompasses not only the narrower experience of former colonial status and lack of self-rule, but also, if to some extent fortuitously, fear of the industrial economies and a mistrust of Europeans and the white race generally. That this mood offers a fertile ground for Communism is evident from the emphasis the Communists themselves have given to the colonial issue. Indeed, considering the extent of the sentiment, and the manifold reasons for its intensity, the United States is fortunate in having only neutralism to deal with and not a continent lined up solidly against the West. To some extent this suggests a weakness in Communism, but it may also reflect an awareness in Asia that, while the European impact brought its ills, it also brought benefits, including the possibility of overcoming some of the ills it introduced.

Nevertheless, very many Asians have an active sense of nonalignment with respect to the issues dividing the Soviet bloc and the Western powers. In part this results from a feeling of weakness, of need to buy time, and from an understandable preoccupation with domestic affairs. It is only natural that regimes which are still consolidating and organizing themselves should desire to avoid "foreign entanglements." But Asian neutralism, especially as embodied in its Indian spokesmen, goes beyond this. Despite the fact that in their domestic politics Asian leaders have frequently come in sharp conflict with the local Communist parties, and despite the fact, too, that on many important questions Asian countries and the United States see eye to eye—as is evident from a comparison of their voting records in the United Nations—Communism is seen by many Asians as a response, albeit a dangerous one at times, to inequities and injustices in the international order which brought it into existence and caused its spread among the nations.

Anticolonialism clearly provides much of the conviction supporting this view, even though, as some Asians have pointed out, the formulations in the main are taken over from non-Communist Western writers who have advanced the same idea. From this strong conviction follows the disconcerting fact that while Asian neutralists may not regard the United States as an active threat to Asian independence, and while we might expect them to try to defend themselves in the event of overt Communist attack, their basic view of what is wrong with the international situation tends to parallel Communist lines of argumentation. As a consequence, there is an inclination to employ a double standard of judgment: to excuse or find mitigating explanations for Communist misdeeds but to regard American or European actions critically and often censoriously.

What should the United States do about it? In so far as

neutralism stands for more than neutrality, and advances an interpretation of the international scene in which American efforts to organize mutual security arrangements in the non-Communist world are regarded as ill-advised, we cannot accept its premises without making nonsense of our own foreign policy. We should not be insensitive to matters directly affecting Asian neutrals—and in areas of tense relations, such as those between India and Pakistan or between Israel and the Arab states, the problem of military aid and cooperation is a very delicate and dangerous one—but even so we could not permit our view of the requirements for Asian security to be reduced to the level of the interpretation of the national interest held by one country. At the same time we must, of course, recognize that the general security of any area depends upon preventing serious rifts within it.

What of India itself and aid to that country? The question of military assistance has not arisen, since India has not wished such aid from the United States. As for economic and technical assistance, the question is frequently asked why the United States should extend aid to a country which is often so opposed to our policy in Asia. Under present circumstances, it is true, we may be unable to achieve a full reciprocity of interests and responsibilities with India. Nevertheless, it is our interest, as it is India's, that the subcontinent not fall to Communism or otherwise suffer political or economic disintegration. If by withholding aid we were to contribute, even in a small degree, to the collapse of the present Indian regime, the outcome would not be to the American advantage. Hence we do have a clear, unambiguous interest in assisting India. This assistance cannot be used as a lever to pry Indian policy from its present course, but if we can have hope that India, during an extremely difficult period of establishment and consolidation, will defend itself, we may be reasonably well satisfied. Meanwhile we should not forgo discussing the major issues with the Indians and finding, where possible, areas of common interest.

No matter how the United States works with the Asian nations, singly or collectively, the problem of neutralism will continue to plague us so long as the residues of "colonialism," in Asia, Africa or elsewhere, can be taken as an attribute of the Western powers, to be weighed against the conduct of the Communist bloc.

While the record of the United States itself is a good one (witness the independence of the Philippines), by and large the United States has teetered uncomfortably between our long-standing national sympathy with the aspirations of subject peoples—aspirations which we popularly identify with our own history—and the need we feel to work in harmony with our European allies—a feeling reinforced by our growing realization that the independence of a politically and economically backward area is not simply a matter of signing a declaration. In the years since the Second World War we have suffered from our uncertainty and our temporizing; we have not gained much credit among the colonial peoples, who tend to interpret our perplexities as a sign that we are, in effect, the major prop of colonialism.

It may be that we must meet and wrestle with each colonial crisis as it arises. Still, certain broad conclusions are possible. The United States must be prepared to harmonize its policies with the growing tide of anticolonialism which is probably as predictable and inexorable a movement, as it moves on from colony to colony, as any human event can be. At the same time, it is indispensable that our actions and policies support European as well as Asian security against Communist aggression. Given the increasing evidence that a colony which can be held only by repeated "pacification" should be written off as a dependency, the European powers in their own interest—as Britain has successfully demonstrated in a number of areas—must also move with the tide. Hence, the desirable goal from the point of view of the United States, and of the European colonial powers as well, is either a) to make it attractive to the colony to preserve its connections with the home country, or b) to release the connection in such a way, and in sufficient time, that the colony will be a friend and not an enemy of the home country. That it can be done is illustrated by the experience with the Philippines and India. It remains to be seen whether it can be realized elsewhere without further unhappy experiences like that of Vietnam.

Policy toward Communist China

When we consider the magnitude of the problem of maintaining the viability and independence of the non-Communist nations of Asia, a problem that is of immediate urgency and yet promises to be very protracted, it is difficult to avoid the conclusion that the interminable, and often bitter, debates over American recognition of the Chinese Communist regime and over Chinese representation in the UN have been something of a distraction. If Communist China were given a seat in the UN or if the United States extended recognition, the basic conflict dividing the Communist and non-Communist worlds would continue unabated. If the United States continues to refuse recognition and if the UN seat is denied the Communists, we will not have advanced a step toward replacing Communist power in China by something else.

Too frequently the debate has been taken to mean a choice between the alternatives of forcibly attempting to overthrow the Communist regime and of letting the Communists have their will on Formosa. But this is an impossible pair of alternatives; neither is acceptable. We cannot initiate, or support, a policy which may provoke general war, nor can we sacrifice the independence of Formosa.

We would not, of course, attempt the *tour de force* of arguing that recognition and UN representation are matters of no concern. Issues creating such heat and controversy are of importance, and when meanings are read into them the meanings are there whether we think they belong or not. We may try, however, to reformulate these issues so as to make them somewhat more manageable.

The problems posed by Communist China are similar in several respects to those raised by the Eastern European satellites. Both are areas of recent, post-1945 Communist expansion. Both are areas for which the United States, during the Second World War, had come to assume definite responsibilities. The Communization of these lands was not just an unpleasant and dangerous event in international affairs; it was quite explicitly a major defeat for American policy, more so, for example, than the Communization of Russia a generation earlier. In addition, the world had, in the course of this generation, become used, if not wholly reconciled, to having the Soviet Union on the scene; one of the underlying issues regarding the Chinese Communists and the Eastern European satellites has been the clash between those who fear and oppose and those who feel it necessary to accept the prospect that the mere passage of time will promote acquiescence in the existence of these new Communist regimes.

There are also differences between Communist China and the Eastern European satellites, differences which explain, in part at least, the considerably sharper dispute concerning United States policy toward Communist China. While the significance of Soviet aid has been debated, the Chinese Communists came to power largely on their own, as clear victors—whatever the means they used and whatever the shortcomings of Chinese Nationalist or American policy—in a hard-fought civil war. The satellite regimes, with the exception of the Yugoslav, were very obviously foisted upon the Eastern European nations by the U.S.S.R. At the same time, the Chinese Communist victory, while far more real, is in a sense less complete, because an alternative Chinese regime remains in acknowledged existence on Formosa, whereas the United States has recognized the satellite governments in Eastern Europe. The natural, if odd, result has been that while opinion in the United States appears to be prepared both to continue recognition of the satellites (and in fact has accepted their admission to the UN) and to aim at the eventual withdrawal of Communist power, in the case of China there is a sharp antithesis: recognition is taken to mean acquiescence, hope for withdrawal is taken to entail nonrecognition.

This difference is reinforced by a difference of general power relations in Europe and Asia. On the one hand, the security of non-Communist Asia is more precarious than that of non-Communist Europe. The acute sense of the weakness of the Asian periphery contributes powerfully to the view that the non-Communist world has more to gain than to lose in trying to stabilize the situation in Asia, to reach some kind of working arrangement with the Chinese Communists.

On the other hand, behind apprehensions about the Chinese Communists there lies also the fear that, once the vast manpower and resources of that great land are mobilized, they will constitute a force of incalculable magnitude, making the Asian situation even more precarious. This fear reinforces the view that Communist power in China simply must not be permitted to consolidate itself.

For these reasons the goal we have expressed above regarding the peoples of East Central Europe—to give them a sense of community with the world which has been shut off from them and to keep alive, or awaken, the belief that Communism is not the only gate to the future, not the world's destiny—may appear either as inadequate or as something we cannot afford in the case of China.

With respect to more active goals, there have been proposals in the direction of active disruption, arming resistance movements and the like. But, as we have remarked already, such activities are most effective, perhaps only effective, in conjunction with military operations, as a part of a hot war—which we do not intend to initiate or provoke. Special operations alone are no substitute for military operations. Although the Communists themselves go in for these activities, we have yet to experience a case in which such methods, by themselves and without the background of real or threatening military force, have achieved productive results.

Somewhat less violent are the proposals for economic warfare. Again, it is problematic whether the cessation of trade with the Soviet bloc would have a decisive effect upon China, either in undermining the regime or in forcing it to make concessions. The results are likely to be marginal and would have to be balanced against costs to the free world—the relative economic gains and losses, the costs of administration and supervision and, in the case of a real blockade, the risks of conflict with the Communists and with non-Communist powers desiring to trade with the Communist bloc. It might be that a rational calculation of these costs would in fact indicate the desirability of trade restrictions, but we should have to be sure that the over-all effect would not be to diminish the comparative strength and cohesion of the non-Communist world.

In general, we conclude that for China, as for the Soviet bloc as a whole, we see no way of forcing a showdown that would not carry with it the high risk of precipitating a conflict that could expand without limit.

The other goal, that of trying to reach some kind of working arrangement, may be approached in two different ways. The first would be directed toward a stabilization of the *de facto* frontiers between the Communist bloc in Asia and the non-Communist areas, a stabilization achieved if possible by mutual arrangement, perhaps with agreed-upon neutralized areas or strips along the contested frontiers. This approach would, in effect, make do with two Chinas, two Koreas and two Vietnams, though such a division could hardly be established *de jure* without the concurrence—which is unlikely—of the opposing Asian parties concerned. The present territorial division, for all its ambiguities, would in this case be prolonged indefinitely as the only workable situation in the absence of profound changes within Communist China. If we can keep border conflicts from erupting, we have more than enough to do to strengthen our side of the line.

An alternative to this approach would be to work for a somewhat more far-reaching and definitive Asian settlement through mutual concessions, for example, the free unification of Korea and Vietnam, the *de jure* recognition of Communist China and Formosa as two independent states, the presence of both in the UN, the neutralization or evacuation of the offshore islands. There are a number of ways these and possibly other aims could be combined, an exercise which we need not go into here. In general, however, any real change would rest on trading a retraction of Communist influence from beyond the mainland frontiers of China in return for a normalization of diplomatic relations and an international agreement concerning the UN. But, as we have found in discussing negotiations on Germany, it is hard to persuade the Communists to trade real estate in their control for such intangibles as recognition and UN representation, which they presumably think theirs of right and likely to come about anyway.

It must be confessed that none of these proposed lines of action is particularly promising, a fact that has certainly contributed to the brittleness of the debates on recognition and UN representation: neither side sees anything useful resulting from the other's position. Those who feel that the United States should not recognize the Communist regime, or support the seating in the UN of a power which has flagrantly violated the basic qualifications for membership, are presented with no convincing evidence of any positive benefits flowing from the contrary course of action. Conversely, those who feel that the tide runs clearly toward the seating of the Chinese Communists in the UN (especially with the recent admission of other Communist powers and the continuing exclusion of Japan) and that we face losing both a pragmatic and a moral battle, in addition to being at odds with a number of our major allies, find no positive gains to be obtained from remaining set in our present course. In a way, both sides are right—at the moment in Asia it is not a matter of our gaining an advantage, but of avoiding the worst disadvantages, a fact we should be prepared to face.

At the same time, the debate should not be seen in terms of principle vs. expediency. When one deals with institutions, inevitably the product of conflicting interests and purposes, principle and expediency are completely intertwined. Some who find it unprincipled to recognize Communist China find it expedient to continue recognizing the Soviet Union, which is just as obnoxious a state and a good deal more dangerous at the moment. The question, in our view, is rather how to make the best use of such instruments as diplomatic recognition or nonrecognition and UN membership, in furthering our proper goals. Among these goals we would include as relevant to our present problem the need to prevent the further advance of Communism in Asia, our human obligation to the Chinese people and the necessity of maintaining as best we can the cohesion of the non-Communist world. All these goals are important, but we cannot predict which at any one time may be in the most immediate need of support.

Hence, we see no absolute answer, either to the question of recognition or to the separate, if related, one of UN representation. They can be answered only in a given setting. With regard to the former, recognition alone need not mean a change of attitude regarding a regime. When the Soviet Union recognized the Bonn Republic the United States did not draw the conclusion that the Soviets had thereby given up any intention of subverting West Germany. Nor is it enough to say that this only proves the unscrupulousness of Soviet foreign policy. The unscrupulousness lies not in the decision to recognize or not, but in the final aim—to subvert. Moreover, the fact that the United States did, whether wisely or unwisely, recognize the satellite regimes of Eastern Europe should not imply, nor has the United States government admitted the implication, a renunciation of our hopes for an eventual retraction of Communist power from that area.

In our judgment, however, so long as illusions remain that recognition will achieve "normalcy" in our relations with the Communist powers, so long as recognition reinforces the impression, whether it should or not, that Communist China is the power of the future for Asia, recognition would not be in the American interest. In other words, to put it as a paradox: the advisability of the United States extending diplomatic recognition to Communist China is probably in inverse ratio to the active demand for it. If recognition were a matter of indifference, a purely formal act which attracted little interest, it might be expedient to grant it, though probably not very useful. We should, perhaps, emphasize again that, whatever the decision on recognition, it must not entail, directly, by implication or by outcome, the loss of Formosan independence.

While American recognition of Communist China would, in all likelihood, have the automatic consequence of leading to a UN seat for the Chinese Communists (though not the expulsion of the Chinese Nationalists), the reverse is not true. It is quite possible for Communist China to be seated even in the absence of American recognition. UN representation is not just a decision for the United States to make; it involves the views of a great many nations as well as the status of the UN itself. Among other things there is the question whether the gain to the UN through having universal representation is more than offset by the presence in it of another Communist power whose actions have not been in accord with the Charter.

Obviously, an American decision on this matter must take account of our relations with other nations: the Japanese, who thus far have been denied membership and who may press vigorously for any formula which may also bring them into the UN; other Asian powers, some of whom see Communist China, incorrectly in our view, as part of the new independence of their continent; and our European allies, many of whom have always regarded the UN, whatever the terms of the Charter, as a forum rather than as an assembly of peace-loving nations. Nor can a decision neglect the tactical aspects of the problem, especially the political cost of trying to block—if it should come to that—the wishes of a majority of UN members. This cost could be great even if the United States gained its point, and much greater if it failed.

Any judgment on this question would have to be tentative, since so much would depend on the particular circumstances of the decision. But whatever the decision—and we are not here attempting to make a recommendation—it is imperative that the United States vigorously oppose any arrangement which would give the Chinese Communists a favored position in the UN over the Nationalist regime or which would give them a basis for justifying a subsequent conquest of Formosa. As for the fear that we might, by our actions regarding recognition or UN representation, write off the Chinese people and consign them to their present regime, in the long run this can be allayed only by measures much more vigorous and creative than either withholding or granting recognition: trying in all possible ways to keep in contact with the Chinese people and at the same time building a sense of security and confidence in the non-Communist world, so that all free people could feel capable of concern for those caught under Communist domination.

It may make all the difference in the world if the peoples of Asia can come to have enough confidence in the future of the free world and of their own societies that they regard the Chinese people as victims needing fellowship and support rather than as the possible vanguard, willing or unwilling, of the world to be. In short, there is no substitute for a healthy and confident periphery in turning the balance in Asia, and it is toward this periphery (including Formosa) that our actions must be primarily directed.

CHAPTER XII
THE OUTLOOK

Our subject is a forbidding one. It is not the less forbidding for the changes that have occurred in the three years since Stalin's death. The surface of international relations has altered somewhat. The style of Soviet behavior is generally less harsh. But we still face two perils, either of which is capable of destroying our civilization: the radical, intransigent hostility of the Soviet Communist outlook and intentions, and the fantastic growth of man's destructive power, which continues to expand apace.

Nor are any certain or final solutions in sight. The presence of the one peril vastly increases the difficulty of mastering the other. Any attempt to precipitate a solution promises only to assure disaster. Above all, we must realize that it is not within the power of the United States alone to bring an end to these dangers, though it could, through stupid actions, guarantee the victory of Soviet Communism or an atomic conflagration.

This does not mean that these problems are out of human control, that we must echo Faust's despair, "Time runs, the clock will strike . . ." We find no inevitability about the triumph of the Soviet Union or the coming of thermonuclear war. More than that, we believe that there are ways whereby we may hope to avert the one without backing into the other. If our trust must lie in an uncertain future, it is not as a frantic effort to buy time, to stall off an inescapable foreclosure. Rather, we believe that the future is yet to be created and that our free actions are a part of that creation.

If we have this measure of effective freedom, it must not be wasted or abused or we shall surely stumble into disaster. There are things we must do and must not do if we are to keep the future open. At the heart of our national policy must be an unqualified determination not to permit Communist world domination. Hence we must have, and if necessary be prepared to use, the capabilities sufficient to break any such attempt. At the same time we must develop these capabilities so as to make any Soviet effort to advance by means of naked power progressively more dangerous to the Communists, and their effort to use concealed or indirect forms of power progressively less rewarding. Our aim, then, must be to give the Soviet leaders powerful and convincing reasons not to play with fire and yet oblige them to work at a disadvantage if they resort to subtler tactics. There are two obvious reasons for this. The first is that we should do our best to keep the conflict from erupting, or degenerating, into a thermonuclear war, to keep the area of active engagement as far from the upper limits of violence as we can. This means having the ability to inflict a damaging defeat at whatever level of force the Soviets may contemplate trying. Historically, to be sure, antagonisms have shown a tendency to build up to increasing pitches of violence as each side strove to outmatch the other. The present fact, however, that the ultimate in physical violence is always close at hand—mutual destruction through thermonuclear exchange—may, paradoxically, provide a means to reverse this tendency, to draw the conflict away from open violence.

The second reason is that the farther from naked violence the issues are fought, the more can constructive rather than destructive elements play a part in determining the outcome. If, as an extreme example, the Soviet effort to expand were in fact, and of necessity, limited to building steel mills in India and promoting good-will tours, and if our sole task were to see to it that the recipients of such favors, while benefiting from the material advantages, were not subverted, made dependent or otherwise brought into the Soviet orbit, such a contest would be greatly preferable to fending off armed attacks, civil uprisings or other violent forms of expansion. It would probably be misleading to call the conflict in this form, if it ever came to be that alone, "peaceful" or "competitive" coexistence. The stakes would remain just as great, the Soviet purposes just as deadly, and the competition certainly not one of mutual emulation or of limited rivalry based on any ground rules. It would be "antagonistic coexistence," if such a term has any use. But in form, at least, it would be far less destructive, provided, of course, that the

United States were able to meet the challenge on this level and did not forget the perils and issues involved in the struggle.

If the United States is to have a policy capable of such modulation, one which can carry out the twofold task of deterring the Soviet Union from open attack and of besting it on other levels of engagement, it must develop the appropriate instruments and means. These have been discussed and explained in earlier chapters and here need only be listed in review:

1. We must maintain the capacity for instant and full retaliation against thermonuclear attack. This is a necessary precondition for survival. It will be expensive, and it may never be used—to which we could only say "Thank God"—but it would not be for that reason a waste of effort. It is an indispensable form of insurance.

2. We must maintain a balanced military force capable of defeating a variety of attacks, under a variety of conditions, with the least danger of forcing recourse, either by our opponents or ourselves, to general thermonuclear fighting.

3. The more we reduce our vulnerability—through defense and warning, dispersal, stockpiling and advance organization for emergencies—the more we reduce the possibility of a surprise attack and increase our ability to carry on a war if we are attacked. In this sphere we have not done nearly enough.

4. We must maintain (and, in some fields, regain) our ability to keep ahead in the continuing technological race. This involves, among other things, a distinct improvement in the training and mobilization of our most talented youths, in the field of science to be sure, but also in the general discipline of the intellect. This will take time and reaches far into our present educational system.

5. Since we are concerned with preventing the outbreak of an atomic war, we must constantly explore the possibilities of arms control and disarmament. We must always, however, remember the role of arms in making our survival possible, and realize that the world cannot unlearn the deadly knowledge it has acquired in the last decade. We must real-

ize, too, that partial disarmament, rather than being a step away from the danger of war, might introduce a perilous element of uncertainty. In other words, we must regard arms in their broadest sense—the possession of the full range of physical capabilities—as being largely coextensive with the whole of the conflict between the Soviet bloc and the alliance of free nations, and not as a separate question to be handled apart from it.

6. Since the chances of Soviet world hegemony are improved with every increase of territory under Communist control, everything should be done which makes it harder for the Soviet Union, or its bloc, to advance.

7. To resist further Communist advance the United States must maintain its overseas commitments and develop them to the best advantage. The value of alliances, however, is not confined to bolstering overseas areas which are threatened; alliances can also be an important source of military, economic and political strength. Above all, if we are successful in our efforts to keep the conflict away from the ultraviolent end of the spectrum, the value of cohesive organizations in the non-Communist world, dedicated to defense and to mutual support in creating a free society, is of highest importance. For this reason we must promote, so far as it is within our power, cooperation and mutual confidence among our allies in Europe and in Asia. In a period in which diplomatic maneuver may be of decisive importance in determining the course of events, it is necessary to check the Soviet effort to split alliances and isolate the United States. There is little question, for example, that disrupting NATO and forcing the United States out of Europe would be a major Soviet victory.

8. In this area of nonmilitary sparring, the United Nations can play an important role, not as a tool of American policy alone—which it is not—but as a clearing house and agency for many types of international cooperation which strengthen and support the nations of the free world. This function is useful despite the presence in the UN of the Communist powers.

9. With regard to the uncommitted and neutral powers, it is in the American interest that they possess the strength and health to keep free of Communist control; we can pro-

vide important assistance to that end. It is also in our interest for them to come to see an advantage in participating in organizations in the non-Communist world, including organizations for defense. For a variety of reasons, however, they may be unable, or unwilling, to go beyond economic and social cooperation. It is not our purpose to impose any penalty, beyond the penalty inherent in their neutrality, namely, the danger that they, as well as the rest of the non-Communist world, are rendered that much more vulnerable to Soviet expansion.

10. Efforts to strengthen the non-Communist world must be accompanied and supported by economic growth, in the United States and elsewhere. While in the extreme case of a thermonuclear assault economic potential might be obliterated, in all the other forms which the conflict may take a continued and, in many areas, a quickened rate of economic growth is indispensable as a support for military expenditures, to provide capital and consumer goods, and most particularly as evidence that the non-Communist world is not stagnating and is capable of meeting the fierce compulsive growth of the Soviet economies.

11. An important factor in the continued expansion of free economies is the free interchange of goods between countries. The case for larger free-trade areas and for a reduction of restrictions and barriers is a sound one. These reductions would not be a cure-all and would certainly not remove all the economic ills of the non-Communist economies, but they would help.

12. With regard to the so-called underdeveloped countries, additional measures are necessary to assist them in achieving self-sustaining economic growth. They require foreign assistance intelligently applied. While their capacity to absorb capital usefully is limited, and varies widely from country to country, the capacity is in most instances greater than the amounts currently available, domestically or from abroad. There is a good case for increasing assistance. Military and economic aid are not wholly distinct from one another, but we should distinguish between emergency aid of a military or economic sort to avert imminent catastrophe (e.g., in Southeast Asia) and the long-run need for encourag-

ing economic growth in areas not in immediate peril. We should certainly not penalize by neglect those nations which are demonstrating the ability to create a healthy political and economic order.

13. Economic and military strength cannot secure the free world unless backed by peoples' confidence and trust in the societies of which they are members. The field of social policy, while it may prove to be the most decisive of all, is also the most difficult to deal with, or even to comprehend, for the reason that social change, the evolution of new cultural and organizational patterns, is not something to be made to order or created by imitation. Each society has its own physiognomy. We want each to be as vigorous and self-reliant as possible, but not replicas of our own, or jerry-built affairs—that is the Communists' role. Our role should be one of assistance and advice in removing obstacles and pointing out dangers which promise to block the free development of these societies. It is, of course, our belief that democracy is a goal to be aimed at, but the democratic spirit can be clothed in many institutional garments, appropriate to different cultures and traditions. If a non-Communist state is undemocratic, it is not our function to penalize it by undermining its ability to remain independent. But we should consistently work for the spread, not the retraction, of political freedom, for the recognition of the individual as a person of infinite worth and not a "thing with one face."

14. There is no question that all these proposed aims will be expensive and that the task of applying them will require some closely considered decisions on priorities and allocations. In general, however, we would stress most strongly that the United States is far from the ceiling of its economic potentialities. We emphatically do not believe that this is any time to slacken our efforts, to cut back our expenditures in this broadly conceived field of defense, either at home or abroad. We see no convincing reason to believe that a continuation or even an increase of these efforts would damage the ability of the national economy to grow or entail any drastic domestic sacrifices. Even if personal sacrifices proved necessary, however—and one can certainly not promise that they never will be—we must remember that these actions are

not being suggested as a diversion. Together they form a set of requirements which must be met if we are to reduce to a minimum the chances of Communist victory or global war. The stakes are fearfully great.

The lines of action proposed above amount to no easy program. Working them out and applying them will be a tremendous undertaking. Admittedly, they are not novel suggestions; all of them have been in the air and under discussion and debate. Many indeed have been a part of United States policy in recent years. This we consider an advantage rather than a disadvantage; it suggests that on the whole the American people and their government have been working in the right directions. In these times of strain and frustration it is tempting to think that complete and final solutions can be found if only we are clever enough. We should not indulge in such fantasies. There is no easy answer, just a great deal of hard work over what may be a long period of time.

The conclusions we have reached thus far largely concern American actions in the non-Communist parts of the world. We believe that this is, in fact, the area where there is the most to be done that can be done. We cannot, however, neglect the problem of direct Soviet-American relations, unpromising though it may appear to be. Any ultimate resolution of the present crisis must depend on the outcome of that relationship.

It seems obvious that no great progress can be made without a profound change on the Soviet side. The peculiarly deep-rooted hostility of Soviet intentions regarding the survival of other societies, Communism's dogmatic conviction of being the sole path to the future, and its willingness to use any available means to advance that conviction—these are the major obstacles to satisfactory Soviet-American relations.

The chief question is what the change must be and what, if anything, the United States can do to promote it. There would be general agreement that change is not out of the question. The world constantly alters; regimes rise and fall, or evolve into new forms with new motivations. What is lacking is agreement on the likely direction of change or the means to promote it. We have put forward some divergent perspectives, each of which envisages a different outcome and different ways to advance it. One would hope for a gradual diminution of Communist zeal through confronting the Soviet bloc with a vigorous free world, fully capable of defending itself but refraining from pressures against the present Communist sphere of control. A second would seek, primarily through negotiation and diplomacy, a more satisfactory and stable basis for a *modus vivendi* than exists at present. A third would seek to exert active pressure against the Soviet bloc with the aim of bringing about a retraction of Communist power and, ideally, its eventual disappearance.

The difficulty with these general perspectives is that none provides more than a problematic chance of achieving its eventual aim, and all fall short as guides in dealing with some of the complex issues—notably the problem of a divided Germany—with which the United States must deal. They are of value, however, in pointing up the need not to engage in incompatible undertakings or to lose sight of the importance of long-run, cumulative effects. While we have found no single perspective able to answer all the needs of our policy toward the Soviet Union in all areas, these divergent approaches are of assistance in framing ranges of policy choices and in indicating some of the implications of our actions.

Although these perspectives are probably irreconcilable in principle—one cannot simultaneously both advance and accept the *status quo* [1]—the differences when they are applied depend very considerably on the kinds of action contemplated. The greater the emphasis on physical power, the more irreconcilable these perspectives appear. Quite evidently there is no way to harmonize a policy of strict nonintervention in, say, East Central Europe with one which might, for example, attempt to detach territory or overthrow satellite regimes by means of armed raids and sabotage. On the level of economic actions the difference in practice be-

[1] At the tactical level, of course, it is possible to hold, or give, ground in one sector and advance in another, but we are here speaking of general objectives.

comes a good deal less acute, whatever the intentions may be. It would be difficult to tell whether a restriction of trade with the Soviet bloc meant an attempt to weaken the regimes or was part of an effort to fortify the West on the basis of the *status quo*. At the political level, in such questions as the free transmission of news or the movement of persons across the Iron Curtain, the distinction becomes even less apparent. Finally, at the opposite pole from physical power—in the conflict of ideas and philosophies—the distinction in perspectives reaches a vanishing point; such terms as *status quo* and forward pressure are hardly applicable to the clash of intellects. In other words, these approaches to direct Soviet-American relations appear in greatest contrast when applied to physical entities: physical power over territory and physical efforts to dislodge it.

For reasons we have given already, the general effort of American policy should be to try to keep the locus of active engagement as far from the range of open violence, of physical power, as it can; to induce the Soviet leaders not to attempt violent experiments, by our having the ability to make these experiments patently unrewarding and costly. The more successful this effort, the better are we able to be flexible in our choice of actions without becoming involved in cross-purposes. Conversely, the closer the locus of engagement is to open violence the greater the need for rigorous correspondence between our actions and our purposes. To take one extreme case, if thermonuclear power were the *only* capability that counted in Soviet-American relations, if all issues hinged solely on the use or nonuse of these weapons, there would be very little room for flexibility, and indeed the need to hold to policies aimed at maintaining the *status quo* would be self-evident. At the other extreme, if the conflict between the Communist and non-Communist worlds were *exclusively* political, if issues could be determined by the outcome of debate, propaganda and persuasion, we could be free, indeed in such a contest we might be obliged, to adopt policies of forward pressure. In other words, our choice of perspectives, as we have called them, is not just a matter of consistency, it also depends on the general state of

Soviet-American relations and on the instruments available to influence them.

Is there not a danger, however, if in actual fact we do go beyond the *status quo* and exert pressure on the Soviet bloc, and if this pressure shows some prospect of success, that the Soviet Union will respond by increasing the pitch of violence to the degree necessary to counteract our efforts? If so, are we not caught in a vicious circle: trying to keep the conflict away from open violence in order to pursue policies which promise, through the Soviet response, to increase rather than diminish the use of violence? This is possible, but the circle, though vicious, is not necessarily closed. If, for example, the Soviet Union, for whatever motive, relaxes its barriers to free communication and travel, and peoples from the West are able to meet with the peoples of the Communist bloc, it is quite possible that the results would be such as to induce the Soviet leaders to restore the barriers. But we cannot conclude from this that we would be back where we started, with no gains and only heightened Communist vigilance. On the contrary, it is our view that all such free movements, even if they are checked, are to the good and may, at one time or another, in one place or another, set new life astir.

It is in conjunction, then, with this effort to keep the conflict of intentions and interests from finding vent in open violence that we may hope to apply two important principles of American policy:

1. The right of people to choose the regime which governs them (in effect, the right of people not to be under Communist domination); and
2. The right of people to unite, if they so desire, to form a single government of their choosing (in effect, the right of Germany, and of Korea and Vietnam, to be reunited under conditions of free elections).

There is no need here to defend these principles; they are at the heart of a democratic foreign policy. To be sure, they cannot be listed as requirements in the sense in which we have been using the term. First, they are not preconditions for preventing the global hegemony of Communism or general war; the free world must be capable of defending itself despite the possible protracted frustration of these principles. Second, we see no definite or assured way of realizing these principles in the immediate circumstances.

Nevertheless, they are not merely expressions of preference or wishful thinking. They indicate what we believe to be necessary conditions for any real compatibility in Soviet-American relations. Nor are they only sops to our moral sensibilities, about which we should do nothing. Within the severe limits of possibility—and among these limits we include the necessity not to incite war or to work hardships on the people whom it is our aim to assist—they are operating principles.

These principles have their cost. However they may be expressed, they are anathema to the Soviet leaders, since they challenge the legitimacy of Communist control over important territories and indicate our trust that this control will not be permanent. We cannot judge with any accuracy the extent to which the effort to realize these principles will stir the Soviet Union to heightened zeal and harsher domination, but a good deal depends on the nature of our actions in this regard. Threats of force would, of course, greatly arouse the Communists' vigor, though even the simple fact that the peoples behind the Iron and Bamboo Curtains look to the United States as their chief hope is itself a provocation, an inevitable one. Clearly our particular actions must be adapted to the international situation as a whole and correspond to the general purposes of American policy, of which these principles are a part. But whatever they may be, the aim is clear: to keep all possible contact with the people in the Soviet orbit, to keep alive the hope that their present status is not irreversible. For at heart this is but a necessary expression of our belief in the free society, a belief which neither we nor the Communists can disregard.

With regard to the instruments, or methods, by which we may work for our several requirements and aims, it is evident from the complexity and movement of events that they must be highly flexible and adaptable. In particular, we should avoid finding final victory or defeat in every act. We are probably in for a long and difficult contest, in which there will be numerous gains and setbacks; we must put up with some developments we do not like, and take the best advantage of others. We are not in full control of the course of events, and there is no substitute for a sense of touch and practical judgment on the part of our statesmen.

Whether this combination of requirements, aims and methods will, in the end, lead us into more tranquil waters, no man can tell. At the very least we can pursue those actions which give us the best chance of averting the worst catastrophes. In so doing, it is of the utmost importance that we do not—at the peril of losing our own humanity—regard our Communist opponents as beyond the pale. We must hold to the distinction between Soviet Communism and its human agents. With the former, as a system of ideas and power, there may be no basis for communication beyond the language of action and facts; with the latter there is always the possibility, if only that, of something more. In the arduous task of meeting the Soviet challenge, we must not fall into the darkest crime of the totalitarians: regarding human beings as objects. We must never forget that we are dealing with fellow men to whom we have something to communicate, even the sense of outrage for the woes we see so senselessly imposed upon the world.

will be numerous traps and setbacks; we must put up with them as patiently as we may like, and take the best advantage of each. We are not in full control of the course of events and there is no substitute for a sense of timing and practical judgment on the part of our statesmen.

Whether this combination of requirements, aims and manners will, in the end, lead us into more tranquil waters, no man can tell. At the very least we can pursue those policies which give us the best chances of averting the worst occurrences. In so doing, it is of the utmost importance that we do not—at the peril of losing our own humanity—regard our communist opponents as beyond the pale. We must hold to the distinction between Soviet Communism and its human agents. With the former, as a system of ideas and power, there may be no basis for conciliation beyond the interplay of action and threat; with the latter there is always the possibility, if only that, of something more. In the arduous task of meeting the Soviet challenge, we must not fall into the earliest crime of the totalitarians, regarding human beings as objects. We must never forget that we are dealing with fellow men to whom we have something to communicate, even the sense of outrage for the woes we see so needlessly imposed upon the world.